Birnbaum's 95
New York

A BIRNBAUM TRAVEL GUIDE

Alexandra Mayes Birnbaum
EDITORIAL CONSULTANT

Lois Spritzer
Editorial Director

Laura L. Brengelman
Managing Editor

Mary Callahan
Senior Editor

David Appell
Patricia Canole
Gene Gold
Jill Kadetsky
Susan McClung
Associate Editors

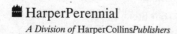

HarperPerennial
A Division of HarperCollinsPublishers

To Stephen, who merely made all this possible.

BIRNBAUM'S NEW YORK 95. Copyright © 1995 by HarperCollins Publishers. All rights reserved. Printed in the United States of America. No part of this book may be used or reproduced in any manner whatsoever without written permission except in the case of brief quotations embodied in critical articles and reviews. For information address HarperCollins*Publishers*, 10 East 53rd Street, New York, NY 10022.

FIRST EDITION

ISSN 0749-2561 (Birnbaum Travel Guides)
ISSN 1056-4446 (New York)
ISBN 0-06-278181-2 (pbk.)

95 96 97 ❖/RRD 5 4 3 2 1

Cover design © Drenttel Doyle Partners
Cover photograph © Jon Ortner/Tony Stone Images
Guggenheim Museum of Art, New York

BIRNBAUM TRAVEL GUIDES

Bahamas, and Turks & Caicos
Berlin
Bermuda
Boston
Canada
Cancun, Cozumel & Isla Mujeres
Caribbean
Chicago
Country Inns and Back Roads
Disneyland
Eastern Europe
Europe
Europe for Business Travelers
France
Germany
Great Britain
Hawaii
Ireland
Italy
London
Los Angeles
Mexico
Miami & Ft. Lauderdale
Montreal & Quebec City
New Orleans
New York
Paris
Portugal
Rome
San Francisco
Santa Fe & Taos
South America
Spain
United States
USA for Business Travelers
Walt Disney World
Walt Disney World for Kids, By Kids
Washington, DC

Contributing Editors

Brenda Fine
Catherine Fredman
Judy Faust Hartnett
Elizabeth Kadetsky
Joanne McGrath
Carole Martin
Elise Nakhnikian
Anita Peltonen
Patricia Schultz
David P. Schulz
Peter Simon

Maps

Mark Carlson
Susan Carlson

Contents

Foreword...vii
How to Use This Guide...5

Getting Ready to Go

Practical information for planning your trip.

When to Go...9
Traveling by Plane...9
On Arrival...12
Package Tours...14
Insurance...17
Disabled Travelers...17
Single Travelers...20
Older Travelers...21
Money Matters...23
Time Zone...23
Business and Shopping Hours...23
Mail...24
Telephone...24
Medical Aid...25
Legal Aid...26
For Further Information...26

The City

A thorough, qualitative guide to New York, highlighting the city's attractions, services, hotels, and restaurants.

Introduction to New York...29

New York At-a-Glance
Seeing the City...31
Special Places...33

Sources and Resources
Tourist Information...60
Getting Around...61
Local Services...63
Special Events...65
Museums...65
Major Colleges and Universities...68
Shopping...69

Sports and Fitness...78
Theater...84
Music and Dance...86
Nightclubs and Nightlife...87

Best in Town
Checking In...90
Eating Out...105
   Sunday Brunch...120
   Taking Tea...121

Diversions

A selective guide to a variety of unexpected pleasures, pinpointing the best places to pursue them.

Exceptional Pleasures and Treasures
Quintessential New York...125
A Few of Our Favorite Things...130
New York Discount Shopping Spree...131
Antiques: New York's Best Hunting Grounds...133
Auction Houses: Best Bids...136
New York Theater: On Broadway and Off...138
Historic Churches and Synagogues...143
A Day at the Races...147
Boating...148
Sailing...150
A Shutterbug's New York...151

Directions

Eight of the most delightful walks through New York.

Introduction...159

Walk 1: Wall Street...161
Walk 2: Little Italy and Chinatown...171
Walk 3: SoHo and TriBeCa...177
Walk 4: Greenwich Village...187
Walk 5: Rockefeller Center and Fifth Avenue...197
Walk 6: The United Nations and the East Side...205
Walk 7: Upper Midtown and Madison Avenue...209
Walk 8: Brooklyn Heights...217

Index...225

Foreword

My husband, Steve Birnbaum, spent most of his free time complaining about New York. To him this was hardly incomprehensible, since the city is unmanageable, unlivable, and unhygienic. Doubtless this is part of the reason why residents find it so irresistible. I, however, am a third generation New Yorker—Manhattan born and bred. Concrete courses through my veins and visions of Big Apples dance in my head.

Love/hate emotions are an intrinsic part of the New York City dynamic; by any objective gauge of quality-of-life standards, New York falls far short of even minimum life-sustaining levels. Still, folks continue to fight to get into the city limits, and are usually dragged from its concrete canyons kicking and screaming.

New York operates at a speed that is all its own—only Hong Kong comes close on this planet—and this pace has an insidious side. Once you have worked or played at New York's pace for any period of time, slowing down becomes almost a physical impossibility. Rather, you find yourself—however reluctantly—straining to get your out-of-town friends and relatives to keep up, and when visiting another town you are likely to spend a disproportionate amount of time trying to get local folks to get on with it.

We have tried to create a guide to New York that's specifically organized, written, and edited for today's demanding traveler, one for whom qualitative information is infinitely more desirable than mere quantities of unappraised data. We realize that it's impossible for any single travel writer to visit thousands of restaurants (and nearly as many hotels) in any given year and provide accurate appraisals of each. And even if it were physically possible for one human being to survive such an itinerary, it would of necessity have to be done at a dead sprint, and the perceptions derived therefrom would probably be less valid than those of any other intelligent individual visiting the same establishments. It is, therefore, both impractical and undesirable (especially in a large, annually revised and updated guidebook *series* such as we offer) to have only one person provide all the data on the entire world. Instead, we have chosen what we like to describe as the "thee and me" approach to restaurant and hotel evaluation and, to a somewhat more limited degree, to the sites and sights we have included in the other sections of our text. What this really reflects is a personal sampling tempered by intelligent counsel from informed local sources.

This guidebook is directed to the "visitor," and such elements as restaurants have been specifically picked to provide the visitor with a representative, enlightening, and, above all, pleasant experience. Since so many extraneous considerations can affect the reception and service accorded a regular restaurant patron, our choices can in no way be construed as an exhaustive guide to resident dining. We think we've listed all the best places, in various price ranges, but they were chosen with a visitor's enjoyment in mind.

Other evidence of how we've tried to tailor our text to reflect modern travel habits is apparent in the section we call DIVERSIONS. Where once it was common for travelers to spend an urban visit seeing only the obvious sights, today's traveler is more likely to want to pursue a special interest or to venture off the beaten path. In response to this trend, we have collected a series of special experiences so that it is no longer necessary to wade through a pound or two of superfluous prose just to find exceptional places and pleasures.

Finally, I also should point out that every good travel guide is a living enterprise; that is, no part of this text is carved in stone. In our annual revisions, we refine, expand, and further hone all our material to serve your travel needs better. To this end, no contribution is of greater value to us than your personal reaction to what we have written, as well as information reflecting your own experiences while using the book. Please write to us at 10 E. 53rd St., New York, NY 10022.

We sincerely hope to hear from you.

Alexandra Mayes Birnbaum

ALEXANDRA MAYES BIRNBAUM, editorial consultant to the *Birnbaum Travel Guides*, worked with her late husband, Stephen Birnbaum, as co-editor of the series. She has been a world traveler since childhood and is known for her travel reports on radio on what's hot and what's not.

New York

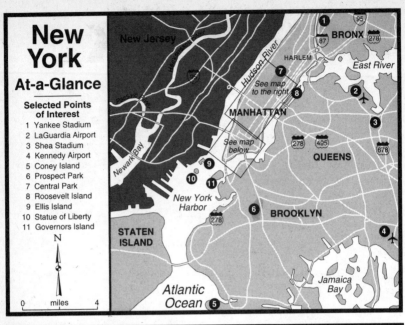
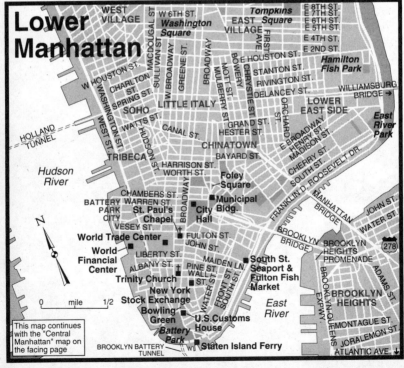

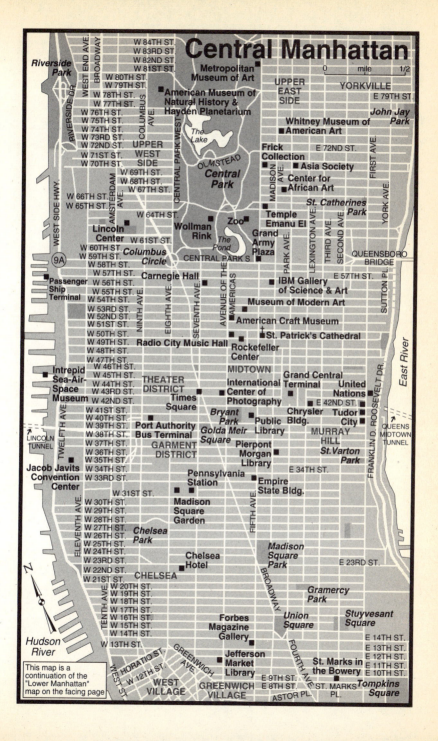

How to Use This Guide

A great deal of care has gone into the organization of this guidebook, and we believe it represents a real breakthrough in the presentation of travel material.

Our text is divided into four basic sections in order to present information in the best way on every possible aspect of a vacation or business trip to New York. Our aim is to highlight what's where and to provide basic information—how, when, where, how much, and what's best—to assist you in making the most intelligent choices possible.

Here is a brief summary of what you can expect in each section. We believe that you will find both your travel planning and en-route enjoyment enhanced by having this book at your side.

GETTING READY TO GO

A mini-encyclopedia of practical travel facts with all the precise data necessary to plan a successful trip to New York City. Here you will find how to get where you're going, plus selected resources—including useful publications and companies and organizations specializing in discount and special-interest travel—providing a wealth of information and assistance useful both before and during your trip.

THE CITY

Our individual report on New York offers a short-stay guide, including an essay introducing the city as a contemporary place to visit; an *At-a-Glance* section that's a site-by-site survey of the most important, interesting, and unique sights to see and things to do; *Sources and Resources,* a concise listing of pertinent tourism information, such as the address of the local tourist office, which sightseeing tours to take, where to find the best nightspot, how to use the subway, which shops have the finest merchandise and/or the most irresistible bargains, and where the best museums and theaters are to be found; and *Best in Town,* which lists our cost-and-quality choices of the best places to eat and sleep on a variety of budgets.

DIVERSIONS

This section is designed to help travelers find the best places in which to engage in a variety of exceptional experiences, without having to wade through endless pages of unrelated text. In every case our particular suggestions are intended to guide you to that special place where the quality of experience is likely to be the highest.

DIRECTIONS

Here are eight walks that cover New York: its main thoroughfares and side streets and its most spectacular landmarks.

To use this book to full advantage, take a few minutes to read the table of contents and random entries in each section to get a firsthand feel for how it all fits together. You will find that the sections of this book are building blocks designed to help you put together the best possible trip. Use them selectively as a tool, a source of ideas, a reference work for accurate facts, and a guidebook to the best buys, the most exciting sights, the most pleasant accommodations, and the tastiest foods—*the best travel experience* that you can possibly have.

Getting Ready to Go

Getting Ready to Go

When to Go

From the standpoint of weather, the best times to visit New York may be spring and early fall, when temperatures are most comfortable. Winters can be bitter, and summers typically are hot and humid. Still, there are good reasons for visiting the city at any time of year. For major cultural institutions, such as the *New York Philharmonic* and the *American Ballet Theater*, the season runs from fall through spring. Even the summer has its attractions—the *Mostly Mozart Festival, Shakespeare in the Park*, and other events—and on weekends many residents head out of town, leaving the city a calmer and less crowded place.

There are no real off-season periods when attractions are closed, and prices stay pretty much within the same range year-round. Bargains are more likely to appear on weekends (when fewer business travelers are in town) rather than during any particular season of the year.

If you have a touch-tone phone, you can call *The Weather Channel Connection* (phone: 900-WEATHER) for current weather forecasts. This service, available from *The Weather Channel* (2600 Cumberland Pkwy., Atlanta, GA 30339; phone: 404-434-6800), costs 95¢ per minute; the charge will appear on your phone bill.

Traveling by Plane

SCHEDULED FLIGHTS

There are three major airports in the New York metropolitan area: *John F. Kennedy International (JFK)* and *LaGuardia* (both in the city, in the borough of Queens), and *Newark International* (across the Hudson River in New Jersey). Leading airlines offering flights to these airports include *America West, American, American Eagle, Carnival, Continental, Continental Express, Delta, Delta Connection, Delta Shuttle, Midwest Express, Northwest, NW Airlink, Tower Air, TWA, TWA Express, United, United Express, USAir, USAir Express,* and *USAir Shuttle.*

FARES The great variety of airfares can be reduced to the following basic categories: first class, business class, coach (also called economy or tourist class), excursion or discount, and standby, as well as various promotional fares. For information on applicable fares and restrictions, contact the airlines listed above or ask your travel agent. Most airfares are offered for a limited time. Once you've found the lowest fare for which you can qualify, purchase your ticket as soon as possible.

RESERVATIONS Reconfirmation is not generally required on domestic flights, although it is wise to call ahead to make sure that the airline has your reservation and any special requests in its computer.

SEATING Airline seats usually are assigned on a first-come, first-served basis at check-in, although you may be able to reserve a seat when purchasing your ticket. Seating charts sometimes are available from airlines and also are included in the *Airline Seating Guide* (Carlson Publishing Co., 11132 Los Alamitos Blvd., Los Alamitos, CA 90720; phone: 310-493-4877).

SMOKING US law prohibits smoking on flights scheduled for six hours or less within the US and its territories on both domestic and international carriers. A free wallet-size guide that describes the rights of nonsmokers under current regulations is available from *ASH (Action on Smoking and Health;* DOT Card, 2013 H St. NW, Washington, DC 20006; phone: 202-659-4310).

SPECIAL MEALS When making your reservation, you can request one of the airline's alternate menu choices for no additional charge. Though not always required, it's a good idea to reconfirm your request the day before departure.

BAGGAGE On major airlines, passengers usually are allowed to carry on board one bag that will fit under a seat or in an overhead bin and to check two bags in the cargo hold. Specific regulations regarding dimensions and weight restrictions vary among airlines, but a checked bag usually cannot exceed 62 inches in combined dimensions (length, width, and depth), or weigh more than 70 pounds. There may be charges for additional, oversize, or overweight luggage, and for special equipment or sporting gear. Check that the tags the airline attaches are correctly coded for your destination.

CHARTER FLIGHTS

By booking a block of seats on a specially arranged flight, charter operators frequently can offer travelers bargain airfares. If you do fly on a charter, however, read the contract's fine print carefully. Federal regulations permit charter operators to cancel a flight or assess surcharges of as much as 10% of the airfare up to 10 days before departure. You usually must book in advance, and once booked, no changes are permitted, so buy trip cancellation insurance. Also, make your check out to the company's escrow account, which provides some protection for your investment in the event that the charter operator fails. For further information, consult the publication *Jax Fax* (397 Post Rd., Darien, CT 06820; phone: 203-655-8746; fax: 203-655-6257).

DISCOUNTS ON SCHEDULED FLIGHTS

COURIER TRAVEL In return for arranging to accompany some kind of freight, a traveler pays only a portion of the total airfare (and sometimes a small registration fee). One agency that matches up would-be couriers with courier companies is *Now Voyager* (74 Varick St., Suite 307, New York, NY 10013; phone: 212-431-1616; fax: 212-334-5243).

Courier Companies

Discount Travel International (169 W. 81st St., New York, NY 10024; phone: 212-362-3636; fax: 212-362-3236; and 801 Alton Rd., Suite 1, Miami Beach, FL 33139; phone: 305-538-1616; fax: 305-673-9376).

F.B. On Board Courier Club (10225 Ryan Ave., Suite 103, Dorval, Quebec H9P 1A2, Canada; phone: 514-633-0740; fax: 514-633-0735).

Halbart Express (147-05 176th St., Jamaica, NY 11434; phone: 718-656-8279; fax: 718-244-0559).

Midnite Express (925 W. Hyde Park Blvd., Inglewood, CA 90302; phone: 310-672-1100; fax: 310-671-0107).

Way to Go Travel (6679 Sunset Blvd., Hollywood, CA 90028; phone: 213-466-1126; fax: 213-466-8994).

Publications

Insiders Guide to Air Courier Bargains, by Kelly Monaghan (The Intrepid Traveler, PO Box 438, New York, NY 10034; phone: 212-569-1081 for information; 800-356-9315 for orders; fax: 212-942-6687).

Travel Unlimited (PO Box 1058, Allston, MA 02134-1058; no phone).

CONSOLIDATORS AND BUCKET SHOPS These companies buy blocks of tickets from airlines and sell them at a discount to travel agents or directly to consumers. Since many bucket shops operate on a thin margin, be sure to check a company's record with the *Better Business Bureau*—before parting with any money.

Council Charter (205 E. 42nd St., New York, NY 10017; phone: 800-800-8222 or 212-661-0311; fax: 212-972-0194).

International Adventures (60 E. 42nd St., Room 763, New York, NY 10165; phone: 212-599-0577; fax: 212-599-3288).

Travac Tours and Charters (989 Ave. of the Americas, New York, NY 10018; phone: 800-872-8800 or 212-563-3303; fax: 212-563-3631).

Unitravel (1177 N. Warson Rd., St. Louis, MO 63132; phone: 800-325-2222 or 314-569-0900; fax: 314-569-2503).

LAST-MINUTE TRAVEL CLUBS Members of such clubs receive information on imminent trips and other bargain travel opportunities. There usually is an annual fee, although a few clubs offer free membership. Despite the names of some of the clubs listed below, you don't have to wait until literally the last minute to make travel plans.

Discount Travel International (114 Forrest Ave., Suite 203, Narberth, PA 19072; phone: 215-668-7184; fax: 215-668-9182).

FLY ASAP (PO Box 9808, Scottsdale, AZ 85252-3808; phone: 800-FLY-ASAP or 602-956-1987; fax: 602-956-6414).

Last Minute Travel (1249 Boylston St., Boston, MA 02215; phone: 800-LAST-MIN or 617-267-9800; fax: 617-424-1943).

Moment's Notice (425 Madison Ave., New York, NY 10017; phone: 212-486-0500/1/2/3; fax: 212-486-0783).

Spur of the Moment Cruises (411 N. Harbor Blvd., Suite 302, San Pedro, CA 90731; phone: 800-4-CRUISES or 310-521-1070 in California; 800-343-1991 elsewhere in the US; 24-hour hotline: 310-521-1060; fax: 310-521-1061).

Traveler's Advantage (3033 S. Parker Rd., Suite 900, Aurora, CO 80014; phone: 800-548-1116 or 800-835-8747; fax: 303-368-3985).

Vacations to Go (1502 Augusta Dr., Suite 415, Houston, TX 77057; phone: 713-974-2121 in Texas; 800-338-4962 elsewhere in the US; fax: 713-974-0445).

Worldwide Discount Travel Club (1674 Meridian Ave., Miami Beach, FL 33139; phone: 305-534-2082; fax: 305-534-2070).

GENERIC AIR TRAVEL These organizations operate much like an ordinary airline standby service, except that they offer seats on not one but several scheduled and charter airlines. One pioneer of generic flights is *Airhitch* (2790 Broadway, Suite 100, New York, NY 10025; phone: 212-864-2000).

BARTERED TRAVEL SOURCES Barter—the exchange of commodities or services in lieu of cash payment—is a common practice among travel suppliers. Companies that have obtained travel services through barter may sell these services at substantial discounts to travel clubs, who pass along the savings to members. One organization offering bartered travel opportunities is *Travel World Leisure Club* (225 W. 34th St., Suite 909, New York, NY 10122; phone: 800-444-TWLC or 212-239-4855; fax: 212-564-5158).

CONSUMER PROTECTION

Passengers whose complaints have not been satisfactorily addressed by the airline can contact the *US Department of Transportation* (*DOT;* Consumer Affairs Division, 400 Seventh St. SW, Room 10405, Washington, DC 20590; phone: 202-366-2220). Also see *Fly Rights* (Publication #050-000-00513-5; *US Government Printing Office,* PO Box 371954, Pittsburgh, PA 15250-7954; phone: 202-783-3238; fax: 202-512-2250). If you have safety-related questions or concerns, write to the *Federal Aviation Administration* (*FAA;* 800 Independence Ave. SW, Washington, DC 20591) or call the *FAA Consumer Hotline* (phone: 800-322-7873).

On Arrival

FROM THE AIRPORTS TO THE CITY

It takes from 45 minutes to an hour to drive to midtown Manhattan from *John F. Kennedy International (JFK)* airport, 30 to 45 minutes from *LaGuardia,* and about 40 minutes from *Newark International.* The cost of a cab ride to Manhattan (not including tolls) is about $30 from *JFK,* about $20 from *LaGuardia,* and $25 to $30 from *Newark.* In New Jersey cabs, there is an extra $1 charge for each bag over 24 inches; in New York, one fare covers up to four passengers and their luggage (regardless of size). At the airports and *Grand Central Station,* pick up cabs at taxi ranks operated by uniformed dispatchers. Beware of hustlers offering to carry your bags and find you a cab—and asking for cash in advance; you could end up losing your money *and* your luggage.

Delta's Water Shuttle (phone: 800-54-FERRY or 908-229-2202) links *Pier 11* at South and Wall Streets to *LaGuardia*'s *Marine Air Terminal,* with a stop at East 34th Street. One-way fare is $20; round-trip fare is $30. There is no service on weekends and major holidays.

Relatively inexpensive transportation is available from the following bus lines: *Carey Transportation* (phone: 718-632-0500) provides service between either *JFK* ($11) or *LaGuardia* ($8.50) and the following locations in Manhattan: near *Grand Central Station* (arrives at Vanderbilt Ave.; departs from Park Ave., just south of 42nd St.); the *Port Authority Bus Terminal;* and the *Holiday Inn Crowne Plaza, Marriott Marquis, New York Hilton,* and *Sheraton Manhattan* hotels ($1.50 extra to hotels). *Carey* also runs a shuttle between the two airports ($9.50). *Gray Line Air Shuttle* (phone: 800-451-0455, 212-757-6840, or 212-315-3006) offers mini-van service between *JFK* ($16), *LaGuardia* ($13), or *Newark* ($18) and midtown hotels. The *Newark Airport Express,* operated by *New Jersey Transit* (phone: 201-762-5100), runs between *Newark Airport* and the *Port Authority Bus Terminal* (Eighth Ave. between W. 40th and W. 42nd Sts.; phone: 212-564-8484) and costs $7 one way ($12 round trip). *Olympia Trails* (phone: 212-964-6233 or 718-622-7700 in New York; 908-354-3330 in New Jersey) provides service (also for $7 one way) between *Newark Airport* and the *World Trade Center, Penn Station,* and *Grand Central Station.*

RENTING A CAR

You can rent a car through a travel agent or national rental firm before leaving home, or from a local company once in New York. Reserve in advance.

Most car rental companies require a credit card, although some will accept a substantial cash deposit. The minimum age to rent a car is set by the company; some also may impose special conditions on drivers above a certain age. If you rent the car at *Newark Airport* (or elsewhere in New Jersey), electing to pay for collision damage waiver (CDW) protection will add to the cost of renting a car, but releases you from financial liability for the vehicle. In New York State, car rental companies are *required* to include CDW in their basic rates—so you won't have a choice—and prices are higher by the amount of this otherwise separate charge. Additional costs include drop-off charges or one-way service fees.

Car Rental Companies

ABC Car Rental (phone: 212-685-5955, 212-734-4100, or 212-989-7260).
Alamo (phone: 800-327-9633).
Avis (phone: 800-331-1212).
Budget (phone: 800-527-0700).
Dollar Rent A Car (phone: 800-800-4000).
Enterprise Rent-A-Car (phone: 800-325-8007).
Hertz (phone: 800-654-3131).
National (phone: 800-CAR-RENT).
Payless (phone: 800-PAYLESS).
Sears (phone: 800-527-0770).
Thrifty (phone: 800-367-2277).
Yorkville Rent-A-Car (phone: 212-410-3100).

> **NOTE**
>
> **Rent-A-Wreck** (phone: 800-421-7253 for locations of local franchises) rents cars that are well worn but (presumably) mechanically sound, and has offices in the Bronx (phone: 718-933-6033), Brooklyn (phone: 718-998-9100), and Queens (phone: 718-784-3302). *Roarin' Roadsters* (phone: 201-569-4793) and *Vogel's Eurocars* (phone: 914-968-8200) both rent luxury models.

Package Tours

A package is a collection of travel services that can be purchased in a single transaction. Its principal advantages are convenience and economy—the cost usually is lower than that of the same services purchased separately. Tour programs generally can be divided into two categories: escorted or locally hosted (with a set itinerary) and independent (usually more flexible).

When considering a package tour, read the brochure *carefully* to determine exactly what is included and any conditions that may apply, and check the company's record with the *Better Business Bureau*. The *United States Tour Operators Association* (*USTOA;* 211 E. 51st St., Suite 12B, New York, NY 10022; phone: 212-750-7371; fax: 212-421-1285) also can be helpful in determining a package tour operator's reliability. As with charter flights, to safeguard your funds, always make your check out to the company's escrow account.

Many tour operators offer packages focused on special interests such as the arts, local history, sports, and other recreations. *All Adventure Travel* (5589 Arapahoe St., Suite 208, Boulder, CO 80303; phone: 800-537-4025 or 303-440-7924; fax: 303-440-4160) represents such specialized packagers. Many also are listed in the *Specialty Travel Index* (305 San Anselmo Ave., Suite 313, San Anselmo, CA 94960; phone: 415-459-4900 in California; 800-442-4922 elsewhere in the US; fax: 415-459-4974). In addition, a number of local companies offer half- or full-day sightseeing tours in and around New York.

Package Tour Operators

Adventure Tours (10612 Beaver Dam Rd., Hunt Valley, MD 21030-2205; phone: 410-785-3500 in the greater Baltimore area; 800-638-9040 elsewhere in the US; fax: 410-584-2771).

American Airlines FlyAAway Vacations (offices throughout the US; phone: 800-321-2121).

American Express Vacations (offices throughout the US; phone: 800-YES-AMEX).

Broadway Theatours (71 Broadway, New York, NY 10006; phone: 800-843-7469 or 212-425-6410; fax: 212-425-6425).

Capitol Tours (PO Box 4241, Springfield, IL 62708; phone: 217-529-8166 for information; 800-252-8924 for reservations; fax: 217-529-5831).

Classic America (1 N. First St., San Jose, CA 95113; phone: 800-221-3949 or 408-287-4550; fax: 408-287-9272).

Collette Tours (162 Middle St., Pawtucket, RI 02860; phone: 800-752-2655 in New England; 800-832-4656 elsewhere in the US; fax: 401-727-4745).

Continental Grand Destinations (offices throughout the US; phone: 800-634-5555).

Corliss Tours (436 W. Foothill Blvd., Monrovia, CA 91016; phone: 800-456-5717 or 818-359-5358; fax: 818-359-0724).

Dailey-Thorp (330 W. 58th St., New York, NY 10019-1817; phone: 212-307-1555; fax: 212-974-1420).

Dan Dipert Tours (PO Box 580, Arlington, TX 76004-0580; phone: 800-433-5335 or 817-543-3710; fax: 817-543-3729).

Delta's Dream Vacations (PO Box 1525, Ft. Lauderdale, FL 33302; phone: 800-872-7786).

Domenico Tours (751 Broadway, Bayonne, NJ 07002; phone: 800-554-8687, 201-823-8687, or 212-757-8687; fax: 201-823-1527).

Educational Adventures (815 North Rd., Westfield, MA 01085; phone: 800-628-9655 or 413-568-2855; fax: 413-562-3621).

Edwards & Edwards (1 Times Square Plaza, 12th Floor, New York, NY 10036-6585; phone: 212-944-0290 in New York State; 800-223-6108 or 800-366-4845 elsewhere in the US; fax: 212-944-7497).

Globetrotters SuperCities (139 Main St., Cambridge, MA 02142; phone: 800-333-1234 or 617-621-0099; fax: 617-577-8380).

Globus/Cosmos (5301 S. Federal Circle, Littleton, CO 80123; phone: 800-221-0090, 800-556-5454, or 303-797-2800; fax: 303-347-2080).

GOGO Tours (69 Spring St., Ramsey, NJ 07446-0507; phone: 201-934-3759).

Jefferson Tours (1206 Currie Ave., Minneapolis, MN 55403; phone: 800-767-7433 or 612-338-4174; fax: 612-332-5532).

Keith Prowse & Co. (USA) Ltd. (234 W. 44th St., Suite 1000, New York, NY 10036; phone: 800-669-8687 or 212-398-1430; fax: 212-302-4251).

Kerrville Tours (PO Box 79, Shreveport, LA 71161-0079; phone: 800-442-8705 or 318-227-2882; fax: 318-227-2486).

Le Ob's Tours (4635 Touro St., New Orleans, LA 70122-3933; phone: 504-288-3478; fax: 504-288-8517).

Liberty Travel (for the nearest location, contact the central office: 69 Spring St., Ramsey, NJ 07446; phone: 201-934-3500; fax: 201-934-3888).

Marathon Tours (108 Main St., Charlestown, MA 02129; phone: 800-444-4097 or 617-242-7845; fax: 617-242-7686).

Maupintour (PO Box 807, Lawrence, KS 66044; phone: 800-255-4266 or 913-843-1211; fax: 913-843-8351).

Mayflower (1225 Warren Ave., Downers Grove, IL 60515; phone: 800-323-7604 or 708-960-3430; fax: 708-960-3575).

MLT Vacations and ***Northwest World Vacations*** (c/o *MLT*, 5130 Hwy. 101, Minnetonka, MN 55345; phone: 800-328-0025 or 612-989-5000; fax: 612-474-0725).

New England Vacation Tours (PO Box 560, West Dover, VT 05356; phone: 800-742-7669 or 802-464-2076; fax: 802-464-2629).

Prestige Programs (136 E. 56th St., New York, NY 10022; phone: 212-759-5821; fax: 212-754-5198).

Smithsonian Study Tours and Seminars (1100 Jefferson Dr. SW, Room 3045, Washington, DC 20560; phone: 202-357-4700; fax: 202-786-2315).

Sutherland Hit Show Tours (370 Lexington Ave., New York, NY 10017; phone: 212-532-7732 in New York State; 800-221-2442 elsewhere in the US; fax: 212-532-7741).

Tours and Travel Odyssey (230 E. McClellan Ave., Livingston, NJ 07039; phone: 800-527-2989 or 201-992-5459; fax: 201-994-1618).

TravelTours International (250 W. 49th St., Suite 600, New York, NY 10019; phone: 800-767-8777 or 212-262-0700; fax: 212-944-5854).

United Airlines Vacations (PO Box 24580, Milwaukee, WI 53224-0580; phone: 800-328-6877).

Yankee Holidays (435 Newbury St., Suite 210, Danvers, MA 01923-1065; phone: 800-225-2550 or 508-750-9688; fax: 508-750-9692).

Companies Offering Day Tours

A TOUR (2329 Hudson Ter., Suite C4, Fort Lee, NJ 07024; phone: 800-STARDOM or 201-944-3394).

Circle Line Sightseeing Yachts (Pier 83, W. 42nd St. and 12th Ave., New York, NY 10036-1095; phone: 212-563-3200).

Gray Line New York Tours (900 Eighth Ave., New York, NY 10019; phone: 800-669-0051 or 212-397-2620; fax: 212-247-6750).

Happy Apple Tours (54-48 82nd St., Elmhurst, NY 11373; phone: 800-421-4518 or 718-639-1106; fax: 718-507-6172).

Harlem Renaissance Tours (34 Hamilton Place, New York, NY 10031; phone: 212-722-9534; fax: 212-996-7563).

Island Helicopter Sightseeing (1 Penn Plaza, Suite 2028, New York, NY 10119; phone: 212-564-9290; 212-683-4575 for recorded information; fax: 212-564-9574; tours depart from the E. 34th St. heliport).

New York Doubledecker Tours (Empire State Building, 350 Fifth Ave., Suite 6104, New York, NY 10118; phone: 800-692-2870 or 212-967-6008; fax: 212-967-5949).

Insurance

The first person with whom you should discuss travel insurance is your own insurance broker. You may discover that the insurance you already carry protects you adequately while traveling and that you need little additional coverage. If you charge travel services, the credit card company also may provide some insurance coverage (and other safeguards).

Types of Travel Insurance

Automobile insurance: Provides collision, theft, property damage, and personal liability protection while driving.

Baggage and personal effects insurance: Protects your bags and their contents in case of damage or theft at any point during your travels.

Default and/or bankruptcy insurance: Provides coverage in the event of default and/or bankruptcy on the part of the tour operator, airline, or other travel supplier.

Flight insurance: Covers accidental injury or death while flying.

Personal accident and sickness insurance: Covers cases of illness, injury, or death in an accident while traveling.

Trip cancellation and interruption insurance: Guarantees a refund if you must cancel a trip; may reimburse you for additional travel costs incurred in catching up with a tour or traveling home early.

Combination policies: Include any or all of the above.

Disabled Travelers

Make travel arrangements well in advance. Specify to all services involved the nature of your disability to determine if there are accommodations and facilities that meet your needs.

Organizations

ACCENT on Living (PO Box 700, Bloomington, IL 61702; phone: 800-787-8444 or 309-378-2961; fax: 309-378-4420).

Access: The Foundation for Accessibility by the Disabled (PO Box 356, Malverne, NY 11565; phone/fax: 516-887-5798).

American Foundation for the Blind (15 W. 16th St., New York, NY 10011; phone: 800-232-5463 or 212-620-2147; fax: 212-727-7418).

Information Center for Individuals with Disabilities (Ft. Point Pl., 27-43 Wormwood St., Boston, MA 02210; phone: 800-462-5015 in Massachusetts; 617-727-5540 elsewhere in the US; TDD: 617-345-9743; fax: 617-345-5318).

Mobility International (main office: 228 Borough High St., London SE1 1JX, England; phone: 44-171-403-5688; fax: 44-171-378-1292; US office: *MIUSA,* PO Box 10767, Eugene, OR 97440; phone/TDD: 503-343-1284; fax: 503-343-6812).

Moss Rehabilitation Hospital Travel Information Service (telephone referrals only; phone: 215-456-9600; TDD: 215-456-9602).

National Rehabilitation Information Center (8455 Colesville Rd., Suite 935, Silver Spring, MD 20910; phone: 301-588-9284; fax: 301-587-1967).

Paralyzed Veterans of America (*PVA;* PVA/ATTS Program, 801 18th St. NW, Washington, DC 20006; phone: 202-872-1300 in Washington, DC; 800-424-8200 elsewhere in the US; fax: 202-785-4452).

Royal Association for Disability and Rehabilitation (*RADAR;* 12 City Forum, 250 City Rd., London EC1V 8AF, England; phone: 44-171-250-3222; fax: 44-171-250-0212).

Society for the Advancement of Travel for the Handicapped (*SATH;* 347 Fifth Ave., Suite 610, New York, NY 10016; phone: 212-447-7284; fax: 212-725-8253).

Travel Industry and Disabled Exchange (*TIDE;* 5435 Donna Ave., Tarzana, CA 91356; phone: 818-368-5648).

Publications

Access for All: A Guide for People with Disabilities to New York City Cultural Institutions (*Hospital Audiences,* 220 W. 42nd St., 13th Floor, New York, NY 10036; phone: 212-575-7663; fax: 212-575-7669).

Access Travel: A Guide to the Accessibility of Airport Terminals (Consumer Information Center, Dept. 578Z, Pueblo, CO 81009; phone: 719-948-3334).

Air Transportation of Handicapped Persons (Publication #AC-120-32; *US Department of Transportation,* Distribution Unit, Publications Section, M-443-2, 400 Seventh St. SW, Washington, DC 20590; phone: 202-366-0039).

The Diabetic Traveler (PO Box 8223 RW, Stamford, CT 06905; phone: 203-327-5832; fax: 203-975-1748).

Directory of Travel Agencies for the Disabled and Travel for the Disabled, both by Helen Hecker (Twin Peaks Press, PO Box 129, Vancouver, WA 98666; phone: 800-637-CALM or 206-694-2462; fax: 206-696-3210).

Guide to Traveling with Arthritis (Upjohn Company, PO Box 989, Dearborn, MI 48121; phone: 800-253-9860).

The Handicapped Driver's Mobility Guide (*American Automobile Association,* 1000 AAA Dr., Heathrow, FL 32746-5080; phone: 407-444-7000; fax: 407-444-7380).

Handicapped Travel Newsletter (PO Box 269, Athens, TX 75751; phone/fax: 903-677-1260).

Handi-Travel: A Resource Book for Disabled and Elderly Travellers, by Cinnie Noble (*Canadian Rehabilitation Council for the Disabled,* 45 Sheppard Ave. E., Suite 801, Toronto, Ontario M2N 5W9, Canada; phone/TDD: 416-250-7490; fax: 416-229-1371).

I Love New York Group Travel Guide for New York State (Attn.: Roy Akins, New York State Department of Economic Development, Division of Tourism, 1 Commerce Plaza, Albany, NY 12245; phone: 800-CALL-NYS, ext. 66322, or 518-474-4116).

Incapacitated Passengers Air Travel Guide (*International Air Transport Association,* Publications Sales Department, 2000 Peel St., Montreal, Quebec H3A 2R4, Canada; phone: 514-844-6311; fax: 514-844-5286).

Ticket to Safe Travel (*American Diabetes Association,* 1660 Duke St., Alexandria, VA 22314; phone: 800-232-3472 or 703-549-1500; fax: 703-836-7439).

Travel for the Patient with Chronic Obstructive Pulmonary Disease (Dr. Harold Silver, 1601 18th St. NW, Washington, DC 20009; phone: 202-667-0134; fax: 202-667-0148).

Travel Tips for Hearing-Impaired People (*American Academy of Otolaryngology,* 1 Prince St., Alexandria, VA 22314; phone: 703-836-4444; fax: 703-683-5100).

Travel Tips for People with Arthritis (*Arthritis Foundation,* 1314 Spring St. NW, Atlanta, GA 30309; phone: 800-283-7800 or 404-872-7100; fax: 404-872-0457).

Traveling Like Everybody Else: A Practical Guide for Disabled Travelers, by Jacqueline Freedman and Susan Gersten (Modan Publishing, PO Box 1202, Bellmore, NY 11710; phone: 516-679-1380; fax 516-679-1448).

The Wheelchair Traveler, by Douglass R. Annand (123 Ball Hill Rd., Milford, NH 03055; phone: 603-673-4539).

Package Tour Operators

Accessible Journeys (35 W. Sellers Ave., Ridley Park, PA 19078; phone: 800-846-4537 or 215-521-0339; fax: 215-521-6959).

Accessible Tours/Directions Unlimited (Attn.: Lois Bonnani, 720 N. Bedford Rd., Bedford Hills, NY 10507; phone: 800-533-5343 or 914-241-1700; fax: 914-241-0243).

Beehive Business and Leisure Travel (1130 W. Center St., N. Salt Lake, UT 84054; phone: 800-777-5727 or 801-292-4445; fax: 801-298-9460).

Classic Travel Service (8 W. 40th St., New York, NY 10018; phone: 212-869-2560 in New York State; 800-247-0909 elsewhere in the US; fax: 212-944-4493).

Evergreen Travel Service (4114 198th St. SW, Suite 13, Lynnwood, WA 98036-6742; phone: 800-435-2288 or 206-776-1184; fax: 206-775-0728).

Flying Wheels Travel (143 W. Bridge St., PO Box 382, Owatonna, MN 55060; phone: 800-535-6790 or 507-451-5005; fax: 507-451-1685).

Good Neighbor Travel Service (124 S. Main St., Viroqua, WI 54665; phone: 800-338-3245 or 608-637-2128; fax: 608-637-3030).

The Guided Tour (7900 Old York Rd., Suite 114B, Elkins Park, PA 19117-2339; phone: 800-783-5841 or 215-782-1370; fax: 215-635-2637).

Hinsdale Travel (201 E. Ogden Ave., Hinsdale, IL 60521; phone: 708-325-1335 or 708-469-7349; fax: 708-325-1342).

MedEscort International (*ABE International Airport*, PO Box 8766, Allentown, PA 18105-8766; phone: 800-255-7182 or 215-791-3111; fax: 215-791-9189).

Prestige World Travel (5710-X High Point Rd., Greensboro, NC 27407; phone: 800-476-7737 or 910-292-6690; fax: 910-632-9404).

Sprout (893 Amsterdam Ave., New York, NY 10025; phone: 212-222-9575; fax: 212-222-9768).

Weston Travel Agency (134 N. Cass Ave., Westmont, IL 60559; phone: 708-968-2513 in Illinois; 800-633-3725 elsewhere in the US; fax: 708-968-2539).

SPECIAL SERVICES

B.S. Mini-Med of New York (1335 Blondell Ave., Bronx, NY 10461; phone: 718-829-2222; fax: 516-374-3353) provides wheelchair and stretcher transportation to and from New York's airports (JFK, LaGuardia, and Newark). Wheelchair Getaways (PO Box 136, Bedminster, NJ 07921; phone: 800-344-5005; fax: 908-781-7238) rents vans designed to accommodate wheelchairs.

Single Travelers

The travel industry is not very fair to people who vacation by themselves—they often end up paying more than those traveling in pairs. There are services catering to single travelers, however, that match travel companions, offer travel arrangements with shared accommodations, and provide information and discounts. Useful publications include *Going Solo* (Doerfer Communications, PO Box 123, Apalachicola, FL 32329; phone/fax: 904-653-8848) and *Traveling on Your Own,* by Eleanor Berman (Random House, Order Dept., 400 Hahn Rd., Westminster, MD 21157; phone: 800-733-3000; fax: 800-659-2436).

Organizations and Companies

Contiki Holidays (300 Plaza Alicante, Suite 900, Garden Grove, CA 92640; phone: 800-466-0610 or 714-740-0808; fax: 714-740-0818).

Gallivanting (515 E. 79th St., Suite 20F, New York, NY 10021; phone: 800-933-9699 or 212-988-0617; fax: 212-988-0144).

Globus/Cosmos (5301 S. Federal Circle, Littleton, CO 80123; phone: 800-221-0090, 800-556-5454, or 303-797-2800; fax: 303-347-2080).

Jane's International and Sophisticated Women Travelers (2603 Bath Ave., Brooklyn, NY 11214; phone: 718-266-2045; fax: 718-266-4062).

Marion Smith Singles (611 Prescott Pl., N. Woodmere, NY 11581; phone: 516-791-4852, 516-791-4865, or 212-944-2112; fax: 516-791-4879).

Partners-in-Travel (11660 Chenault St., Suite 119, Los Angeles, CA 90049; phone: 310-476-4869).

Singles in Motion (545 W. 236th St., Riverdale, NY 10463; phone/fax: 718-884-4464).

Singleworld (401 Theodore Fremd Ave., Rye, NY 10580; phone: 800-223-6490 or 914-967-3334; fax: 914-967-7395).

Solo Flights (63 High Noon Rd., Weston, CT 06883; phone: 800-266-1566 or 203-226-9993).

Suddenly Singles Tours (161 Dreiser Loop, Bronx, NY 10475; phone: 718-379-8800 in New York City; 800-859-8396 elsewhere in the US; fax: 718-379-8858).

Travel Companion Exchange (PO Box 833, Amityville, NY 11701; phone: 516-454-0880; fax: 516-454-0170).

Travel Companions (Atrium Financial Center, 1515 N. Federal Hwy., Suite 300, Boca Raton, FL 33432; phone: 800-383-7211 or 407-393-6448; fax: 407-451-8560).

Travel in Two's (239 N. Broadway, Suite 3, N. Tarrytown, NY 10591; phone: 914-631-8301 in New York State; 800-692-5252 elsewhere in the US).

Umbrella Singles (PO Box 157, Woodbourne, NY 12788; phone: 800-537-2797 or 914-434-6871; fax: 914-434-3532).

Older Travelers

Special discounts and more free time are just two factors that have given older travelers a chance to see the world at affordable prices. Many travel suppliers offer senior discounts—sometimes only to members of certain senior citizens organizations (which provide benefits of their own). When considering a particular package, make sure the facilities—and the pace of the tour—match your needs and physical condition.

Publications

The Mature Traveler (PO Box 50820, Reno, NV 89513-0820; phone: 702-786-7419).

The Senior Citizen's Guide to Budget Travel in the US and Canada, by Paige Palmer (Pilot Books, 103 Cooper St., Babylon, NY 11702; phone: 516-422-2225; fax: 516-422-2227).

Take a Camel to Lunch and Other Adventures for Mature Travelers, by Nancy O'Connell (Bristol Publishing Enterprises, PO Box 1737, San Leandro, CA 94577; phone: 510-895-4461 in California; 800-346-4889 elsewhere in the US; fax: 510-895-4459).

Unbelievably Good Deals & Great Adventures That You Absolutely Can't Get Unless You're Over 50, by Joan Rattner Heilman (Contemporary Books, 1200 Stetson Ave., Chicago, IL 60601; phone: 312-782-9181; fax: 312-540-4687).

Organizations

American Association of Retired Persons (*AARP;* 601 E St. NW, Washington, DC 20049; phone: 202-434-2277).

Golden Companions (PO Box 754, Pullman, WA 99163-0754; phone: 208-858-2183).

Mature Outlook (Customer Service Center, 6001 N. Clark St., Chicago, IL 60660; phone: 800-336-6330).

National Council of Senior Citizens (1331 F St. NW, Washington, DC 20004; phone: 202-347-8800; fax: 202-624-9595).

Package Tour Operators

Elderhostel (75 Federal St., Boston, MA 02110-1941; phone: 617-426-7788; fax: 617-426-8351).

Evergreen Travel Service (4114 198th St. SW, Suite 13, Lynnwood, WA 98036-6742; phone: 800-435-2288 or 206-776-1184; fax: 206-775-0728).

Gadabout Tours (700 E. Tahquitz Canyon Way, Palm Springs, CA 92262; phone: 800-952-5068 or 619-325-5556; fax: 619-325-5127).

Grand Circle Travel (347 Congress St., Boston, MA 02210; phone: 800-221-2610 or 617-350-7500; fax: 617-423-0445).

Grandtravel (6900 Wisconsin Ave., Suite 706, Chevy Chase, MD 20815; phone: 800-247-7651 or 301-986-0790; fax: 301-913-0166).

Interhostel (*University of New Hampshire,* Division of Continuing Education, 6 Garrison Ave., Durham, NH 03824; phone: 800-733-9753 or 603-862-1147; fax: 603-862-1113).

Mature Tours (c/o *Solo Flights,* 63 High Noon Rd., Weston, CT 06883; phone: 800-266-1566 or 203-226-9993).

OmniTours (104 Wilmot Rd., Deerfield, IL 60015; phone: 800-962-0060 or 708-374-0088; fax: 708-374-9515).

Saga International Holidays (222 Berkeley St., Boston, MA 02116; phone: 800-343-0273 or 617-262-2262; fax: 617-375-5950).

Money Matters

CREDIT CARDS AND TRAVELER'S CHECKS

Most major credit cards enjoy wide domestic and international acceptance; however, not every hotel, restaurant, or shop in New York accepts all (or in some cases any) credit cards. It's also wise to carry traveler's checks while on the road, since they are widely accepted and replaceable if stolen or lost. You can buy traveler's checks at banks and some are available by mail or phone. Keep a separate list of all traveler's checks (noting those that you have cashed) and the names and numbers of your credit cards. Both traveler's check and credit card companies have international numbers to call for information or in the event of loss or theft.

CASH MACHINES

Automated teller machines (ATMs) are increasingly common worldwide, and most banks participate in international ATM networks such as *CIRRUS* (phone: 800-4-CIRRUS) and *PLUS* (phone: 800-THE-PLUS). Cardholders can withdraw cash from any machine in the same network using either a "bank" card or, in some cases, a credit card. Additional information on ATMs and networks can be obtained from your bank or credit card company.

SENDING MONEY

Should the need arise, you can have money sent to you in New York via the services provided by *American Express MoneyGram* (phone: 800-926-9400 for information; 800-866-8800 for money transfers) or *Western Union Financial Services* (phone: 800-325-6000 or 800-325-4176).

Time Zone

New York is in the eastern standard time zone. Daylight saving time is observed from the first Sunday in April until the last Sunday in October.

Business and Shopping Hours

New York maintains business hours that are fairly standard throughout the US: 9 AM to 5 PM, Mondays through Fridays. Banks generally are open weekdays from 9 AM to 3 PM, although some may open at 8 or 8:30 AM and stay open until 5:30 or 6 PM at least one day a week. Some banks also offer Saturday morning hours. Most retail stores are open from 9:30 or 10 AM to 5:30 or 6 PM, Mondays through Saturdays, and some also are open on Sundays. Department stores may stay open until 7 PM on most weekdays and until 8:30 or 9 PM on Thursdays.

Mail

The main post office in New York, *James A. Farley General Post Office (JAF;* 421 Eighth Ave., New York, NY 10199; phone: 212-967-8585), provides window service 24 hours a day. For information on other branches, call the main office or check the yellow pages. Stamps also are available at most hotel desks, some supermarkets and other stores, and from public vending machines.

For rapid, overnight delivery to other cities, use *Express Mail* (available at post offices), *Federal Express* (phone: 800-238-5355), or *DHL Worldwide Express* (phone: 800-225-5345).

You can have mail sent to you care of your hotel (marked "Guest Mail, Hold for Arrival") or the main post office (sent "c/o General Delivery" to the address above). Some *American Express* offices in New York City also will hold mail for customers ("c/o Client Letter Service"); information is provided in their pamphlet *Travelers' Companion*.

Telephone

New York City has two area codes: 212 for Manhattan, and 718 for the Bronx, Brooklyn, Queens, and Staten Island. To make a long-distance call, dial 1 + the area code + the local number. (Calls between numbers in the 212 and 718 area codes are dialed like long distance calls, and cost more than calls within a single area code.) The nationwide number for information is 555-1212; you also can dial 411 for local information. If you need a number in another area code, dial 1 + the area code + 555-1212. (If you don't know an area code, dial 555-1212 or 411 for directory assistance.) The nationwide number for emergency assistance is 911.

Although you can use a telephone company calling card number on any phone, pay phones that take major credit cards (*American Express, MasterCard, Visa,* and so on) are increasingly common. Also available are combined telephone calling/bank credit cards, such as the *AT&T Universal Card* (PO Box 44167, Jacksonville, FL 32231-4167; phone: 800-423-4343). Similarly, *Sprint* (8140 Ward Pkwy., Kansas City, MO 64114; phone: 800-THE-MOST or 800-800-USAA) offers the *VisaPhone* program, through which you can add phone card privileges to your existing *Visa* card. Companies offering long distance phone cards without additional credit card privileges include *AT&T* (phone: 800-CALL-ATT); *Executive Telecard International* (4260 E. Evans Ave., Suite 6, Denver, CO 80222; phone: 800-950-3800); *MCI* (323 Third St. SE, Cedar Rapids, IA 52401; phone: 800-444-4444; and 12790 Merit Dr., Dallas, TX 75251; phone: 800-444-3333); *Metromedia Communications* (1 International Center, 100 NE Loop 410, San Antonio, TX 78216; phone: 800-275-0200); and *Sprint* (address above).

Hotels routinely add surcharges to the cost of phone calls made from their rooms. Long-distance telephone services that may help you avoid this added expense are provided by a number of companies, including *AT&T* (International Information Service, 635 Grant St., Pittsburgh, PA 15219; phone: 800-874-4000); *MCI* (address above); *Metromedia Communications* (address above); and *Sprint* (address above). Note that even when you use such long-distance services, some hotels still may charge a fee for line usage.

Useful resources for travelers include the *AT&T 800 Travel Directory* (phone: 800-426-8686 for orders); the *Toll-Free Travel & Vacation Information Directory* (Pilot Books, 103 Cooper St., Babylon, NY 11702; phone: 516-422-2225; fax: 516-422-2227); and *The Phone Booklet* (Scott American Corporation, PO Box 88, W. Redding, CT 06896; no phone).

Medical Aid

In an emergency: Dial 911 for assistance, 0 for an operator, or go directly to the emergency room of the nearest hospital.

Hospitals

Bellevue Hospital (462 First Ave. at 27th St.; phone: 212-561-4141).
Lenox Hill Hospital (100 E. 77th St.; phone: 212-434-3300).
Mount Sinai Hospital (Fifth Ave. at 100th St.; phone: 212-241-6500).
New York University Medical Center (560 First Ave. at 34th St.; phone: 212-263-7300).
St. Luke's–Roosevelt Hospital Center (428 W. 59th St. at Ninth Ave.; phone: 212-523-4000).
St. Vincent's Hospital and Medical Center of New York (153 W. 11th St. at Seventh Ave.; phone: 212-790-7000).

Pharmacies

Duane Reade (350 Fifth Ave. at 33rd St.; phone: 212-714-2417). Open weekdays from 8 AM to 6:30 PM and Saturdays from 10 AM to 6 PM.
Duane Reade (51 W. 51st St.; phone: 212-582-8525). Open weekdays from 8 AM to 6:30 PM.
Kaufman Pharmacy (557 Lexington Ave. at 50th St.; phone: 212-755-2266). Open 24 hours daily.

Additional Resources

International SOS Assistance (PO Box 11568, Philadelphia, PA 19116; phone: 800-523-8930 or 215-244-1500; fax: 215-244-2227).
Medic Alert Foundation (2323 Colorado Ave., Turlock, CA 95382; phone: 800-ID-ALERT or 209-668-3333; fax: 209-669-2495).
Travel Care International (*Eagle River Airport*, PO Box 846, Eagle River, WI 54521; phone: 800-5-AIR-MED or 715-479-8881; fax: 715-479-8178).

Legal Aid

If you don't have, or cannot reach, your own attorney, most cities offer legal referral services maintained by county bar associations. These services ensure that anyone in need of legal representation gets it and can match you with a local attorney. In New York City, the *Legal Referral Service* (phone: 212-626-7373; fax: 212-575-5676) is located at the offices of the *Association of the Bar of the City of New York* (42 W. 44th St., New York, NY 10036; phone: 212-382-6600; fax: 212-575-5676), and is co-sponsored by the bar association and the *New York County Lawyers Association* (14 Vesey St., New York, NY 10007; phone: 212-267-6646; fax: 212-285-4482). If you must appear in court, you are entitled to court-appointed representation if you can't obtain a lawyer or can't afford one.

For Further Information

The best sources of tourist information are the *New York Convention and Visitors Bureau* (2 Columbus Circle, New York, NY 10019; phone: 212-397-8222; fax: 212-245-5943) and the *New York State Department of Economic Development, Division of Tourism* (1 Commerce Plaza, Room 301, Albany, NY 12245; phone: 800-CALL-NYS or 518-474-4116; fax: 518-486-6416). For additional sources of tourist information in New York City, see *Sources and Resources* in THE CITY.

The City

New York City

Any visitor's first impression of this enormously diverse city can be distorted easily by the specific neighborhood in which he or she happens to land. An uninitiated tourist in the Tottenville section of Staten Island would likely surprise neighbors back home with descriptions of rolling farmland, rural ambience, and settings seemingly more appropriate to Iowa than to this country's most cosmopolitan center. That same stranger standing in parts of the South Bronx would horrify friends with tales of a "war zone" reminiscent of Dresden after the World War II firebombings. And seeing the corner of Fifth Avenue and 59th Street for the first time, our fledgling traveler couldn't help but be impressed with surroundings whose incredible elegance and opulence have few equals in the world. The question, then, is: Which is the real New York?

The answer is that New York is all these things. In a way visitors have their choice of the New York City they wish to visit, and it's a fairly simple matter to be insulated from most potential unpleasantness. A tourist's terrain in New York is limited traditionally to Manhattan, and within this relatively narrow geographic area, especially between 34th and 96th Streets, stand New York's most famous hotels, the majority of its elegant restaurants, and its most celebrated theaters, movie houses, museums, and fine shops.

It is, therefore, sometimes difficult for a visitor to reconcile the entertaining New York of his or her own experience with the troubled and troublesome New York so luridly described in the tabloids. It is hard to understand matters of want and welfare while window shopping in the chic, dramatic boutiques of Madison Avenue or craning one's neck up the canyon of Park Avenue. The visitor's New York and the most crowded residential areas of the city seldom intersect, and unless a traveler specifically sets out to see the city's other faces, the only aspect of New York's malaise likely to intrude will be the large number of homeless people and panhandlers—they are found all over town.

New York offers an array of distractions unequaled anywhere on earth. Nowhere are there more museums of such a consistently high quality. Nowhere are there restaurants of such striking ethnic diversity. Nowhere is there more varied shopping for more esoteric paraphernalia, and nowhere in the world do the pace of life and the activities of the populace more dramatically accent a city's vitality and appeal.

Just as US citizens hardly ever refer to themselves simply as Americans—they are Southerners, Texans, Californians, and so on—New York's nearly eight million residents are similarly chauvinistic about the specific enclaves of their city. Though in theory New York is composed of five boroughs—Manhattan, Queens, Brooklyn, the Bronx, and Richmond (Staten Island)—

everyone understands that Manhattan is "The City." (New York's daytime population swells to something close to 20 million, which is the total figure of New Yorkers plus residents of the outlying commuter communities.)

Indeed, New York feels like the capital of this country in almost every way, and the presence of the United Nations complex in the middle of Manhattan makes it possible to describe the city as the capital of the world. There may be more Frenchmen in Paris, more Japanese in Tokyo, and more Africans in Dakar, but in New York these ethnic entities come together in a single, singular place. And then there are the movers and shakers who live and/or work here; as you sit down to lunch in a midtown restaurant, you may find yourself dining next to people deeply involved in discussing anything from the future of world commerce to the maintenance of world peace.

New York also is the communications capital of the planet. While the majority of TV production facilities are based in California, a vast number of the decisions about what will be produced (and seen) are made in executive offices in Manhattan—which happens to be the country's advertising hub. New York also dominates radio broadcasting and magazine and book publishing, and though the city is now down to only a handful of citywide daily newspapers, one of them—*The New York Times*—is considered a (if not *the*) standard-bearer of contemporary journalism. Books, CDs and tapes, and even motion pictures often reflect New York values, giving the literary and media world a northeastern US bias of which people elsewhere often do not feel a part.

There is, in addition, a widespread perception that for any creative artist to succeed, he or she must gain recognition in New York. In the theater every actor, writer, director, designer, singer, dancer, musician, and composer feels the magnetic pull of Broadway. Painters, sculptors, novelists, cartoonists, jingle writers, poets, charlatans—all focus their creative and financial yearnings on New York. Whether one wants to make it on the stage, screen, airwaves, bookshelves, or billboards, the path to success almost always crosses New York.

Just as hard to characterize as the geography of this city is the attempt to stereotype a typical New Yorker. The city is notable, first of all, for its immense ethnic diversity, and there are large areas where the English language is hardly ever heard. From the obvious examples of Spanish Harlem, Chinatown, and Little Italy to the smaller Slavic and Hasidic enclaves, centuries-old traditions are kept up, as are the ethnic ghettos in which they thrive. (See *Walk 2: Little Italy and Chinatown* in DIRECTIONS.)

Other New Yorkers visit these districts to buy food and clothing not available elsewhere, or to attend ethnic festivals throughout the year. The *Chinese New Year* is celebrated intensely on Mott Street, and one would be hard pressed to develop a more authentic case of Italian indigestion than can be suffered during the *San Gennaro Festival* on Mulberry Street each fall. New Yorkers, whose culinary horizons probably reach farther afield than those of any other civic population on earth, regularly feast on such exotica as Greek stuffed grape leaves, Lebanese shish kebabs, Slavic piroshki, spicy Latino stews, and German wursts. The visitor who does not sample as many ethnic cuisines as possible is indeed wasting a special opportunity.

New York's cultural and gastronomic leadership is only slightly less important to the nation and the world than its financial ascendancy. Just walking through the Wall Street area dramatically reaffirms that the city has a secure hold on world commerce. Visitors' galleries at the *New York Stock Exchange* and the commodity exchanges provide a unique opportunity to watch capitalism in action, and nowhere is the sense of the enormity of American industry and the scope of financial trading more keenly felt. (See *Walk 1: Wall Street* in DIRECTIONS.)

Trading has a long history in New York City, where $24 worth of trinkets and baubles bought Manhattan Island from the Native Americans who may (or may not) have been its owners. Depending on one's point of view about this city, the Native Americans were either boldly deceived on the price or made one of the best real estate deals of all time.

The dimensions of the original island of Manhattan—a wilderness traversed by several streams and rivers which is recalled in some of its larger parks—bear little resemblance to the island today. Various landfill and reclamation projects have enlarged it over the years, and just a brief glance at the *Battery Park* area (at Manhattan's southernmost tip) indicates that expanding the island's real estate is still very much an active enterprise.

In all the world, New York has no equal. Its ability to prosper despite monumental problems testifies to its strength and resilience more dramatically than can any analytic essay. That its residents choose to continue to live with its shortcomings shows that New York's excitement and challenges outweigh its imperfections, a formula that must also work for most visitors here, whether on a mission of obligatory business or frivolous pleasure.

New York At-a-Glance

SEEING THE CITY

New York is one of the most complex cities in the world. Even people who have lived here all their lives don't know all of it; its size and diversity challenge even the most ambitious. For the visitor who wants to feel the magic of New York and to understand how the city is laid out, the best bet is to take it in from several vantage points. For more information on city views, see *Quintessential New York* in DIVERSIONS.

BROOKLYN HEIGHTS PROMENADE Standing on this walkway at dusk, with the lights of Manhattan shimmering across the East River, you'll get an idea of the magnitude and beauty of the city. In lower Manhattan the towers of the *World Trade Center* rise before you, and the Brooklyn Bridge spans the river to your right. Farther north stand the *Empire State Building* and the *UN Secretariat Building,* landmarks of midtown. The easiest way to get here is via the *IRT* Seventh Avenue subway line (No. 2 or No. 3 train), Clark Street stop. For detailed information, see *Walk 8: Brooklyn Heights* in DIRECTIONS.

WORLD TRADE CENTER Note: Although the terrorists' bomb that exploded here in February 1993 led to fatalities (four men were found guilty and sentenced to life in prison in connection with the bombing), the building itself miraculously escaped structural damage. Security in the buildings is, however, stricter than ever. The elevator to the observation deck of *2 World Trade Center* whisks you more than a quarter of a mile above the street. There is an enclosed deck on the 107th floor and a promenade on the roof above the 110th floor. Manhattan spreads out to the north, Brooklyn is to the east, to the west is New Jersey, and to the south lies New York Harbor, leading to the Atlantic Ocean. Open daily from 9:30 AM to 9:30 PM; to 11:30 PM June through September. The roof promenade may be closed during inclement weather and strong winds; check beforehand. Tickets are sold on the mezzanine level of the building. Liberty and West Sts. (phone: 435-7397). See also *Special Places.*

EMPIRE STATE BUILDING Although many visitors prefer the newer and higher *World Trade Center* observation deck, the old queen of New York, which turned 60 in 1991, attracts more than two million people a year. You can feel the breeze from the 86th floor or ascend to the glass-enclosed 102nd floor. Open daily from 9:30 AM to midnight (the last ascending elevator is at 11:30 PM). Admission charge. Fifth Ave. from W. 33rd to W. 34th Sts. (phone: 736-3100). See also *Special Places.*

VIEWS FROM THE ROAD Some of the most dramatic views of New York are visible when entering the city by car. The three western access routes have special features: The Holland Tunnel access road from the New Jersey Turnpike, leading into lower Manhattan, offers a panorama of the southern tip of the island; the Lincoln Tunnel access road offers a view of Manhattan's West Side; and the George Washington Bridge, linking New Jersey and the Upper West Side, has spectacular views of the Hudson, the city's long shore along the river, and the New Jersey Palisades. The bridge is a work of art itself, best seen from a distance, from the river, or while driving north on the West Side Highway.

BUS, BOAT, AND FLIGHT TOURS Many of the tour companies in the city will help you get your bearings before setting out on your own. *Gray Line* (900 Eighth Ave., between W. 53rd and W. 54th Sts., and 166 W. 46th St., near Seventh Ave.; phone: 397-2600) provides good bus tours. For a higher perspective, *NY Double Decker Tours* operates old-fashioned double-decker buses from the *Empire State Building* at Fifth Avenue and West 34th Street (phone: 967-6008). The *Manhattan Neighborhood Trolley* now includes Ellis Island (in the summer only) among its escorted tours of popular sites (phone: 677-

7268). *NYC Downtown Tours!* gives minibus tours of areas not usually covered by mainstream tour operators; these include lower Manhattan districts like Little Italy, SoHo, and the Lower East Side, with specialty tours centered around downtown nightlife, art, restaurants, and theater (phone: 932-2744). *Circle Line Sightseeing Yachts* offers an interesting three-hour guided boat trip around Manhattan and a new two-hour twilight voyage from early March until December 27. Boats leave from Pier 83 at the foot of W. 42nd Street and the Hudson River (phone: 563-3200). Most spectacular is *Island Helicopter*'s ride around Manhattan. Though the price is considerable ($47 to $119 for flights covering from seven to 34 air miles), you won't soon forget this trip. At E. 34th St. and the East River (phone: 683-4575).

WALKING TOURS Seeing New York on foot is probably the best way to get acquainted with this complex city: You can do it on your own or take a guided tour. A number of excellent walking tours are available, led by guides who are knowledgeable in everything from architecture and ethnic neighborhoods to literary history, the jazz circuit, movie locations, and noshing spots. Try *Adventures on a Shoestring,* which offers 40 or more walking tours and other activities around Manhattan year-round (phone: 265-2663); *Sidewalks of New York,* which conducts theme tours such as "Ghosts After Sunset," "Writers' New York," and "Hollywood on the Hudson" (phone: 517-0201); *Urban Explorations,* whose walks are organized around such themes as "The Art Deco Era" and "Atriums of New York," with the focus on the city's history, architecture, and ethnic neighborhoods as well as its parks and gardens (phone: 718-721-5254); or *Big Onion Walking Tours,* run by two doctoral candidates in New York history who give lively tours reflecting the history of immigration during trips to Harlem, Chinatown, Ellis Island, and Governors Island, to name a few; Irish and Jewish New York tours are also specialties, as are multiethnic eating tours (phone 439-1090). Also try the *Municipal Art Society* (phone: 935-3960), the *Museum of the City of New York* (phone: 534-1672), the *92nd Street YM/YWHA* (phone: 996-1105), or the *Lower East Side Tenement Museum* (phone: 431-0233), which offers a choice of 11 "living history" tours that explore the city's colorful ethnic heritage. For additional walks, see DIRECTIONS.

SPECIAL PLACES

Manhattan is a 12½-mile-long island stretching 2½ miles across at its widest point. Avenues run north and south; streets run east and west. Fifth Avenue is the dividing line between addresses designated east and those designated west. For example, 20 E. 57th Street is in the first block of 57th east of Fifth Avenue; 20 W. 57th Street is in the first block west of Fifth Avenue. New York grew from south to north, street by street and neighborhood by neighborhood; the oldest parts of the city are around the docks in lower Manhattan and in the financial district.

You will want to take taxis or public transport between areas—distances can be great—but, in general, the well-populated, active areas of the city offer an interesting environment for walking, so don't hesitate, unless the neighborhood is unfamiliar or it's late at night (see our choices on foot in DIRECTIONS). The much-touted reputation of New Yorkers as aloof and unfriendly simply isn't true. Just watch what happens when you ask directions on a bus or subway (except during rush hours, when things are, admittedly, a bit primitive). We suggest a copy of *Flashmaps! Instant Guide to New York* (Flashmaps; $5.95), which has the most accessible and best-organized series of maps of New York neighborhoods we've seen. It's available at bookstores and newsstands around the city. The new 36-by-42-inch *New York Identity Map* ($25), a double-sided, highly detailed map of Manhattan south of 65th Street, identifies major buildings by name and provides a color-coded legend for easy identification—yellow for hotel, blue for office, gray for residential, and so on. There are also symbols to pinpoint public sites such as police stations, movie theaters, and law courts. Contact the *Identity Map Co.* (55 Bethune St., Suite 1207; phone: 627-1994; fax: 627-5718).

LOWER MANHATTAN

STATUE OF LIBERTY Given by France as a symbol of friendship with the United States, this great lady has been guarding the entrance to New York Harbor since its dedication in 1886. The *Statue of Liberty Ferry* (phone: 269-5755) from *Battery Park* to Liberty Island runs from 9:30 AM to 3:30 PM, every 45 minutes on weekdays, every half-hour on weekends. The ferry ticket includes admission to the statue and to the *Ellis Island Immigration Museum* on Ellis Island (see below). You can see the statue from a distance as well as the southern tip of the city by riding the *Staten Island Ferry* (phone: 718-390-5253), still one of the world's great transportation bargains at 50¢. The ferry terminal is next to *Battery Park* (the South Ferry stop on the *IRT* Seventh Avenue subway local line, No. 1 or No. 9 train). For more details, see *Quintessential New York* in DIVERSIONS.

ELLIS ISLAND Visible from the *Statue of Liberty* or *Battery Park,* Ellis Island served as a processing center for more than 17 million immigrants from 1892 to 1954. Their dramatic experience is painstakingly portrayed at the *Ellis Island Immigration Museum* (phone: 363-3200), featuring dozens of exhibits of native costumes, instruments, and household implements as well as a film and a series of photographs that eloquently document the tension, terror, and joy of the immigrants' ordeal. The *American Immigrant Wall of Honor* is inscribed with the names of more than 420,000 immigrants to the United States who were commemorated by their descendants through a donation. These donations helped pay for the $160 million, six-year Ellis Island restoration project spearheaded by Lee Iacocca. The *Statue of Liberty Ferry* departs from *Battery Park* at regular intervals every day (see *Statue of Liberty* entry, immediately above) for the statue and then Ellis Island. Admission charge is included in the boat fare. For more details, see also *Quintessential New York* in DIVERSIONS.

GOVERNORS ISLAND Now a coast guard base, the island's two pre-1800 structures are the *Governor's House* and *Fort Jay; Castle Williams* was completed in 1811 and has been both a fort and a prison. Here you will also find great oceangoing views, oak, hickory, and chestnut trees, and a Gothic stone chapel hung inside with battle flags from the Mexican War. The island is open to visitors once a month (first or second Saturday) only with *Big Onion Walking Tours* (phone: 439-1090). Off Manhattan's southern tip, it is otherwise accessible only to officials by boat.

BATTERY PARK Twenty-one acres of green overlooking New York Harbor, this is the spot for picnics on hot summer days. There's a statue of Giovanni da Verrazano, who piloted the *Dauphine,* the ship that reached Manhattan in 1524, and there's also a monument to World War II dead. *Castle Clinton,* built as a fort in 1812, has functioned as an opera house, an immigrant landing depot, and an aquarium at various times. Its latest incarnation is as a ticketing center for the *Statue of Liberty Ferry.* Bordered by State St., Battery Pl., and the harbor (phone: 344-7220). Nearby, in *Battery Park City,* is *South Cove,* a three-acre park directly on the Hudson River.

BATTERY PARK TO WALL STREET This area is a lovely and usually safe place to wander on weekends, when the empty streets emphasize the incongruity of the *Merrill Lynch building,* the *World Trade Center,* and the *World Financial Center* (where free concerts are held in a magnificent indoor courtyard), surrounded by the 17th- and 18th-century buildings on Pearl Street, *Bowling Green,* and Hanover Square. Two buildings of particular note are *India House,* on the south side of Hanover Square (built in 1837), and the old *US Custom House* (the new *Custom House* is in the *World Trade Center*) on *Bowling Green,* which was erected in 1907 in Beaux Arts style.

NEW YORK STOCK EXCHANGE A tree growing in front of the stock exchange commemorates the one under which the first trading transaction took place in 1792. Today more than 1,600 corporations are listed on the Big Board. You can observe the action from a glass-enclosed gallery reached via the visitors' entrance at 20 Broad Street. Open weekdays; no admission charge, but tickets are required and are distributed at 9 AM on a first-come, first-served basis (phone: 656-5168). Large groups should call in advance for special arrangements. Cameras are prohibited. The *American Stock Exchange* (86 Trinity Pl.) no longer has a visitors' gallery. If you want to see real emotion, head for the *Coffee, Sugar, and Cocoa Exchange,* which makes the *New York Stock Exchange* look like a London tea party. The visitors' gallery is open weekdays; no admission charge. *4 World Trade Center* (phone: 938-2025).

FEDERAL HALL This *National Historic Site* served as the British headquarters during the Revolution and later was the seat of American government for about a year. George Washington was sworn in as president here in 1789. Open weekdays. No admission charge. At the corner of Wall and Broad Sts. (phone: 264-8711).

TRINITY CHURCH This church was first granted a charter by King William III in 1697. The present rose-colored stone building was completed in 1846 (it got a cleaning in the early 1990s), but the graveyard beside it is even older. For years the *Trinity Church* steeple was the highest point on the New York skyline. On Broadway at the head of Wall St. (phone: 602-0800). See also *Historic Churches and Synagogues* in DIVERSIONS.

ST. PAUL'S CHAPEL The oldest public building in continuous use in Manhattan, this fine example of colonial architecture was erected in 1766 on what was then a field outside the city. George Washington worshiped here. Classical concerts are held in the chapel on Mondays and Thursdays at noon from September through June. Suggested donation for concerts is $2. On the corner of Broadway and Fulton St. (phone: 602-0874).

BATTERY PARK CITY This $4-billion complex includes apartments, tree-lined streets, public parks and squares, and a sumptuous centerpiece, the *World Financial Center* (not related to the neighboring *World Trade Center*). The *WFC* is the home of the *Winter Garden* (not to be confused with the Broadway theater of the same name), a must-visit while in this part of town, where a variety of free concerts are held and artwork is displayed amid towering Royal palm trees in the soaring atrium. A true city within a city, this landfill development on the Hudson River is logically designed and decidedly not ostentatious. There is a wealth of other diversions, among them a spa, a 1950s rock 'n' roll club, the *Hudson River Club* restaurant (phone: 786-1500), and numerous shops. The views from the 1.2-mile Esplanade are spectacular. The *Winter Garden* is open from 8 AM to midnight. No admission charge. For general *Battery Park City* information, call 416-5300; for *Winter Garden* information, call 945-0505.

WORLD TRADE CENTER An unprecedented terrorist bomb attack in the *WTC*'s garage in early 1993 left several dead and all of New York traumatized. Although there was no structural damage, much reconstruction was necessary, and there is now a higher level of security here than in most New York buildings. The "Twin Towers," at 1,350 feet each, are not quite the tallest buildings in the world (the *CN Tower* in Toronto is, at 1,821 feet), but spectacularly set at the southern tip of Manhattan, they are a must-see landmark. In order to build the center, 1.2 million yards of earth and rock were excavated (they're now in the Hudson River). The concourse has a variety of shops and eateries. The *Custom House* is here, as are the *Commodity, Cotton, and Mercantile Exchanges*. Open daily. Admission charge for the *Observation Deck* (see *Seeing the City*, above). Bounded by West, Church, Liberty, and Vesey Sts. (phone: 435-7000).

CITY HALL This is the third *City Hall* in New York; it was built in 1803 and houses the office of the mayor and the City Council chamber. The original construction cost half a million dollars, and in 1956 the restoration cost some $2 million (times change). The building was a site of great importance to New York and US history: Lafayette visited in 1824; Lincoln's body lay in state here in 1865; and in the 1860s *City Hall* and *Tammany Hall* (Park Row and Frankfort St.) were controlled by Boss Tweed, the powerful, corrupt man who dominated New York politics until the 1870s.

Other city government buildings nearby include the *Municipal Building* on the northeast corner of *City Hall Park,* the *United States Court House,* across from Foley Square, the *New York County Courthouse* next door, the *Federal Office Building* on the other side of Lafayette Street, and the *Hall of Records.* In *City Hall Park* is a statue of Nathan Hale, a patriot of the Revolution who was executed here in 1776. Today protestors of every persuasion gather in the park to "fight *City Hall."* Closed weekends. No admission charge. In the triangle formed by Park Row, Broadway, and Chambers St. (phone: 788-7165).

SOUTH STREET SEAPORT AND THE FULTON FISH MARKET Completed in the 1980s, stage one of the *South Street Seaport* redevelopment program enlivened the area with shops and restaurants and additional space for the *South Street Seaport Museum.* The Museum Block is an entire row of rejuvenated buildings (some dating to the 1700s), with room for exhibitions, shops, and offices. The Schermerhorn Row of renovated 19th-century warehouses is also alive with retail outlets and the *South Street Seaport Museum Visitors' Center.* All of these changes have not substantially altered the area's famous old *Fulton Fish Market,* where, from about 2 to 8 AM, trucks still deliver fresh fish to the wholesale outdoor market.

But the old market is now joined by another building called the *Fulton Market,* with restaurants, cafés, and food stalls. Among the many eateries is one of New York's oldest seafood restaurants, *Sloppy Louie's* (92 South St.; phone: 509-9694). Prices are reasonable, but the portions remain hearty and the fish is as fresh as ever. Also of interest are the historic boats docked at Piers 15 and 16, where summertime pop and jazz concerts are staged. The three-story *Pier 17 Pavilion* adds even more shops and restaurants. Fulton St., between South and Water Sts.

BROOKLYN BRIDGE You can stroll from Manhattan to Brooklyn by crossing the Brooklyn Bridge on a pedestrian walk. You'll get a good view of the city and a close look at this engineering feat. The 6,775-foot-long bridge, which spans the East River at a height of 133 feet, was completed in 1883 and cost $25 million; it's considered by many to be one of the most beautiful bridges in the world. Free (unless someone succeeds in selling you title to it). Take the *IRT* Lexington Avenue subway line (No. 4, No. 5, or No. 6 train) to the Worth Street–Brooklyn Bridge–City Hall station.

CHINATOWN The best way to get the feel of New York's Chinese neighborhood is to hit the streets, especially Mott, Bayard, and Pell. The despair of census takers, this crowded, ever-expanding ethnic neighborhood which seeps into Little Italy is loosely estimated to be home to more than 100,000 people. Some say the Chinese community here is not as large as the one in San Francisco, but it is equally authentic. You'll know when you reach Chinatown by the pagoda-shaped telephone booths and stores that sell shark fins, duck eggs, fried fungi, and squid. Herbs are lined up next to aspirin in the pharmacies. Don't miss the good, inexpensive restaurants, the tea parlors, or the bakeries. At lunchtime try dim sum (steamed or fried dumplings filled with seafood, pork, or beef are just some of the choices). Favorite spots among New Yorkers are the *Golden Unicorn,* whose dim sum are the best in town (see *Eating Out*); *Peking Duck House* (22 Mott St.; phone: 227-1810); *Bo Ky* (80 Bayard St.; phone: 406-2292); and *Sun Hop Kee* (13 Mott St.; phone: 285-9856). Sundays are a good time to visit the area, but if you can, come during the *Chinese New Year* (held on the first full moon after January 21). The celebration is wild and woolly, with fireworks, dancing dragons, and throngs of people. For more information, see *Walk 2: Little Italy and Chinatown* in DIRECTIONS.

LITTLE ITALY Italian music wafting from tenement windows, old men playing *bocce,* old women dressed in black checking the vegetables in the markets, store windows with religious articles, pasta factories, and the ubiquitous aroma of Italian cooking give character to this ever-shrinking neighborhood, which has the reputation of being one of the safest in the city. Mulberry Street is the center of Little Italy (stop for an espresso at *Caffè Roma,* 385 Broome St.; phone: 226-8413), but the area stretches for blocks surrounding and blending into parts of SoHo and Greenwich Village. Even the section of Bleecker Street near the Avenue of the Americas has a decidedly Italian flavor, with bakeries that sell cannoli and cappuccino sandwiched between Middle Eastern restaurants and stores that sell Chinese window shades. Little Italy is thronged during the festivals of *San Gennaro* and *St. Anthony.* In September *San Gennaro* covers Mulberry Street from Spring Street to Park Row; *St. Anthony* fills Sullivan Street from Houston to Spring in June. The festivals attract people from in and out of the city with game booths, rides, and, most of all, enough food and drink (both Italian and "foreign") for several armies. Bordered by Canal and Houston Sts., the Bowery, and the Ave. of the Americas. For more information, see *Walk 2: Little Italy and Chinatown* in DIRECTIONS.

THE BOWERY There is nothing romantic about New York's Skid Row. On this strip are people who are decidedly down on their luck—both old and young. If you drive west on Houston Street, you'll get a look at some of the inhabitants—they'll wipe your windshields whether you like it or not and expect some change for their trouble. The area has a few theaters and music places and some good shopping spots; specialties include lighting and restaurant supplies. The stores have relocated here because of the proximity to one of the most interesting shopping markets in the world: the Lower East Side. Between Cooper Sq. and Chatham Sq.

LOWER EAST SIDE This area is probably the largest melting pot in the city. Eastern European Jews, many of whom are Hasidim (an ultra-religious sect, recognizable by the men's earlocks, called *peyes,* and their broad-brimmed hats and long black coats), sell their wares—everything from designer fashions to bedspreads—at discounted prices; you'll have to bargain if you want the best prices, and these merchants are formidable opponents. Everything is closed on Saturdays, the Jewish sabbath, but it's business as usual on Sundays, the busiest day of the week. The area also is home to Hispanics, African-Americans, Asian-Americans, and various other minority groups; you will hear an assortment of languages spoken, including Yiddish, Spanish, and even some Yiddish-accented Spanish.

The Lower East Side was where the Eastern European Jews, fleeing czarist persecution and deadly pogroms, first settled during their massive migration from 1880 to 1918. Many of the streets, including Rivington, Hester, Essex, and Grand, still look much as they did then. To get a real taste of the area, try the knishes at *Yonah Schimmel's* (137 E. Houston St.; phone: 477-2858); hot dogs at *Katz's* delicatessen (205 E. Houston St.; phone: 254-2246); or the Romanian "broilings" at *Sammy's* (see *Eating Out*).

SOHO The name stands for "*S*outh of *Ho*uston Street" (pronounced *How*-stun). SoHo leads a double life. On weekends uptown New Yorkers and out-of-towners fill the streets to explore its trendy stores, restaurants, and art galleries. During the week SoHo is a very livable combination of 19th-century cast-iron buildings, spillovers from adjacent Little Italy, off-off-Broadway theater groups, and practicing artists. At night the streets are empty, and you can see into the residential lofts of the old buildings; some are simple, open spaces, others are jungles of plants and Corinthian columns. *Fanelli's* (Mercer and Prince Sts.; phone: 226-9412) is one of the oldest bars around and a hangout for residents. Many local artists also have moved to TriBeCa, which is south and west of SoHo. SoHo is between Canal and Houston Sts., and Broadway and Hudson St. For more information, see *Walk 3: SoHo and TriBeCa* in DIRECTIONS.

TRIBECA Once neglected, TriBeCa (the name stands for "*Tri*angle *Be*low *Ca*nal Street") has made a flashy comeback. The current artist residents have spawned a plethora of trendy art galleries on White and Franklin Streets and lower Hudson Street. This is where Robert De Niro has his film production studio, and there are also many discount clothing stores, nightclubs, restaurants, and theaters here. Historical oddities worth visiting include the *Bond* hotel (125 Chambers St.), reputedly Manhattan's oldest; Stanford White's "Clocktower" building (346 Broadway); and the Art Deco *Western Union Building* (60 Hudson St.). TriBeCa extends from Canal St.

to Chambers St. and from West Broadway to the Hudson River. For more information, see *Walk 3: SoHo and TriBeCa* in DIRECTIONS.

EAST VILLAGE Still the center of New York's counterculture, this section has become gentrified, with a growing number of art galleries, restaurants, and nightspots competing for space with poor artists and various ethnic groups (the largest of which is Ukrainian, but there also are Armenians, Czechs, Germans, Russians, Poles, Jews, African-Americans, and Hispanics, many of whom live in low-income housing projects). Famous during the 1960s as the city's psychedelic capital, St. Mark's Place, between Second and Third Avenues, is still a lively block, lined with inexpensive restaurants and shops featuring styles from hippie to punk; it's generally hopping (sometimes with the help of controlled substances) at all hours of the day and night. Two streets south is "India Row," where numerous Indian restaurants line East Sixth Street between First and Second Avenues. Astor Place, on the border of the East and Greenwich Villages, is the site of *Cooper Union,* a liberal arts institute (good for free concerts and lectures); nearby is the *New York Shakespeare Festival* (also called the *Joseph Papp Public Theater;* 425 Lafayette St.; phone: 598-7150), where you'll find both contemporary and classical drama as well as experimental theater. You can have a drink at *McSorley's Old Ale House* (15 E. Seventh St.; phone: 473-9148); established in 1854, it is one of the oldest bars still in operation in New York. A few blocks north is the spiritual home of the Village, *St. Mark's-in-the-Bouwerie* (Second Ave. and E. 10th St.). The church still sponsors community activities, especially poetry readings by some of the best bards in New York. The East Village has housed many writers, from James Fenimore Cooper (6 St. Mark's Pl.; he also lived at 145 Bleecker St. in Greenwich Village) to W. H. Auden (77 St. Mark's Pl.) to Amiri Baraka, born LeRoi Jones (27 Cooper Sq.). Note: Some parts of the East Village, especially east of Avenue A, remain seedy; don't wander here after dark unless you know where you're going—and don't go unaccompanied. Bounded by Lafayette St. and the East River, Houston and 14th Sts.

GREENWICH VILLAGE

You can—and definitely should—stroll around the heart of the Village at night. The area is filled with surprises. You've probably heard of Bleecker Street, the slightly tawdry gathering place of tourists and the high school crowd from the suburbs, or of *Washington Square Park,* with its musicians, mimes, and street people. But you might not have pictured Grove Court, the lovely and secluded row of 19th-century houses near the corner of Grove and Bedford Streets (where O. Henry lived), or the Morton Street pier on the Hudson River, from which you can see the *Statue of Liberty* on a clear day. There are meat-packing factories from the 1920s, old speakeasies turned into restaurants, a miniature Times Square on West Eighth Street, and immaculate (and expensive) brownstones on quiet, tree-lined streets.

Get a map (you'll need it—there's nowhere else in Manhattan where West Fourth Street could bisect West 12th) and wander. Or you can ask directions—Villagers love to help, and it's a nice way to meet them. You can eat, go to the theater, sip cappuccino in an outdoor café, hear great jazz, and find your own special places. Bounded by Broadway on the east, the Hudson River on the west, Houston St. on the south, and W. 14th St. on the north. For more information, see *Walk 4: Greenwich Village* in DIRECTIONS.

WASHINGTON SQUARE Actually a park, this is a gathering place for students from *New York University,* Frisbee aficionados, volleyball players, modern bohemians, and people who like to watch them all. The Fifth Avenue entryway, the *Washington Square Arch,* is New York's answer to the *Arc de Triomphe.* Buildings surrounding the square include the *NYU* library, administration buildings, and law school. The north side of the square has some lovely homes, including No. 7, where Edith Wharton lived. Bounded by extensions of W. Fourth St., MacDougal St., Waverly Pl., and University Pl.

BLEECKER STREET Strolling down Bleecker Street (James Fenimore Cooper once made his home at No. 145) from La Guardia Place to Eighth Avenue, you'll pass outdoor cafés, falafel parlors, jazz clubs, Italian specialty stores, and myriad restaurants. Be sure to wander down some of the side streets, like Thompson, MacDougal (Bob Dylan's old stomping ground), and Sullivan. Have a cappuccino at *Caffè Dante* (79 MacDougal St.; phone: 982-5275), then pay homage to Eugene O'Neill at the *Provincetown Playhouse* (133 MacDougal St.; phone: 477-5048; seasonal). Beyond Seventh Avenue, the side streets become more residential; try Charles Street, West 10th Street, and Bank Street for examples of how the upper middle class lives in the Village. You'll also pass Christopher Street, the center of gay life in Manhattan.

LOWER FIFTH AVENUE This is where wealthy Villagers live. The *Salmagundi Club,* built in 1853 (47 Fifth Ave., near 12th St.), is the last of the imposing private mansions that once lined the avenue. On the streets between Fifth and the Avenue of the Americas (which the natives persist in calling Sixth Avenue) are expensive brownstones. The *New School for Social Research* (66 W. 12th St.; phone: 229-5600 or 800-544-1078, ext. 18, for general information) offers courses in everything from fixing a leak to ethnomusicology. From Waverly Pl. to 14th St.

AVENUE OF THE AMERICAS New Yorkers know it as Sixth Avenue. One of the most unusual buildings in the Village is the *Jefferson Market Library* (Sixth Ave. and W. 10th St.), with a small garden alongside. Built in 1874–78 in Italian Gothic style, it served as a courthouse and prison for many years. Across the street is *Balducci's,* an incredible international market (see *Shopping*). *Famous Ray's of Greenwich Village* (465 Sixth Ave. at W. 11th St.; phone: 243-2253)—the place on the corner with the long lines—is considered the source of some of the best pizza in the city. (Note that many pizza places in the city have "Ray's" in their names, but this is the one that gets the raves.) From W. Fourth to W. 14th St.

WEST VILLAGE Farther west (between Seventh Ave. S. and the Hudson River) is a series of small winding streets with some especially interesting places to visit. At 75½ Bedford Street is the house in which Edna St. Vincent Millay and John Barrymore once lived (not at the same time)—it's only nine feet wide. *Chumley's* (86 Bedford St.; phone: 675-4449) used to be a speakeasy during Prohibition and still has no sign on the door—but it does have good food and poetry readings inside. Commerce Street is a small side street lined with lovely old buildings, including the *Cherry Lane Theater* (38 Commerce St.; phone: 989-2020), one of the city's oldest. Two blocks south is Leroy Street with St. Luke's Place, a row of 19th-century houses. No. 6 Leroy was built in 1880 and was once the home of the city's flamboyant Mayor Jimmy Walker. If you walk to the end of the block and north on Hudson, you'll come to the *White Horse Tavern* (567 Hudson St.; phone: 243-9260), Dylan Thomas's hangout on his trips to New York City. Go in and have a drink.

14TH STREET TO 34TH STREET

UNION SQUARE For many years this was a place to avoid—particularly at night, when it was populated by drug pushers and other undesirables. Now, after a major face-lift, it's beginning to resemble itself in the halcyon days of the 19th century, when the square was the core of upper-crust Manhattan life. The open-air produce market on Mondays, Wednesdays, Fridays, and Saturdays and several new cafés, restaurants, discos, and theaters fill the side streets and the lower reaches of Park Avenue South; stop in at the trendy *Coffee Shop* (29 Union Sq. W.; phone: 243-7969) or the more upscale *Union Square Café* (see *Eating Out*). E. 14th to E. 17th St., between University Pl. and Fourth Ave.

GRAMERCY PARK A few blocks northeast of Union Square, *Gramercy Park* is one of the few places where visitors can experience the graciousness of old Manhattan. The park itself is open only to residents on the perimeter streets (they have their own keys), but on a sunny day you can see nannies with their privileged charges sitting on the benches in the shadows of the 19th-century mansions that surround the park. Stop in for a beer on Irving Place, south of the park, at cozy (if frayed), historic *Pete's Tavern* (129 E. 18th St.; phone: 473-7676); one of the oldest bars in New York City and formerly the *Portman* hotel, it is where local resident O. Henry is said to have written some of "The Gift of the Magi." Teddy Roosevelt's birthplace (28 E. 20th St.; phone: 260-1616) is a museum. Closed Mondays and Tuesdays; admission charge. Other well-known park sons and daughters include Herman Melville and Stephen Crane. A few blocks north of *Gramercy Park* on Lexington Avenue are dozens of little Indian shops selling splendid assortments of spices, saris, cotton blouses, jewelry, and food. E. 20th to E. 21st St., between Park Ave. S. and Third Ave.

CHELSEA In this eclectic residential neighborhood in the West 20s, between Seventh and 10th Avenues, you'll find elegant brownstones next door to run-down, four-story, walk-up tenements. The *Chelsea* hotel (222 W. 23rd St., between Seventh and Eighth Aves.; phone: 243-3700) has earned an important place in literary history. Thomas Wolfe, Brendan Behan, Dylan Thomas, and Arthur Miller slept and wrote in its rooms. Andy Warhol made a four-hour movie about its raunchier inhabitants. For a sojourn into tranquillity, step into the inner courtyard of the *General Theological Seminary,* a gift to the city in 1817 by Clement C. Moore, author of "A Visit from Saint Nicholas." The grounds are open daily in the early afternoons (from 2 to 4 PM on Sundays), except during special functions. No admission charge. 175 Ninth Ave. (phone: 243-5150).

MIDTOWN (34TH STREET TO 59TH STREET)

WEST 34TH STREET Still a major shopping street, this is the home of *Macy's* (Broadway from W. 34th to W. 35th St.), the mercantile giant; the nearby multilevel mall known as *A & S Plaza* (Ave. of the Americas from W. 32nd to W. 33rd Sts.; see *Shopping* for both); and scores of boutiques selling inexpensive blue jeans, blouses, shoes, tapes and CDs, and electronic gear. The hub of 34th Street is Herald Square, where Broadway intersects the Avenue of the Americas (Sixth Ave.). The main shopping district runs along 34th Street from Eighth Avenue to Madison Avenue, with a number of smaller shops lining the street as far east as Third Avenue.

MADISON SQUARE GARDEN, THE PARAMOUNT THEATER, AND PENNSYLVANIA STATION This is a huge coliseum-arena, office building, and transportation complex. The *Garden*'s seats (19,800 maximum capacity) usually are fully packed when the New York *Knicks* (*NBA* basketball) or the New York *Rangers* (*NHL* hockey) play home games, when the *Ringling Brothers and Barnum & Bailey Circus* comes to town, or whenever there is a major exhibition, concert, or convention. Formerly the *Felt Forum*, the *Paramount Theater* (not to be confused with the old movie house of the same name), a 5,600-seat subsidiary hall that's part of the *Garden*, is the site of boxing matches, concerts, and smaller exhibitions. The current *Penn Station,* which dates from the mid-1960s, is *Amtrak*'s major New York terminal and also serves the *Long Island Rail Road (LIRR)* and *New Jersey Transit* commuter lines; the original *Pennsylvania Station* on the same site, a vaulted and columned neoclassical structure, opened in 1910 and was demolished in 1963. No guided tours. W. 31st to W. 33rd St., from Seventh to Eighth Aves. (phone: 465-6741 for *Garden* and *Paramount Theater* information).

GARMENT DISTRICT Here is the nation's center of the clothing and fashion design industries (Seventh Avenue street signs here actually say "Fashion Avenue").

On any weekday during office hours, racks of the latest apparel are pushed through the teeming streets. From W. 30th to W. 42nd St., between Seventh and Eighth Aves.

EMPIRE STATE BUILDING The first skyscraper in New York to be attacked by King Kong, this 102-story Art Deco edifice was erected in 1931 and has been the symbol of the city for decades. There is an open-air observation deck on the 86th floor, to which millions of tourists have ascended over the years to gaze in awe at the surrounding New York skyline; there is another glass-enclosed viewing area on the 102nd floor. Don't be surprised if the top of the building is bathed in colored lights in the evening (red, white, and blue on *July 4th,* for example, or orange on *Halloween*)—it's the city's way of commemorating holidays and special occasions. Open daily from 9:30 AM to midnight (last elevator up at 11:30 PM). Admission charge. Fifth Ave. from W. 33rd to W. 34th St. (phone: 736-3100).

JACOB K. JAVITS CONVENTION CENTER This glass-and-steel monolith with a 15-story atrium, designed by eminent architect I. M. Pei, hosts the bigger conventions that outgrew the old *New York Coliseum.* The complex covers five square blocks between 11th and 12th Avenues and encompasses 1.8 million square feet of space, making it one of the world's largest buildings. The kitchens can produce banquet meals for up to 10,000, while the cafeteria serves 1,500 people an hour. State-of-the-art facilities include a sophisticated audiovisual system and soundproofing throughout its 131 separate meeting rooms, with simultaneous interpretation in up to eight languages. There's also a VIP lounge, press room, video information center, and cocktail lounge. The only thing missing is a garage. 655 W. 34th St. (phone: 216-2000).

TIMES SQUARE Every *New Year's Eve,* Times Square is where hundreds of thousands of New Yorkers and visitors congregate. Although Times Square is always crowded, the quality of the crowds leaves something to be desired. In spite of its reputation as one of the major crossroads of the world, Times Square is still struggling to shake its attraction for pickpockets, drug pushers, pimps, hookers, junkies, religious fanatics, and assorted street peddlers attempting to fence stolen goods. It is no longer wall-to-wall triple-X cinemas and porn shops, but the sex industry still has a grip on the area. Proposals for rehabilitation have been numerous: Signs of a possibly brighter future for the area included the completion in 1985 of the 50-story *Marriott Marquis* convention hotel (1535 Broadway at W. 45th St.; phone: 398-1900 or 800-228-9290; fax: 704-8930). This led to a resurgence of hotels that now include the *New York Renaissance, Macklowe, Paramount,* and *Embassy Suites* (see *Checking In* for all four). Although the overall seediness of Times Square has diminished slightly due to the presence of these upscale hotels, many New Yorkers are skeptical that any of the various cleanup projects their tax money has financed will turn the area completely around. The Times Square area is centered from West 42nd Street to West 46th Street, where Broadway and Seventh Avenue converge. The building at 229 West 43rd Street is the home of the *The New York Times,* after which the district is named (the newspaper formerly had its headquarters on Times Square).

BROADWAY AND THE THEATER DISTRICT On and just north of Times Square are the colorful marquees and billboards for which New York is famous. The lights are still pretty dazzling, twinkling on and off in a glittering electric collage. On most nights the streets are jammed with theatergoers, taxis, and limos; most curtains go up at 8 PM. The main theaters are between West 42nd and West 53rd Streets, east and west of, as well as on, Broadway.

NEW YORK PUBLIC LIBRARY A couple of blocks east of Times Square, this dignified neoclassical building is a good place to relax and catch your breath. Sit on the front steps, between the famous lion statues, or in *Bryant Park,* behind the library. Inside the library is New York's (and one of the world's) largest collection of books and periodicals as well as a gift store; there also are various exhibitions and public programs. Tours are given Tuesdays through Saturdays at 11 AM and 2 PM. Closed Sundays and Mondays. No admission charge. Fifth Ave. from W. 40th to W. 42nd St. (phone: 930-0800).

GRAND CENTRAL STATION This magnificent Beaux Arts relic is worth seeing, and there is a one-hour tour Wednesdays at 12:30 PM (phone: 935-3960); contribution suggested. Otherwise, be sure to check out the illuminated zodiac dotting the immense vaulted ceiling. The *Café at Grand Central,* principally a bar, also offers good food and a great view of the terminal. It is located on the west balcony (phone: 883-0009). The main station entrance is on E. 42nd St., between Vanderbilt and Lexington Aves., although access can be gained from all four sides.

CHRYSLER BUILDING This is the princess of the New York skyline. Its distinctive, graceful spire, decorated with stainless steel, sparkles with more than usual brilliance because of the installation of hand-blown fluorescent lights around its pinnacle. Although it long ago ceded the title of tallest in the city, this Art Deco building completed in 1930 remains, to many New Yorkers, the most beautiful of all. There are no tours and the observatory was closed long ago, but a visit to the small lobby, with its ceiling murals and exquisite inlaid elevator doors, is worth the trip. 405 Lexington Ave. at E. 42nd St.

FORD FOUNDATION BUILDING If you happen to be wandering through New York at sunrise and climb the stairs between First and Second Avenues on 42nd Street, you'll see the bronzed windows of the *Ford Foundation Building* catch the first rays, reflecting copper-colored light into the sky. At other times the building is just as dramatic. Built around a central, glass-enclosed courtyard containing tropical trees and plants, it is the only place in Manhattan where you can feel as if you're in a jungle. It's one of the great New York experiences—especially on snowy afternoons. Open weekdays. No admission charge. 320 E. 43rd St. (phone: 573-5000).

TUDOR CITY A nearly forgotten pocket of Manhattan, this 1920s neo-Tudor apartment complex is one of its most romantic parts. An esplanade overlooks the East River and the nearby *United Nations*. The home of many diplomats and UN employees, *Tudor City* serves as an international campus. (According to local legend, it used to be where executives and industrialists housed their mistresses in the 1930s and 1940s.) The long, curved staircase leading to the sidewalk opposite the *United Nations* is known as the *Isaiah Steps,* because of the biblical quote carved into the wall. Between E. 41st and E. 43rd Sts. at Tudor City Pl. (near First Ave.). For more information, see *Walk 6: The United Nations and the East Side* in DIRECTIONS.

UNITED NATIONS Although the *UN* is open all year, the best time to visit is between September and December, when the General Assembly is in session. Delegates from about 200 nations gather to discuss the world's problems, and there are a limited number of free tickets available to the public. The delegates' dining room also is open to the public for lunch, weekdays throughout the year; overlooking the East River, it offers a lovely international menu and the chance to overhear intriguing conversations. Reservations are essential; pick up a pass in the lobby. The *UN* is open daily. Charge for a guided tour. The visitors' entrance is on First Ave. between E. 45th and E. 46th Sts. (phone: 963-4440). For more information, see *Walk 6: The United Nations and the East Side* in DIRECTIONS.

ROCKEFELLER CENTER A group of skyscrapers built in the 1930s, *Rockefeller Center* is best known for its giant *Christmas* tree in December; for its ice skating rink open October through April; for *Radio City Music Hall,* a theatrical landmark and home of the *Rockettes* (phone: 247-4777); and for the romantic *Rainbow Room,* where dinner for two becomes a Fred Astaire and Ginger Rogers fantasy. After dinner, visit *Rainbow and Stars* for sophisticated cabaret entertainment (see *Nightclubs and Nightlife*). There are tours of the NBC television studios in 30 Rockefeller Plaza daily except Sundays. Admission charge; children under six not permitted. Fifth Ave. from W. 49th to W. 51st St. (phone: 664-4000). For more information, see *Walk 5: Rockefeller Center and Fifth Avenue* in DIRECTIONS.

ST. PATRICK'S CATHEDRAL A refuge from the crowds on Fifth Avenue, this is the most famous church in the city. Dedicated to Ireland's patron saint, it stands in Gothic splendor across the street from *Rockefeller Center* in the shadow of skyscrapers. Catholic services are held daily. See also *Historic Churches and Synagogues* in DIVERSIONS. Fifth Ave. from E. 50th to E. 51st St. (phone: 753-2261).

SIXTH AVENUE It's officially known as the Avenue of the Americas, but no true New Yorker calls it that. The stretch of Sixth Avenue between 42nd and 57th Streets is lined with skyscrapers and is particularly imposing at dusk, when the giant glass and steel buildings light up.

MUSEUM OF MODERN ART Possibly the most complete repository of 20th-century art in the world, its permanent collection includes the work of cubists, abstractionists, expressionists, conceptualists, and others. Among the many great paintings housed here are Wyeth's *Christina's World,* Monet's *Water Lilies* (housed in its own gallery), and van Gogh's *Starry Night.* A four-story glass Garden Hall overlooks the sculpture garden. The museum's permanent collection is installed in chronological order, and by following a suggested route, visitors can see the history of modern painting, photography, and sculpture unfold. The *William S. Paley Collection* (Paley was the founder of CBS) consists of 82 major works by Cézanne, Degas, Matisse, and Picasso, among others. The museum's film department and its leadership in film preservation are internationally renowned. Hollywood classics, award-winning foreign films, and the works of lesser-known directors are screened here regularly. Keep your eye out for the shows in the popular "Projects Series," dedicated to installations by contemporary young artists. Closed Wednesdays. Admission charge; on Thursday and Friday evenings, though, when the museum is open until 8:30 PM, admission is on a pay-as-you-wish basis. 11 W. 53rd St. (phone: 708-9400; 708-9480 for recorded information).

FIFTH AVENUE Although the street runs from Washington Square straight up to Spanish Harlem, when New Yorkers refer to Fifth Avenue, they usually mean the stretch of the world's most opulent shops between *Rockefeller Center* at 49th Street and the *Plaza* hotel opposite the southeastern corner of *Central Park* at Central Park South (59th Street). *Saks Fifth Avenue, Gucci, Tiffany, Cartier, Henri Bendel,* and *Bergdorf Goodman* make walking along the street an incredible test in temptation. Stop in at *Steuben Glass* on the corner of East 56th Street and marvel at its permanent collection of sculpted glass in mythological and contemporary themes. And whether you decide to go in or not, *Trump Tower*'s golden façade across East 56th Street is quite a spectacle, housing luxury apartments and some of the most exclusive (read: expensive) stores in the city.

GRAND ARMY PLAZA This square, with its central fountain just across the street from the southeast corner of *Central Park,* faces *Bergdorf Goodman,* the regal *Plaza* hotel, the General Motors Building, and the hansom cabstand where horse-drawn carriages (some with drivers in top hat and tails) wait to carry clients through the park. If you have a lover, be sure to arrange to meet here at least once. Be sure, too, to take at least one ride through the park in a hansom cab, preferably at dusk. In the southern part of the plaza, Pomona, the Roman Goddess of Abundance, stands atop the *Pulitzer Fountain.* Regilded in 1989, the statue of General Sherman shines brightly (to many New Yorkers, too brightly) in the northern part of the plaza. Three times the quantity of gold used on the flame of the *Statue of Liberty* was used to brighten him. Fifth Ave. and Central Park S.

CENTRAL PARK More than 50 blocks in length but only three lengthy blocks wide, this beloved stretch of greenery, designed by Frederick Law Olmsted and Calvert Vaux in the 1860s, is now a *National Historic Landmark.* New Yorkers use it for everything—jogging, biking, walking, ice skating (at *Wollman Rink*), roller-blading, riding in horse-drawn hansom cabs, listening to concerts (including the *Free Concerts in the Park* series every summer, courtesy of the *New York Philharmonic*) and opera, watching Shakespeare's plays, demonstrating against injustice, flying kites, boating, gazing at sculpture, and playing all kinds of ball games. Although city officials claim that the park is now safer due to increased security efforts, you should definitely avoid it at night; and even when you visit it during the day, be cautious, and don't wander into densely wooded areas, especially on weekdays. In the evenings and on weekends car traffic through the park is reduced or prohibited, leaving the considerable non-vehicular crowd to wend its way around the loop road inside the park much more peacefully. The pretty and very manageably sized *Central Park* zoo, recently renamed the *Central Park Wildlife Conservation Center* (entrance on Fifth Ave. between E. 61st and E. 65th Sts., in the southeast corner of the park), is run by the *New York Zoological Society* (phone: 861-6030), which also oversees the Bronx zoo, now called the *International Wildlife Conservation Park.* Despite the renamings, to New Yorkers, their zoos will always—and most affectionately—be zoos. Admission charge. *Central Park* is bounded by Central Park S. (W. 59th St.) on the south, W. 110th St. on the north, Fifth Ave. on the east, and Central Park W. on the west. Urban rangers offer free walking tours (phone: 427-4040), and there even are guides who describe which items growing in the park are edible. For information on park events, call 360-1333.

UPPER EAST SIDE

For the art lover, upper Fifth Avenue offers "Museum Mile," including the *Metropolitan Museum of Art* and the *Guggenheim* (see below), as well as the *Cooper-Hewitt,* the *Frick,* the *International Center of Photography,* and the *Jewish Museum* (see *Museums* for all four), plus the *Whitney Museum of American Art,* nearby on Madison Avenue (see below).

METROPOLITAN MUSEUM OF ART Usually considered the finest museum this side of the *Louvre,* it is visited by more than 4.5 million people every year. Here are works by the great masters from the Middle Ages to the present day, a vast assemblage of Greek and Roman sculpture, the most comprehensive collection of Islamic art anywhere, Oriental art, prints and photographs, musical instruments, decorative arts from all ages, and special exhibitions of stunning quality. The *Sackler Wing* contains the *Temple of Dendur;* the *Lila Acheson Wallace Gallery* in the wing of the same name has an extensive Egyptian collection; and 21 more galleries are devoted to 20th-century works. The *American Wing* comprises three centuries of American period rooms, paintings, sculpture, and decorative arts. The *Michael C. Rockefeller Wing* has works from Africa, the Pacific Islands, and pre-Columbian Americas. Asian art galleries include a Buddhist shrine and a Chinese garden court. The *Nineteenth-Century European Paintings and Sculpture Galleries* (formerly the *André Meyer Gallery,* on the second floor) house an unrivaled collection of French Impressionist paintings, including works by Degas and van Gogh. A permanent installation containing 1,300 works created between the third millenium BC and the early 19th century opened last year in 18 of the *Florence and Herbert Irving Galleries for the Arts of South and Southeast Asia.*

A sculpture-filled roof garden offers staggering views. There is also an outdoor sculpture garden overlooking *Central Park* (open May through October). There's a good cafeteria, a restaurant, and two superb, large gift shops. Films and lectures are presented throughout the year, and a distinguished concert series (phone: 570-3949) is held from September through May. The optimum times to visit the museum are Friday and Saturday evenings, when it is open until 9 PM. Closed Mondays and some major holidays. (Note: Some wings occasionally close due to lack of funds.) Suggested donation. The main entrance is at Fifth Ave. and 82nd St. (phone: 535-7710 or 879-5500).

SOLOMON R. GUGGENHEIM MUSEUM Designed in 1959 by Frank Lloyd Wright, this white circular building has an interior quarter-mile-long ramp that spirals upward for seven floors, allowing you to travel through the collections by following the curves of the building. While it is given over primarily to exhibitions of contemporary art (including a large collection of works by Kandinsky, Chagall, and Picasso), some patrons feel that the architecture is more impressive than what it houses. The museum reopened in 1992 after extensive renovations, which included a 10-story tower and a redesign of the interior space to bring it more in line with Wright's original vision. The fourth level of this new addition was recently designated the *Robert Mapplethorpe Gallery;* the museum's primary space for photography, it includes periodic exhibitions drawn from the Mapplethorpe collection and other objects belonging to the late controversial photographer, all donated to the museum by the *Mapplethorpe Foundation.* The on-site *Dean & DeLuca Café* (423-3657) offers a varied menu ranging from full meals to scrumptious desserts. Besides additional gallery space in the annex, the museum also has the *Guggenheim Museum SoHo* gallery (575 Broadway at Prince St.; phone: 423-3500; closed Mondays and Tuesdays; open until 8 PM Saturdays), which features exhibitions from the museum's permanent collection and some traveling shows. The main museum is closed Thursdays; open until 8 PM Fridays and Saturdays. Admission charge for both. 1071 Fifth Ave., between E. 88th and E. 89th Sts. (phone: 423-3500 for both the main museum and the SoHo gallery).

WHITNEY MUSEUM OF AMERICAN ART The permanent collection includes works by Calder, de Kooning, Hopper, Johns, O'Keeffe, Nevelson, Prendergast, Segal, Sheeler, and Warhol, among others. About 15 exhibitions are mounted each year, exclusively featuring 20th-century American art, with the emphasis on the work of living artists. Known locally as the *"Whitney,"* the museum presents an ambitious film and video series focusing on some of the work displayed in the galleries. *Sarabeth's Kitchen* (phone: 570-3670), a branch of the popular Upper East Side eatery, is set in an atrium on the lower level. In addition to the museum's midtown branch in Manhattan (see addresses below), there is one in Stamford, CT (1 Champion Plaza; phone: 203-358-7630) and a third, the *Whitney Museum at Philip Morris* at 120 Park Ave. at E. 42nd St. (phone: 878-2550). Closed Mondays and Tuesdays. Admission charge. 945 Madison Ave. at E. 75th St. (phone: 570-3600; 570-3676 for recorded information).

YORKVILLE AND GRACIE MANSION In this interesting ethnic neighborhood of mostly German and Eastern European families, a lot of high-rise apartment towers now are diluting the character somewhat. Nonetheless there are still a number of restaurants and delicatessens selling Wiener schnitzel, sauerbraten, goulash, and kielbasa—plus some splendid bakeries. *Gracie Mansion*, the 1799 official residence of the Mayor of New York, sits in a fenced garden in *Carl Schurz Park*, alongside the East River. The park is popular with joggers and dog walkers and is most attractive at dawn, when the eastern sky comes to life. Yorkville stretches from E. 80th to E. 89th St., between Lexington and York Aves. *Gracie Mansion* and *Carl Schurz Park* are at East End Ave. and E. 88th St. The mansion can be visited by appointment only, on Wednesdays from mid-March to mid-November (phone: 570-4751); suggested donation.

ROOSEVELT ISLAND A self-contained housing development in the middle of the East River, Roosevelt Island is accessible from Manhattan by tramway or subway (the Q train weekdays, the B on weekends), or from Queens by bus and subway. A loop bus encircles the island, which has restricted automobile traffic. Visitors also can stroll the main street from end to end. A landscaped riverside promenade has benches for relaxing while enjoying the unique view of midtown Manhattan. The aerial tramway leaves each side every 15 minutes daily, except during rush hours, when it leaves every seven and a half minutes. The fare at press time was $1.40. The Manhattan terminal is at Second Ave. and E. 60th St. (phone: 832-4543).

UPPER WEST SIDE

LINCOLN CENTER The pulsing water and light of the *Lincoln Center* fountain, the centerpiece of this 14-acre complex, are dramatically framed by the *Metropolitan Opera House,* a contemporary hall with two giant murals by Marc Chagall. The performing arts complex also contains *Avery Fisher Hall,* the *New York State Theater,* the *Vivian Beaumont Theater,* the *Mitzi E. Newhouse Theater, Alice Tully Hall,* the *Juilliard School of Music,* the new *Walter Reade Theatre,* and the *New York Public Library for the Performing Arts* (see *Theater* and *Music and Dance,* below, and *New York Theater: On*

Broadway and Off in DIVERSIONS). Guided tours through the major buildings are conducted daily and last about an hour. Admission charge except for children under six. Columbus Ave. from W. 62nd to W. 66th St. (phone: 875-5400 for *Lincoln Center;* 769-7000 for the *Metropolitan Opera Guild*).

AMERICAN MUSEUM OF NATURAL HISTORY With its $45-million face-lift scheduled for completion later this year, this museum will be an even greater cornucopia of curiosities. The anthropological and natural history exhibitions in the form of life-size dioramas showing people and animals in realistic settings have made this one of the most famous museums in the world. The new dinosaur and fossil halls, due to open this year, will feature such prehistoric creatures as the baurosaurus (better known as the brontosaurus) and the Tyrannosaurus rex in the largest freestanding dinosaur exhibit in the world. The popular *Naturemax Theater,* with its four-story screen, often shows double features of nature films (phone: 769-5200 or 769-5650). The museum has three cafeterias and three gift shops. Free guided tours leave from the main floor information desk daily at 15 past each hour. Closed *Thanksgiving* and *Christmas.* Donation suggested. Central Park W. and W. 79th St. (phone: 769-5000; 769-5100 for recorded information).

HAYDEN PLANETARIUM Housed here is an amazing collection of astronomical displays on meteorites, comets, space vehicles, and other galactic phenomena. The sky show, in which constellations are projected onto an observatory ceiling, is one of New York's greatest sights. Subjects include lunar expeditions, the formation of the solar system, and UFOs. There are also special children's shows on weekends. Open daily. Admission charge. W. 81st St., between Central Park W. and Columbus Ave. (phone: 769-5920).

CATHEDRAL OF ST. JOHN THE DIVINE The largest Gothic-style cathedral in the world, it has seating capacity for 10,000. A chronic shortage of funds (and skilled stonemasons) has allowed only two-thirds of the impressive church to be completed since work began in 1892. According to current projections, it may be nearly the 22nd century before construction is completed. Nonetheless, religious services (Episcopal), packed-out concerts, and poetry readings continue, as does the community spirit for which this imposing church has become known. There is a stunning Renaissance and Byzantine art collection as well. Free guided tours of the cathedral and the stone yard are conducted every day except Mondays. Open daily. Amsterdam Ave. and W. 112th St. (phone: 316-7540). See also *Historic Churches and Synagogues* in DIVERSIONS.

COLUMBIA UNIVERSITY This is the Big Apple's member of the Ivy League. Although more than 27,000 students attend classes here, the campus is spacious enough to dispel any sense of crowding. Around it are a number of interesting bookstores, restaurants, and bars, including the *West End Gate Café* (2911 Broadway at W. 113th St.; phone: 662-8830), a student favorite. Guided tours of the campus leave from 201 Dodge Hall; call ahead for schedules. No admission charge. The main gate is at Broadway and W. 116th St. (phone: 854-2845).

RIVERSIDE CHURCH Perched on a cliff overlooking the Hudson River, *Riverside* is an interdenominational Christian church with a functioning carillon tower and an amazing statue of the angel Gabriel blowing his trumpet. The tower is open on Sundays only from 12:30 to 3:30 PM; free guided tours of the church also are given on Sundays at 12:30 PM. W. 120th St., between Riverside Dr. and Claremont Ave. (phone: 222-5900). See also *Historic Churches and Synagogues* in DIVERSIONS.

GRANT'S TOMB Who is buried in Grant's tomb? Suffice it to say, the general and his wife are entombed in a gray building topped with a rotunda, set in *Riverside Park*. The interior was inspired by Napoleon's burial place in the *Invalides* in Paris. A word about the park: Don't wander here after dark. Known officially as the *General Grant National Memorial,* the tomb is closed Mondays and Tuesdays. No admission charge. Riverside Dr. and W. 122nd St. (phone: 666-1640).

THE CLOISTERS AND FORT TRYON PARK One of the most unusual museums in the country, if not the world, the *Cloisters* is a branch of the *Metropolitan Museum* and consists of sections of cloisters originally belonging to monasteries in southern France. It houses an inspiring collection of medieval art from different parts of Europe, of which the *Unicorn Tapestries* are the most famous. Recorded medieval music echoes through the stone corridors and courtyards daily; medieval and Renaissance concerts are held on selected Sundays throughout the year. Set in *Fort Tryon Park* along the Hudson River, the *Cloisters* offers a splendid view of the New Jersey Palisades, the George Washington Bridge, and the Hudson River. Closed Mondays. Suggested admission charge. The closest intersection is Washington Ave. and W. 193rd St. (phone: 923-3700).

HARLEM Some visitors to New York—black or white—are uncomfortable at the thought of entering Harlem, and like any unfamiliar place, it can be intimidating. But there is much to see here, and a visit can dispel the negative image many people have of the neighborhood. Starting at 120th Street and stretching to about 160th Street, it is a community of families who are just as concerned about local problems as in anywhere else in the city.

The most pleasant part of Harlem is "Strivers Row"—138th Street between Seventh and Eighth Avenues—two blocks of turn-of-the-century brownstones, some designed by Stanford White. Quite a lot of Harlem, however, is undergoing a revival. *Mart 125* (260-262 W. 125th St.; phone: 316-3340) is a shopping center offering handicrafts from developing countries, and there is always a constant flow of activities held on Harlem's 10-block waterfront that includes African-American, Latin, and Caribbean arts, music, entertainment, and food stalls. In August *Harlem Week* is actually 20 days of music, food, and cultural happenings; in the fall the main event is the *Harlem Jazz Festival*; and the famous *Apollo Theater* (253 W. 125th St.; phone: 749-5838) is well worth a visit year-round. The *Harlem Festival Orchestra* performs at the *Church of the Intercession* (550 W. 155th St.; phone: 283-6200) once or twice a year. Condos are going up in the area, and a multi-screen cinema has opened.

In the words of a New York police officer: "The best way to see Harlem is by driving or in a cab. Take a bus rather than a subway if you are using public transportation." Among the reliable tour operators are *Harlem Spirituals* (phone: 757-0425) and *Harlem Your Way* (phone: 690-1687 or 866-6997). Worthwhile sights include the *Morris-Jumel Mansion,* once the home of Aaron Burr and Washington's headquarters (Edgecombe Ave. and W. 160th St.; phone: 923-8008); the *Schomburg Center for Research in Black Culture* (515 Malcolm X Blvd. at W. 135th St.; phone: 491-2200); *Aunt Len's Doll and Toy Museum,* with its collection of more than 5,000 dolls, by appointment only (6 Hamilton Ter. at W. 141 St.; phone: 281-4143); the *Abyssinian Baptist Church* (132 W. 138th St.; phone: 862-7474), where the late Adam Clayton Powell Jr. preached; the *Studio Museum of Harlem* (144 W. 125th St.; phone: 864-4500); and the *Black Fashion Museum,* the country's only museum devoted to black contributions to fashion (155-157 W. 126th St.; phone: 666-1320). For more information on Harlem, call the *Uptown Chamber of Commerce* (phone: 427-7200) or the *New York Convention and Visitors' Bureau* (phone: 397-8222).

BROOKLYN

People who do not know the borough (and that includes many Manhattanites) think purely in terms of the book *A Tree Grows in Brooklyn* or 1930s gangster movies in which Brooklyn-born thugs make snide remarks out of the sides of their mouths while chewing on cigars. Actually, Brooklyn has a lot of trees (more than Manhattan) and some charming neighborhoods that are more European than American in character. Not only is it greener, it is also considerably more rural than Manhattan, even though it has more than four million people and bills itself as the "fourth largest city in America."

BROOKLYN HEIGHTS The most picturesque streets of classic (and expensive) brownstones and private gardens are found in this historic district. Not only does the Promenade facing the skyline offer a traditional picture-postcard view of Manhattan, but the area behind it retains an aura of dignity that characterized a more gracious past. Montague Street, a narrow thoroughfare lined with restaurants and shops selling ice cream, candles, old prints, flowers, and clothing, runs from the East River to the *Civic Center,* a complex of federal, state, and municipal government buildings. To get to Brooklyn Heights from Manhattan, take the *IRT* Seventh Avenue line (No. 2 or No. 3 train) to Clark Street station; or better yet, walk across the Brooklyn Bridge and bear right. The district extends from the bridge to Atlantic Avenue and from Court Street to the Promenade. For information on events, contact the *Brooklyn Heights Association* (55 Pierrepont St.; phone: 718-858-9193). For more information, see *Walk 8: Brooklyn Heights* in DIRECTIONS.

ATLANTIC AVENUE Lebanese, Yemeni, Syrian, and Palestinian shops, bakeries, and restaurants line the street, where purveyors of tahini, Syrian bread, baklava, halvah, other assorted foodstuffs, Arabic recordings, and books are to be found. There is even an office of the *Palestinian Red Crescent,* an official branch of the *International Red Cross* that has been helping victims of the wars in Lebanon. Occasionally, women in veils make their way to and from the shops, some incongruously carrying transistor radios. The most active street scene takes place between the waterfront and Court Street.

PARK SLOPE This restored district resembles London's borough of Chelsea, with its many beautiful shade trees and gardens. A large part of Park Slope has been designated a historic district, and there are some truly impressive townhouses here. Grand Army Plaza, with its colossal arch commemorating those who died in the Civil War, stands at the end of the Slope that extends along the western edge of *Prospect Park*. On Sundays you can climb the inside stairway to the top—the view is stupendous. Seventh Avenue, two blocks from the park, is an intriguing shopping street for old furniture, stained glass, ceramics, housewares, flowers, health food, vegetables, and toys. Saturday afternoons get pretty lively. To get to Park Slope from Manhattan, take the *IRT* Seventh Avenue line (No. 2 or No. 3 train) to Grand Army Plaza, or the *IND* line (D or Q train) to the Seventh Avenue station.

PROSPECT PARK AND THE BROOKLYN BOTANIC GARDENS *Prospect Park,* an Olmsted and Vaux creation (as is Manhattan's *Central Park*), is comprised of more than 500 acres of gracefully landscaped greenery with fields, fountains, lakes, a concert band shell, an ice skating rink in winter, a bridle path, and a zoo. The *Botanic Gardens* (1000 Washington Ave.; phone: 718-622-4433) contain 50 acres of serene rose gardens and hothouses with orchids and other tropical plants, as well as an impressive bonsai collection, cherry trees, an herb garden, and hundreds of other flowers and shrubs. Closed Mondays. No admission charge. From Manhattan, take the *IRT* Seventh Avenue line (No. 2 or 3 train) to the Eastern Parkway station, or take the *IND* line (D or Q train) to the Prospect Park station.

BROOKLYN MUSEUM In addition to its outstanding anthropological displays devoted to Native Americans of both the Northern and Southern Hemispheres, the museum's 1.5-million-object permanent collection also includes fine exhibits of Oriental arts, American painting and decorative arts, and European painting by the likes of van Gogh, Rodin, Toulouse-Lautrec, Gauguin, Monet, and Chagall. The recently renovated *West Wing* contains extensive Egyptian and primitive art collections. This museum hosts excellent traveling exhibitions as well. Closed Mondays and Tuesdays. Suggested donation. From Manhattan take the *IRT* Seventh Avenue line (No. 2 or No. 3

train) to the Eastern Parkway station. 200 Eastern Pkwy. and Washington Ave. (phone: 718-638-5000).

BAY RIDGE Although Brooklynites have long been fond of this onetime Scandinavian-dominated waterfront community, it took the movie *Saturday Night Fever* to bring it to national attention. Bay Ridge is one of the two anchor points for the world's longest suspension bridge, the Verrazano-Narrows Bridge, which connects Brooklyn with Staten Island. Those moviegoers still suffering from bouts of night fever can revisit the world of the film, although it was in the 1970s that John Travolta tripped down Fourth Avenue. Meanwhile, there is the timeless backdrop of the bridge looming over the tops of houses, shops, restaurants, and discos. A bike path runs along the edge of the Narrows (the body of water that connects New York City's rivers to the Atlantic) from Owl's Head Pier, the pier of the now-defunct Brooklyn–Staten Island ferry, all the way to the bridge. The pier has been renovated and is a great place for fishing, watching the ships come in, and catching a wide-angle view of lower Manhattan. To get to Bay Ridge from Manhattan, take the *BMT* line (R train) to the 95th Street station.

CONEY ISLAND Formerly a summer resort where generations of working class New Yorkers came for a day of sun and fun, *Coney Island* is now a long strip of garish amusement park rides, penny arcades, food stands, honky-tonk bars along the boardwalk where country-and-western singers compete with the sound of the sea, and low-income housing complexes. It is jam-packed in the summer, eerily deserted in winter. Summer weekends are the worst time to visit; weekday evenings are considerably less frenetic. You can ride the Cyclone, one of the most terrifying roller coasters on the East Coast, and the Wonder Wheel, a giant Ferris wheel alongside the ocean; the parachute jump, a highly visible *Coney Island* landmark, is no longer operational. The actual amusement park is called *Astroland Park* (phone: 718-265-2100) and is open mid-April through mid-June on weekends only, and from mid-June through early September seven days a week, noon to midnight. The famous belugas (white whales) are the stars of the *New York Aquarium,* officially called the *Aquarium for Wildlife Conservation* (Surf Ave. and W. Eighth St.; phone: 718-265-3400). If you get a sudden craving for Italian food, head for *Gargiulo's* (2911 W. 15th St.; phone: 718-266-4891) for some good Neapolitan dishes. Another New York treat is to have hot dogs at *Nathan's Famous* (1310 Surf Ave.; phone: 718-946-2202), an institution generally referred to simply as *Nathan's.* The area's most recent ethnic flavor is provided by a second wave of Russian immigrants, and nearby Brighton Beach has been affectionately dubbed "Little Odessa." From Manhattan take the *IND* line (F, D, or N train) to the Stillwell Avenue station. For further information, call the *Chamber of Commerce* (phone: 718-266-1234).

SHEEPSHEAD BAY This area operates more at the pace of a New England fishing village than a part of New York City. A few anglers sometimes sell their catch on the dock in the early afternoon; charter boats that take people out for the day leave very early in the morning. For the best view of the scene, cross the wooden footbridge at Ocean Avenue and walk along the mile-long esplanade. A few blocks south of the bay is Manhattan Beach, a neighborhood of tree-lined streets and rather elegant homes. Brighton Beach, a few blocks to the east, joins Manhattan Beach with *Coney Island*. From Manhattan take the *IND* line (D or Q train) to the Sheepshead Bay station.

THE BRONX

With almost two million inhabitants, the Bronx is smaller than Brooklyn, and it's the only New York borough on the mainland. Although all the points of interest listed here are safe for visitors, some sections of the Bronx are among the most dangerous in the city. The South Bronx has been nicknamed "Fort Apache" by the police, and officers advise staying clear of any place south of Fordham Road.

BRONX ZOO (INTERNATIONAL WILDLIFE CONSERVATION PARK) In 1993 this zoo's name, along with those of all the *New York Zoological Society's* facilities, was changed to include the word "conservation." Whatever you choose to call it, this is one of the most famous facilities of its kind in the world, with over 265 acres inhabited by more than 4,000 animals. Elephants, tigers, chimps, seals, rhinos, hippos, birds, and buffalo are the favorites. Ride the *Bengali Express* monorail through Wild Asia; visit Jungle World or a children's petting zoo; or survey it all from the *Skyfari* tramway. To get here from Manhattan, take the *IRT* Seventh Avenue line express train (No. 2) to the Pelham Parkway station; walk west to the Bronxdale entrance (for other routes, call the zoo). Open daily. Admission charge, except on Wednesdays; parking charge. Fordham Rd. and Bronx River Pkwy. (phone: 718-367-1010).

NEW YORK BOTANICAL GARDENS Adjoining the zoo to the north, these 250 acres of flowering hills, valleys, woods, and gardens are set in an unspoiled natural forest. The site comprises the only surviving remnants of the original woodland that once covered the city. The *Enid A. Haupt Conservatory* (closed Mondays), a crystal palace with 11 pavilions—each with a totally different environment—is a special treat; call to find out its post-renovation reopening date, scheduled for this summer. Other highlights include a rose garden, azalea glen, daffodil hill, botanical museum, and restaurant. It's well worth the trip, especially in the spring. From Manhattan take the *IND* line (D train) to the Bedford Park station and walk eight blocks east (for other routes, call the gardens). Closed Mondays. Suggested donation; parking charge. Southern Blvd. and E. 200th St. (phone: 718-817-8705).

BRONX MUSEUM OF THE ARTS This museum's changing exhibitions have two themes: contemporary art and the artistic expression of the many ethnic groups who live in the borough. Classical music concerts, film programs, poetry readings, and dance performances are held throughout the year.

From Manhattan take the *IRT* Lexington Avenue line (No. 4 train) to 161st Street, or the *IND* line (C or D train) to 167th Street. Closed Mondays and Tuesdays. Donation suggested. 1040 Grand Concourse at E. 165th St. (phone: 718-681-6000).

EDGAR ALLAN POE COTTAGE Adequately cramped to inspire claustrophobia in anyone larger than a raven, this tiny cottage sits incongruously in the middle of the Grand Concourse. Poe lived here during his last years, and the home contains his personal belongings. Open Sunday afternoons and Saturdays. Admission charge. Grand Concourse at E. Kingsbridge Rd. (phone: 718-881-8900).

WAVE HILL This country mansion set on 28 acres has been a home to Mark Twain, Teddy Roosevelt, Arturo Toscanini, William Thackeray, T. H. Huxley, and Social Darwinist Herbert Spencer. It was eventually donated to the city and features a Gothic Armor Hall and beautiful gardens, as well as a considerable mix of dance, jazz, and classical music performances; call for the schedule. Closed Mondays. No admission charge weekdays. In the elegant, residential Riverdale section of the Bronx at 675 W. 252nd St. (phone: 718-549-3200).

YANKEE STADIUM The home of the *"Bronx Bombers,"* this 55,745-seat stadium is where Babe Ruth, Lou Gehrig, Joe DiMaggio, and dozens of other baseball stars played the national sport. From Manhattan take the *IND* line (C or D train) or the *IRT* Lexington Avenue line (No. 4 train) to East 161st Street. Open during baseball season. River Ave. and E. 161st St. (phone: 718-293-6000).

HALL OF FAME OF GREAT AMERICANS About 100 bronze-cast busts of American presidents, poets, and people noted for achievement in the sciences, arts, and humanities are set atop columns outdoors on the *Bronx Community College* campus. From Manhattan take the *IND* line (D train) to West 183rd Street, or the *IRT* Lexington Avenue line (No. 4 train) to Burnside Avenue. Open daily. No admission charge. University Ave. and W. 181st St. (phone: 718-220-6450).

QUEENS

Manhattanites used to think of Queens as outer suburbia—until Manhattan's skyrocketing rents prompted many middle class folks to take a second look. Actually, Queens is less than a five-minute subway ride from Manhattan's eastern edge and is the largest of the five boroughs. It boasts 118.6 square miles that include major sports facilities, 196 miles of waterfront, numerous parks, cultural centers, universities, two of the metro area's three airports, and even a growing motion picture industry. Queens also is one of the most ethnically diverse areas in the nation, though nationalities tend to congregate in specific pockets. Greeks have settled in Astoria; Hispanics in Corona and Jackson Heights; Asians in Flushing. The largest Hindu temple in North America is found on Bowne Street in Flushing, and Flushing's Chinatown now rivals Manhattan's. These neighborhoods offer a fascinating assortment of restaurants, groceries, and bakeries—Filipino, Italian, Peruvian, Ecuadoran, Colombian, Argentinian, Greek, German—and also sponsor a number of festivals featuring their own foods, crafts, music, and dancing. For information on these activities, call *Queens Borough Hall* (phone: 718-286-3000).

Queens's architectural ambience can change literally from block to block—from pretty Kew Gardens to elegant Jamaica Estates and Bayside Hills, from the quiet row houses of Flushing to the Victorian homes in Richmond Hill, Old Woodhaven, and College Point. Historical sites abound, including the *Friends Meeting House* (137-16 Northern Blvd., Flushing; phone: 718-358-9636). Built in 1694, it is the oldest house of worship in the US.

Sports buffs flock to Queens to see the *Mets* at *Shea Stadium,* the horse races at *Aqueduct* and *Belmont,* and the *US Open Tennis Championships* at the *USTA National Tennis Center* in *Flushing Meadow Park.* There are abundant facilities for golf, tennis, swimming, ice skating, horseback riding, boating, hiking, and bird watching. Lovers of the great outdoors enjoy the borough's wetlands and woodlands, including the two-mile Pitobik Trail; Turtle Pond; *Alley Pond Environmental Center* (phone: 718-229-4000); *Forest Park* (phone: 718-520-5900); *Jamaica Bay Wildlife Refuge* (phone: 718-318-4340); and the *Queens Botanical Gardens,* in Flushing (phone: 718-886-3800).

BOWNE HOUSE Dating from 1661, this was the home of John Bowne, a Quaker credited with winning religious freedom in the Dutch colony of New Amsterdam from Governor Peter Stuyvesant. The house is now a museum, featuring 17th- and 18th-century furnishings, pewter, and paintings. Officially open 2:30 to 4:30 PM, Tuesdays, Saturdays, and Sundays; call ahead to confirm. Admission charge. 37-01 Bowne St., Flushing (phone: 718-359-0528).

KINGSLAND HOUSE AND THE QUEENS HISTORICAL SOCIETY The sole survivor of what was once the prevalent architectural style in Queens, this Dutch colonial/English house dating to circa 1785 contains antique china and assorted memorabilia. Open 2:30 to 4:30 PM, Tuesdays, Saturdays, and Sundays. Admission charge. 143-35 37th Ave., Flushing (phone: 718-939-0647).

KING MANSION Built in the early 18th century, this home was bought by Rufus King, one of the signers of the Constitution, in 1805. Much of the present structure, a fine example of Georgian-Federal architecture, dates from the 19th century, during which time three generations of King descendants added to it. Tours are available by appointment only. Admission charge. Jamaica Ave. and 153rd St., Jamaica (phone: 718-291-0282).

AMERICAN MUSEUM OF THE MOVING IMAGE A national landmark that pays tribute to New York's revitalized film industry, this museum is located in a building that once housed Paramount Pictures' East Coast facilities and is now home to Kaufmann Astoria Studios. In the 1930s and 1940s the Marx

Brothers movies (among others) were produced here; today directors such as Woody Allen, Spike Lee, and Sidney Lumet regularly use this second-largest soundstage in the country. The museum offers lectures and seminars on film and television. An excellent permanent exhibit, "Behind the Screen: Producing, Promoting, and Exhibiting Motion Pictures and Television," displays old movie sets, posters, costumes, and more. Closed Mondays. Admission charge. 35th Ave. and 36th St., Astoria (phone: 718-784-4520).

FLUSHING MEADOW–CORONA PARK The site of the *1939* and *1964 World's Fair*s and the original headquarters of the *UN,* the park is now a center for cultural and outdoor activities (phone: 718-760-6565). The *Queens Museum* hosts a variety of changing exhibitions and includes in its permanent collection a 15,000-square-foot scale model of New York City, updated last year. Closed Mondays; open afternoons only on weekends. Suggested donation (phone: 718-592-2405). The park's *New York Hall of Science* has several permanent exhibits—everything from laser displays to cow's-eye dissections. Closed Mondays and Tuesdays. Admission charge (phone: 718-699-0005). From Manhattan take the *IRT* Flushing line (No. 7 train) to Willets Point/Shea Stadium.

STATEN ISLAND

Much closer to New Jersey than New York, Staten Island is the Big Apple's most remote borough and, with only about 375,000 people, its least populous. This is the borough that keeps threatening to "secede" from the others in New York City's union. In 1993 the island's residents voted two to one in favor of secession, but legislators in Albany, the state capital, have yet to work out what kind of status the borough can be given. Since the Verrazano-Narrows Bridge opened in 1964, Staten Island has been filling up with suburban housing developments and shopping centers, but a few farms remain in the southern reaches. To find them, you can take the bus marked "Richmond Avenue" at the ferry terminal, but getting around by public transportation takes a long time; driving is recommended if at all possible.

STATEN ISLAND ZOO Considerably smaller than the *Bronx Zoo,* this animal house covers eight wooded acres near a lake in *Barret Park.* Its specialty is reptiles of all descriptions. Open daily. Admission charge. 614 Broadway at Clove Rd. (phone: 718-442-3101).

JACQUES MARCHAIS CENTER OF TIBETAN ART One of the more unusual treasures of the city, this is also one of its best-kept secrets. A reconstructed Tibetan prayer hall, featuring an adjoining library and gardens with Oriental sculpture, the center sits on a hill overlooking a pastoral, un–New York setting of trees. *The Tibetan Book of the Dead,* other esoteric tomes, prayer wheels, statuary, and weavings are on display. Open Wednesday through Friday December through March; Wednesday through Sunday April through

November; also open by appointment for group tours. Admission charge. 338 Lighthouse Ave. (phone: 718-987-3478).

CONFERENCE HOUSE Now a national landmark, this manor house was built circa 1680 and hosted such Revolutionary War notables as Benjamin Franklin. Crafts demonstrations are frequently offered; call ahead. Open Wednesday through Sunday afternoons. Admission charge. 7455 Hylan Blvd. (phone: 718-984-6046).

RICHMONDTOWN RESTORATION In this 96-acre park, exhibits and crafts demonstrations depict three centuries of local culture, harking back to the early Dutch settlers. Open Wednesday through Sunday afternoons. Admission charge. 441 Clarke Ave. (phone: 718-351-1617).

Sources and Resources

TOURIST INFORMATION

The *New York Convention and Visitors' Bureau Information Center* (2 Columbus Circle, New York, NY 10019; phone: 397-8222) is an excellent source for hotel and restaurant information, subway and bus maps, descriptive brochures, and current listings of entertainment, special events, and other activities; the office is staffed by multilingual aides. *Big Apple Greeter* (Manhattan Borough President's Office, 1 Centre St., New York, NY 10007; phone: 669-8159) is a program in which New York citizens—from students to seniors—serve as volunteer guides for out-of-towners. Greeters, who are first screened and trained, are matched with a visitor based on the volunteer's expertise and the visitor's interests, needs, and language requirements. During the two- to four-hour neighborhood tours (which usually require at least 24 hours' notice), greeters share their insights and knowledge of their particular slice of the Big Apple. A subscribers-only hotline called *Manhattan Intelligence* provides information on anything from where to pet a lion cub to more mundane data such as cultural events, making restaurant reservations, and finding a parking space for your car (phone: 925-0900 for more information). Call the *New York State Travel Information Center Hotline* (phone: 800-CALL-NYS) for maps, calendars of events, health updates, and travel advisories.

Visitors who require assistance in an emergency—anything from a lost wallet to a lost child—should stop at the *Traveler's Aid Services* office (1481 Broadway; phone: 944-0013); open weekdays from 9 AM to 6 PM (Wednesdays to 1 PM), weekends from 9:30 AM to 3 PM. There is also a branch in the International Arrivals Building at *John F. Kennedy International Airport* (phone: 718-656-4870); open weekdays from 10 AM to 8 PM, weekends from 1 to 8 PM.

Numerous excellent guides to the city's architecture and history are available at most good-size bookstores.

LOCAL COVERAGE *The New York Times,* the *Daily News, New York Newsday,* and the *New York Post* all are morning dailies; the *Village Voice* comes out weekly on Wednesdays. Other publications include the weekly *New Yorker* and *New York* magazines.

TELEVISION STATIONS Channel 2–WCBS; Channel 4–WNBC; Channel 5–WNYW (Fox); Channel 7–WABC; Channel 9–WOR (local); Channel 11–WPIX (local); Channel 13–WNET (PBS).

RADIO STATIONS AM: WFAN 660 (sports/talk); WOR 710 (news/talk); WABC 770 (talk); WCBS 880 (news); WRHD 1570 (oldies). FM: WBGO 88.3 (jazz); WXRK 92.3 (classic rock); WNYC 93.9 (classical); WQXR 96.3 (classical); WNEW 102.7 (rock); WBLS 107.5 (urban contemporary).

FOOD A food-seeker's bible is the *Zagat New York City Restaurant Guide* (Zagat Survey; $9.95). *Restaurants of New York,* by Seymour Britchky (Fireside Paperbacks; $11.95); *Bryan Miller's New York Times Guide to Restaurants in New York City* (Times Books; $12.95); and Mimi Sheraton's *Favorite New York Restaurants* (Simon & Schuster; $9.95) are also excellent.

The *Food Phone* can assist callers in selecting a dining spot according to the neighborhood, type of cuisine, ambience, and price range preferred. Dial 777-FOOD and press the touch-tone buttons as instructed; a recording will deliver brief descriptions of several eateries that meet your specifications. *Menufax* (phone: 800-545-MENU) provides the caller with similar information via fax machine. There is no charge for either service.

TELEPHONE The area code for Manhattan is 212. The area code for the Bronx, Brooklyn, Queens, and Staten Island is 718. The area code for Long Island is 516. Unless otherwise noted, all telephone numbers in this chapter are in Manhattan—area code 212.

SALES TAX New York City's sales tax is 8.25%. The hotel tax is 14.25% plus a $2 per night occupancy tax. Restaurant meals also are taxed 8.25%.

GETTING AROUND

BUS New York City buses run frequently. There are more than 220 routes and over 3,800 buses in operation. Although considerably slower than subways, buses often bring you closer to your destination, stopping about every two blocks, except on express routes, which stop only at major crossings. The main routes in Manhattan are north-south on the avenues and east-west (crosstown) on major cross-streets (such as 14th, 34th, 42nd, 57th, and 72nd Streets), as well as some crisscross and circular routes. Check both the sign on the front of the bus and the one at the bus stop to make sure the bus goes where you want and stops where you are waiting. Be sure to have exact change for the fare or a subway token. *Bus drivers do not make change, nor do they accept bills.* The multiple-use *MetroCard,* introduced early last year, may be used on buses and at some subway stops; it is intended to be in use system-wide by the end of this year. The size of a credit card, the *MetroCard* is run through a scanner, and one fare is deducted each time you use it. Cards are sold at values of $5 to $80.

At press time the per-trip transit fare was $1.25, no matter what the length of your trip or method of payment; on buses a transfer is necessary for any change of bus on a continuous journey and is free, but there is no free transfer from bus to subway or vice versa. Most bus routes operate 24 hours a day, seven days a week, but service is less frequent late at night and on Sundays. For information on buses to points outside Manhattan from the *Port Authority Bus Terminal* (Eighth Ave. and W. 42nd St.), call 564-8184 or 564-1114. Free bus maps are available at *Grand Central* and *Penn Stations* or by sending a self-addressed, stamped legal-size (#10) envelope to the *New York Transit Authority,* Room 875, 370 Jay St., Brooklyn, NY 11201, Attn.: Maps.

CAR RENTAL For information on renting a car, see GETTING READY TO GO.

SUBWAY The New York subway system has a reputation for being dangerous, dirty, and confusing. The reality is not quite so harrowing as most people fear. The past several years have brought many new trains, tracks, and station improvements to this extensive underground network, as well as an increased transit police presence. The system's convenience and speed can't be duplicated by any other form of transportation. Pick up free subway maps at token booths or at the *New York Convention and Visitors' Bureau Information Center* (see above); system maps are in most cars—but usually not outside on the platforms. Keep in mind that certain interchange stations are large and confusing, so if you don't find a sign that confirms you are on the right platform, double-check with another passenger or any transit worker. Also double-check that you don't board an express if you are better served by a local; the map makes the distinctions relatively clear, but even New Yorkers occasionally whiz 50 or more blocks beyond a desired stop when they don't pay attention to which train they are boarding.

Basically, there are three different subway lines, with express and local routes serving all city boroughs except Staten Island (reached via the *Staten Island Ferry*). The most extensive is the *IRT,* which originates in Brooklyn and travels north through Manhattan en route to the Bronx. The *IRT* has two main divisions: the Seventh Avenue line, which serves the West Side of Manhattan, and the Lexington Avenue line, which covers the East Side. You can go from east to west (crosstown) on the shuttle (S) or *IRT* No. 7 train (which goes to Flushing, Queens) between *Grand Central Station* and Times Square, and the L train will take you crosstown at 14th Street. The *IND* line serves Brooklyn, Queens, Manhattan, and the Bronx. The *BMT* line serves Brooklyn, Queens, and Manhattan.

The subway is the most heavily used means of city transportation (about four million people ride it daily on 722 miles of track) and so is mobbed during rush hours—weekdays from 7:30 to a little after 9 AM and from

4:30 to 7 PM. The fare at press time was $1.25 (no matter how far you travel or how many times you change trains without exiting), but there have been some rumblings about a possible fare hike. Tokens or a *MetroCard* are required to enter. Buy them at booths in the subway stations, and insert them in turnstiles to gain access to the trains. Buy a 10-pack of tokens to save time (but not money); the introduction of the multiple-fare *MetroCard* last year (see *Buses*, above) should also streamline subway entry.

The subway system operates 24 hours a day, although most schedules are cut back between midnight and 6 AM. At night the lights outside many stations indicate accessibility: A red light means the station is closed; a yellow light indicates that the station is open but no one is on duty at the token booth; and a green light means both the station and token booth are open. Whenever possible, try to avoid traveling alone late at night when stations and train cars are more deserted and transit police officers are few and far between. For general bus and subway information, call the *New York Transit Authority* (phone: 718-330-1234).

TAXI The handiest—albeit one of the most expensive—ways to get around the city is by taxi. Cabs can be identified by their yellow color and are available if the center portion of the roof light is on (if the *entire* roof light is either on or off, this means that the cab is off-duty, on call, or already occupied). They can be hailed almost anywhere and if on-duty, they are required by law to pick you up and deliver you to your specified destination. New Yorkers generally tip cabbies about 20% of the metered fare. There is a 50¢ surcharge on most cab fares between 8 PM and 6 AM and all day Sundays. Passengers must pay any bridge and/or tunnel tolls. The *New York City Taxi and Limousine Commission* (phone: 221-TAXI) publishes a pamphlet called "How to Use a New York City Taxi." It lists rates, sample fares to common destinations, and other useful information.

New York also has dozens of companies that provide conventional sedans with drivers and can be called by phone (known locally as "car services"). Fares run somewhere between those of yellow street cabs and limousines, but are usually cheaper than both for long-distance runs, such as to airports, because a fixed fee is charged. Two such companies are *Dialcar* (phone: 718-743-8383) and *Love* (phone: 718-633-3338).

LOCAL SERVICES

AUDIOVISUAL EQUIPMENT *Ace Sound Rental Co.* (13 E. 31st St.; phone: 685-3344); *Select Audio Visual* (460 W. 34th St.; phone: 290-4800).

BABY-SITTING Ask at your hotel desk for recommendations.

BUSINESS SERVICES *QED Transcription Service* (phone: 563-0740) or *Wordflow* (phone: 725-5111) for taping and immediate transcription of meetings and seminars.

COMPUTER AND TYPEWRITER RENTAL *Cavalier,* two-week minimum (phone: 682-1780); *Business Office Equipment,* from computers to office tables and chairs, weekly rate only (phone: 265-4550).

DRY CLEANER/TAILOR *Newman Cleaners & Dyers* (914 Seventh Ave., between W. 57th and W. 58th Sts.; phone: 247-5207); *S & A Cleaners & Tailors* (134½ E. 62nd St.; phone: 838-0630). There is a high density of dry cleaners in Manhattan, especially in residential areas, and almost all hotels have cleaning and tailoring services.

FORMALWEAR RENTALS *Baldwin Formals* (phone: 245-8190) for classic and designer tuxedos and men's formal accessories, including collapsible top hats; *One Night Stand* (phone: 772-7720) has designer gowns and women's accessories, priced from $120 to $350 per evening. Note: Many rental outlets require appointments.

LIMOUSINE SERVICES *Gotham Limousine* (phone: 868-8860 or 800-227-7997); *London Town Cars* (phone: 988-9700; 800-221-4009 outside of New York); *SoHo Car and Limo Service* (phone: 431-9090 or 800-441-7646).

MECHANIC *Express Auto* (276 Seventh Ave.; phone: 242-5811) for 24-hour road service and repairs.

MEDICAL EMERGENCY For information on area hospitals and pharmacies, see GETTING READY TO GO.

MESSENGER SERVICES *Accurate Messenger Service* (phone: 688-5450); *Bullit Messenger Manpower,* 24-hour service (phone: 983-7400).

PHOTOCOPIES *Amal Printing* (630 Fifth Ave., in *Rockefeller Center;* phone: 247-3270); *Commerce Photo-Print,* open late and weekends by appointment (106 Fulton St., in the Wall Street area; phone: 964-2256).

POST OFFICES For information on local branch offices, see GETTING READY TO GO.

PROFESSIONAL PHOTOGRAPHER *Matar Studio* (101 Maiden La.; phone: 809-0080).

SECRETARY/STENOGRAPHER *A Steno Service* (phone: 682-4990); or inquire at your hotel.

TELECONFERENCE FACILITIES The *New York Hilton, Sheraton Manhattan, Sheraton New York,* and the *Waldorf-Astoria* have facilities available to guests (see *Checking In* for all four).

TRANSLATORS *Berlitz* (phone: 777-7878); *Lawyers & Merchants* (phone: 344-2930); *Translation Aces* (phone: 269-4660).

WESTERN UNION/TELEX *Western Union* (phone: 661-9595; 800-325-6000) has many offices in the city. For information on money transfers, see GETTING READY TO GO.

OTHER *ETX Corp.,* simultaneous teleprocessing (phone: 927-8555); *HQ, Headquarters Company,* word processing, telex, fax, and conference rooms (phone: 949-0722); *International Conference Group,* meeting and conference planners (phone: 941-0022); *Miller Associates,* videotaping of meetings (phone: 741-8011); *Manhattan Passport,* a private concierge enterprise providing travel arrangements and customized shopping and sightseeing tours, among other services (phone: 744-0203); *Video Monitoring Service,* for broadcast information, tapes, and transcripts (phone: 736-2010).

SPECIAL EVENTS

January or February (the first full moon after January 21), *Chinese New Year Celebration and Dragon Parade,* Chinatown; March 17, *St. Patrick's Day Parade,* Fifth Avenue; *Easter Sunday, Easter Parade,* Fifth Avenue; May, *Ninth Avenue International Food Festival;* May, *Washington Square Outdoor Art Show,* Greenwich Village; first Sunday in June, *Puerto Rican Day Parade,* Fifth Avenue; late June to early July, *JVC Jazz Festival; July 4th, Macy's* fireworks along the East River; July and August, free *Shakespeare Festival, Delacorte Theater, Central Park,* and free performances of the *New York Philharmonic* and *Metropolitan Opera,* all boroughs; August, *Harlem Week;* late August and September, *US Open Tennis Championships, USTA National Tennis Center, Flushing Meadow Park,* Queens; September, *African-American Day Parade;* September, the 10-day *Festival of San Gennaro,* patron saint of Neapolitans, Mulberry Street, Little Italy; September and October, *New York Film Festival, Lincoln Center;* October, *Columbus Day Parade,* Fifth Avenue; October 31, *Halloween Parade,* Greenwich Village; November, *NYC Marathon, Central Park* (finish line); November, *Veterans Day Parade,* Fifth Avenue; November, *Macy's Thanksgiving Day Parade,* Broadway; December, *Christmas Tree Lighting,* Rockefeller Plaza; November through January, the *Great Christmas Show, Radio City Music Hall.*

For borough-by-borough information on parades, festivals, exhibits, and free events, call 360-1333 (Manhattan); 718-625-0080 (Brooklyn); 718-590-3500 (Bronx); 718-447-4485 (Staten Island); and 718-291-ARTS (Queens).

MUSEUMS

The city boasts more than 150 museums. In addition to those described in *Special Places,* other notable New York museums include the following:

AMERICAN CRAFT MUSEUM Jewelry, rugs, textiles, metal crafts, and other exhibits. Closed Mondays. Admission charge; under 12, free. 40 W. 53rd St. (phone: 956-6047).

ASIA SOCIETY Changing exhibits of ancient and contemporary Asian art. Closed Mondays. Admission charge except Thursday evenings; under 12, free. 725 Park Ave. at E. 70th St. (phone: 288-6400).

CHILDREN'S MUSEUM OF THE ARTS Hands-on, interactive exhibits with arts-related themes. Children are encouraged to design and make their own collages, clay models, and paintings. Closed Mondays. Admission charge except for children 18 months or younger. 72-78 Spring St. (phone: 941-9198).

COOPER-HEWITT MUSEUM The *National Museum of Design* branch of the *Smithsonian Institution,* featuring a full range of decorative arts. Closed Mondays. Admission charge except for children under 12. 2 E. 91st St. at Fifth Ave. (phone: 860-6868).

FORBES MAGAZINE GALLERIES World's largest collection of Fabergé Imperial Russian *Easter* eggs plus model boats and soldiers. Closed Sundays and Mondays; Thursdays are reserved for guided tours. No admission charge. 62 Fifth Ave. at 12th St. (phone: 206-5548).

FRAUNCES TAVERN MUSEUM This landmark building, the site of Washington's farewell to his officers in 1783, contains memorabilia of the American Revolution (including Washington's hat). Open weekdays and Saturday afternoons. Admission charge. The *Fraunces Tavern* restaurant (269-0144) occupies the ground floor. 54 Pearl St. at Broad St. (phone: 425-1776).

FRICK COLLECTION This magnificent mansion, the former home of Pittsburgh industrialist Henry Clay Frick, houses his staggering collection of sculpture, porcelain, furniture, antiques, and Old Master paintings—among them Renoir's *Mother and Children,* Fragonard's *The Progress of Love,* Rembrandt's *Polish Rider* and a self-portrait, Giovanni Bellini's *St. Francis in Ecstasy,* three canvases by Vermeer, Holbein's portraits of Sir Thomas More and Thomas Cromwell, and works by El Greco, David, Gainsborough, Goya, Lawrence, Reynolds, and Turner. Closed Mondays. Admission charge; children under 10 not permitted. 1 E. 70th St. at Fifth Ave. (phone: 288-0700).

GUINNESS WORLD OF RECORDS Displays featuring feats and strange facts from the *Guinness Book of Records.* The exhibits include life-size models of the tallest, fattest, and shortest men in the world, videos of records being reached, and computer-generated displays. Open daily. Admission charge except for children under three. In the *Empire State Building,* 350 Fifth Ave., from W. 33rd to W. 34th St. (phone: 947-2335).

INTERNATIONAL CENTER OF PHOTOGRAPHY Rotating exhibits of the latest works by internationally renowned photographers; occasionally, these are arranged around particular themes, such as the Holocaust. Closed Mondays. Admission charge. 1130 Fifth Ave. at 94th St. (phone: 860-1777) and 1133 Sixth Ave. at W. 43rd St. (phone: 768-4683).

INTREPID SEA-AIR-SPACE MUSEUM This World War II aircraft carrier has exhibits on the navy, pioneers in aviation, and technology. A lightship (a seagoing lighthouse) and a MiG-21 fighter jet are part of the "fleet," which also includes a submarine and a battleship. Open daily from *Memorial Day* through *Labor*

Day; closed Mondays and Tuesdays the rest of the year. Admission charge except for children under six. Permanently moored at Pier 86 in the Hudson River, 12th Ave. and W. 46th St. (phone: 245-0072 or 245-2533).

JEWISH MUSEUM Reopened in 1993 after a $50-million expansion and renovation, this museum houses a permanent collection of more than 27,000 works of art, artifacts, ceremonial objects, and more, spanning 4,000 years of Jewish history. Closed Fridays, Saturdays, and major Jewish holidays. Admission charge except for children under 12. 1109 Fifth Ave. at 92nd St. (phone: 423-3200).

LOWER EAST SIDE TENEMENT MUSEUM Reopened last year, America's first urban "living history" museum features a restored replica of a 19th-century tenement building, as well as photographs, drawings, and documents recounting the lives of immigrants. Walking tours and a Wednesday slide show are also offered. Closed Mondays and Saturdays. Donation suggested; admission charge for the slide show. 97 Orchard St. (phone: 431-0233).

MUSEO DEL BARRIO Dedicated to the arts and culture of Puerto Rico, including painting, sculpture, concerts, photography, and films. Closed Mondays and Tuesdays. Donation suggested. 1230 Fifth Ave. at 104th St. (phone: 831-7272).

MUSEUM FOR AFRICAN ART A recently enlarged facility featuring sculpture, paintings, and crafts in both contemporary and traditional styles. The emphasis is on artisans from Zaire, Cameroon, Ghana, and the Ivory Coast. There are also art-history seminars. Closed Mondays. Admission charge. 593 Broadway, between Houston and Prince Sts. (phone: 966-1313).

MUSEUM OF AMERICAN FOLK ART Educational programs, exhibits, and publications devoted to American folk art from the 18th century to the present. Closed Mondays. Donation suggested. Columbus Ave. and W. 66th St. (phone: 595-9533).

MUSEUM OF TELEVISION AND RADIO Formerly the *Museum of Broadcasting,* this repository of over 40,000 radio and television programs and commercials hosts frequent seminars and has excellent research facilities. Closed Sundays and Mondays. Suggested admission charge. 25 W. 52nd St. (phone: 621-6600).

MUSEUM OF THE CITY OF NEW YORK A free video show, "The Big Apple," is a permanent attraction here; there are also temporary exhibits focusing on the city. Closed Mondays and Tuesdays. Donation suggested. Fifth Ave. and 103rd St. (phone: 534-1672).

NATIONAL MUSEUM OF THE AMERICAN INDIAN A comprehensive collection of artifacts linked to the indigenous peoples of all the Americas, this museum, part of Washington, DC's *Smithsonian Institution,* also is known as the *George Gustav Heye Center,* named after a major collector. Last year it relocated from West 155th Street to the *Alexander Hamilton US Custom House* at the southern tip of the island. The new facility, which features changing displays of its one million objects, also stages educational workshops, film and video festivals, and performances of Native American dance, music, and theater. Although the focus is on North, Central, and South American peoples, there are ethnological materials from as far away as Siberia. Open daily year-round except *Christmas Day.* No admission charge. 1 *Bowling Green* (phone: 668-NMAI).

NEW-YORK HISTORICAL SOCIETY Established in the early 19th century, this institution is a repository of paintings by the Hudson River School, and more; it houses a library of some 700,000 volumes on the history of New York City and New York State. Sadly, most of the society closed in 1993 due to lack of funding, but the library remains open. Closed weekends. No admission charge. 170 Central Park W. at W. 76th St. (phone: 873-3400).

NEW YORK TRANSIT MUSEUM Old subway cars and other nostalgic and informative metropolitan memorabilia plus changing exhibitions (including some very imaginative ones geared to children), a lecture series, and tours. Closed Mondays. Admission charge except for children under two. Boerum Pl. and Schermerhorn St., Brooklyn (phone: 718-330-3060).

NOGUCHI MUSEUM This garden museum features more than 300 of Isamu Noguchi's works, including sculptures in stone, clay, and wood; paper lamps; and plans for fountains and playgrounds. Open Wednesdays and Saturdays from April through November. Donation suggested. 32-37 Vernon Blvd., Long Island City, Queens (phone: 718-204-7088).

PIERPONT MORGAN LIBRARY AND ANNEX These elegant buildings house Old Masters' drawings, early printed books, music manuscripts, plus a private research library. A superb collection of medieval and Renaissance illuminated manuscripts is also on display. The facility includes the adjacent *Morgan House;* the two buildings are linked by the beautifully designed, glass-enclosed Garden Court—a pleasant place to take a breather from viewing exhibits. Closed Mondays. Donation suggested. 29 E. 36th St. at Madison Ave. (phone: 685-0610).

STUDIO MUSEUM OF HARLEM An impressive collection of works by African-American artists. Closed Mondays and Tuesdays. Admission charge. 144 W. 125th St. (phone: 864-4500).

MAJOR COLLEGES AND UNIVERSITIES

New York City is the home of many leading institutions of higher education, some offering a broad-based liberal arts curriculum, others concentrating in areas of specialization, and all enriching the city as a center of culture and learning. Among them are *Barnard College* (Broadway and W. 117th St.; phone: 854-5262); *Brooklyn College* (Bedford Ave. and Ave. H; phone: 718-951-5000); *City College of New York* (Convent Ave.

and W. 138th St.; phone: 650-7000); *Columbia University* (Broadway and W. 116th St.; phone: 854-1754); *Cooper Union* (Third Ave. and Seventh St.; phone: 254-6300); *Fashion Institute of Technology* (227 W. 27th St.; phone: 760-7700); *Fordham University* (Columbus Ave. and W. 60th St.; phone: 636-6000; and Third Ave. and E. Fordham Rd, Bronx; phone: 718-579-2000); *Hunter College* (695 Park Ave.; phone: 772-4000); *Jewish Theological Seminary of America* (Broadway and W. 122nd St.; phone: 678-8000); *Juilliard School of Music* (Lincoln Center; phone: 799-5000); *Manhattan School of Music* (120 Claremont Ave.; phone: 749-2802); *Mannes College of Music* (105 W. 85th St.; phone: 580-0210); *Marymount Manhattan College* (221 E. 71st St.; phone: 517-0400); *New School for Social Research* (66 W. 12th St.; phone: 229-5600); *New York Institute of Technology* (1855 Broadway at W. 61st St.; phone: 399-8300); *New York University* (Washington Sq.; phone: 998-1212); *Pace University* (1 Pace Plaza, near *City Hall;* phone: 346-1200); *Parsons School of Design* (Fifth Ave. and 12th St.; phone: 229-5600); *Pratt Institute* (200 Willoughby Ave., Brooklyn; phone: 718-636-3600); *Queens College* (65-30 Kissena Blvd., Flushing; phone: 718-520-7000); *St. John's University* (Jamaica, Queens; phone: 718-990-6750); *Union Theological Seminary* (3041 Broadway at W. 120th St.; phone: 662-7100); and *Yeshiva University* (500 W. 185th St. at Amsterdam Ave.; phone: 960-5400).

SHOPPING

This city is like no other for acquiring material possessions. It is the commercial center and the fashion capital of the country, and styles that originate here set the trends for fashionable folk from Portland, Maine, to Portland, Oregon. The scope of merchandise available approaches the infinite, and the best part of all is that there are goodies for every budget.

ANTIQUES "Antiques Row" is a district extending from E. 10th Street to E. 14th Street, from Broadway to University Place, with many former wholesalers now open to the public. Elsewhere, there is the *Chelsea Antiques Building* (110 W. 25th St.; phone: 929-0909); the year-round, weekends-only *Indoor Antiques Fair* (122 W. 26th St.; phone: 627-4700), with two floors and 65 vendors; and the nearby *Annex Flea Market,* which spreads from W. 24th to W. 26th St. along the Avenue of the Americas (Sixth Avenue), with more than 150 vendors (this is not for ultraserious museum collectors, but a discerning eye can ferret out some exquisite pieces from an extensive collection that includes jewelry, decorative objects, and furniture). Much further west is *John Koch Antiques* (514 W. 24th St., between 10th and 11th Aves., Third Floor; phone: 243-8625), which sells estate objects from the everyday to the elegant. A down-market, downtown source is the *Soho Antiques Fair and Collectibles* (Broadway and Grand St.; phone: 682-2000); this weekend outdoor flea market sells an enormous variety of trinkets, clothes, photographic and electronic equipment, furniture, art, housewares, and oddities. For a selection of other good antiques districts and shops, like East

60th Street between Second and Third Avenues, see *Antiques: New York's Best Hunting Grounds* in DIVERSIONS.

BED AND TABLE LINENS For good buys on top-quality and designer sheets and pillowcases, New York is definitely the place. At *H & G Cohen Bedding* (306 Grand St.; phone: 226-0818), all the major brands are available at a 25 to 30% discount. (This, like most Lower East Side shops, is closed Saturdays but open Sundays.) *D. Porthault* (18 E. 69th St.; phone: 688-1660) is the French master of extraordinary table and bed linens, many in magnificent floral prints; *Léron* (750 Madison Ave.; phone: 753-6700) imports exquisite bed and table linens and lingerie. *Pratesi* (829 Madison Ave.; phone: 288-2315) and *Frette* (799 Madison Ave.; phone: 988-5221) offer a wide selection of the finest bed, bath, and table linens manufactured at the companies' factories in Italy. The third floor at *ABC Carpet & Home* (888 Broadway; phone: 473-3000) is stocked with hundreds of down comforters, blankets, pillows, tablecloths and napkins, and sheets and pillowcases from the most prestigious domestic and European houses; the nine-floor emporium, which underwent expansion last year, also sells a large selection of furniture and home textiles and accessories. In the Wall Street vicinity, *Century 21* (22 Cortland St., between Broadway and Church St.; phone: 227-9092), which is better known for clothing, has a large collection of discounted linens.

BOOKSTORES The publishing capital of the world, New York is a bibliophile's delight. *Barnes & Noble* (105 Fifth Ave. at W. 18th St.; phone: 807-0099; 675 Ave. of the Americas at 21st St.; phone: 727-1227; 600 Fifth Ave. at W. 48th St.; phone: 765-0590; 2289 Broadway at W. 82nd St.; phone: 362-8835; and 1280 Lexington Ave., between 86th and 87th Sts.; phone: 423-9900) carries wide selections, some at discounted prices. *B. Dalton* (666 Fifth Ave. at W. 53rd St.; phone: 247-1740; and 396 Ave. of the Americas at W. Eighth St.; phone: 674-8780) and *Doubleday* (724 Fifth Ave., between W. 56th and W. 57th Sts.; phone: 397-0550) carry a broad variety of new titles and trade books, as does *Coliseum Books* (1771 Broadway at W. 57th St.; phone: 757-8381). The *Strand* (828 Broadway at E. 12th St.; phone: 473-1452) has eight miles of old and used books and even some rare manuscripts. *Rizzoli* (31 W. 57th St.; phone: 759-2424; 454 West Broadway; phone: 674-1616; and in the *Winter Garden* of the *World Financial Center* at 200 Vesey St.; phone: 385-1400) is best known for its collection of art, music, and photography books. *Kitchen Arts & Letters* (1435 Lexington Ave. at E. 93rd St.; phone: 876-5550) is a bookstore and gallery devoted exclusively to food and wine. *Forbidden Planet* (821 Broadway at E. 12th St.; phone: 473-1576) has the wackiest bunch of comics, science fiction books, masks, and monsters you're liable to find this side of Mars. The *New York Astrology Center* (545 Eighth Ave.; phone: 947-3609) claims to have the country's largest selection of books on astrology. The *Complete Traveller Bookstore* (199 Madison Ave. at E. 35th St.; phone: 685-9007) and the *Traveller's Bookstore* (22 W. 52nd St., in *Rockefeller Center;* phone: 664-0995) have enviable troves of travel guides and books. Architecture buffs should head to *Perimeter* (146 Sullivan St.; phone: 529-2275), and bookish toddlers will be delighted by *Books of Wonder* (132 Seventh Ave.; phone: 989-3270).

BOUTIQUES AND SPECIALTY SHOPS Fifth Avenue in the 50s, the adjacent blocks east (especially East 57th Street), and Madison Avenue in the East 60s and 70s are lined with boutiques that carry haute couture at haute prices, but looking is free. The names are an encyclopedia of style: *Armani, Chanel, Daniel Hechter, Emanuel Ungaro, Gucci, MaxMara, Saint Laurent, Sonia Rykiel, Valentino, Versace,* and the like. Also on the cutting edge of fashion are the styles at *Charivari* (441 Columbus Ave. at W. 81st St.; phone: 496-8700; and five other locations around town). For the finest in rainwear and traditional British tailoring, there's *Burberrys* (9 E. 57th St.; phone: 371-5010) and *Aquascutum of London* (680 Fifth Ave. at W. 54th St.; phone: 975-0250). *Ashanti* (872 Lexington Ave. at E. 65th St.; phone: 535-0740) specializes in stylish clothes for fuller-figured women. *Polo/Ralph Lauren* (867 Madison Ave. at E. 72nd St.; phone: 606-2100), in the 19th-century *Rhinelander Mansion,* is a showcase for the designer's men's, women's, and boys' collections; across the street is *Polo Sport* (888 Madison Ave.; phone: 434-8000). *Fendi* (720 Fifth Ave. at W. 56th St.; phone: 767-0100) features exclusive leather goods and clothes.

CDS, TAPES, AND RECORDS There are a number of places where you can get good prices. *Tower Records* (692 Broadway at E. Fourth St.; phone: 505-1500; 215 E. 86th St.; phone: 369-2500; and 1965 Broadway at W. 66th St.; phone: 799-2500) has enormous music stores open until midnight every day of the year. *J&R Music World* (33 Park Row, near *City Hall;* phone: 349-0062) has the best selection of new and hard-to-find jazz records at good prices. The *House of Oldies* (35 Carmine St.; phone: 243-0500) specializes in records from the past; the *Gryphon Record Shop* (251 W. 72nd St., between Broadway and West End Ave.; phone: 874-1588) has 60,000 out-of-print recordings. *HMV* (1280 Lexington Ave. at E. 86th St.; phone: 348-0800; and 2081 Broadway at W. 72nd St.; phone: 721-5900), another gigantic music retailer, has an extensive selection of jazz, blues, gospel, rock, pop, New Age, and new and vintage Broadway show music. For sheet music try the *Music Exchange* (151 W. 46th St.; phone: 354-5858) or the *Joseph Patelson Music House* (160 W. 65th St.; phone: 582-5840).

CHINA, CRYSTAL, AND PORCELAIN The retail branch of *Villeroy & Boch* (974 Madison Ave. at E. 76th St.; phone: 535-2500) carries a full line of elegant tableware. *Royal Copenhagen* (683 Madison Ave. at E. 61st St.; phone: 759-6457) has all that's best in contemporary Danish crystal and porcelain. *Michael C. Fina* (3 W. 47th St.; phone: 869-5050), suitably located in the diamond district, carries a wide selection of the top names in china, crystal, and silver at reasonable prices. For splendid glass sculpture, bowls, and goblets, head for *Steuben Glass* (717 Fifth Ave. at E. 56th St.; phone: 752-1441).

DEPARTMENT STORES *Bloomingdale's* (Lexington Ave. from E. 59th to E. 60th St.; phone: 355-5900 or 705-2073), a world unto itself known affectionately to New Yorkers as *"Bloomie's,"* is considered by many to be the ultimate in Upper East Side chic. *Macy's* (Broadway from W. 34th to W. 35th St.; phone: 695-4400) is the largest New York department store, where you can choose from a huge assortment of high-quality goods. *Macy's* basement emporium, *The Cellar,* is designed as a street of shops carrying everything from fruits and vegetables to housewares, plus restaurants, including the *Cellar Grill,* which serves pizza, pasta, and grilled meats. *Lord & Taylor* (Fifth Ave. from W. 38th to W. 39th St.; phone: 391-3344) has stylish, if conservative, clothing and a bright, airy atmosphere that makes browsing enjoyable. *Saks Fifth Avenue* (Fifth Ave. from E. 49th to E. 50th St.; phone: 753-4000) is where you can be sure to get whatever is fashionable this season. *Bergdorf Goodman* (Fifth Ave. and W. 58th St.) is the epitome of elegant shopping for women; *Bergdorf Goodman Men* is directly across the street (phone: 753-7300 for both). *Henri Bendel* (Fifth Ave. and W. 56th St.; phone: 247-1100) carries an impressively stylish yet often whimsical selection of women's clothes, accessories, and miscellany.

Forward-looking *Barneys New York* is a major fashion player, and the flagship Seventh Avenue store's arty *Christmas* windows are a big draw. The oh-so-posh uptown and *Financial Center* branches carry the same upscale goods (106 Seventh Ave., from W. 16th to W. 17th St.; phone: 929-9000; 225 Liberty St., in the *World Financial Center;* phone: 945-1600; and 660 Madison Ave. at E. 61st St.; phone: 826-8900). *Abraham & Straus (A & S;* Sixth Ave. and W. 33rd St.; phone: 594-8500; and 420 Fulton St. in downtown Brooklyn; phone: 718-875-7200) carries a complete stock of moderately priced goods.

FABRICS AND TRIMMINGS Fabulous silks, imported woolens, and dazzling cotton prints for home decorating or homemade haute couture are available, often at greatly discounted prices, at a number of fascinating and abundant fabric emporiums. *Silk Surplus* (235 E. 58th St.; phone: 753-6511); its nearby annex (223 E. 58th St.; phone: 759-1294); and a third location on the Upper East Side (1147 Madison Ave., between E. 85th and E. 86th Sts.; phone: 794-9373) carry closeouts from their parent company, Scalamandre. While discounts generally are only about 15%, better bargains can be had during June and October sales. A small branch of *Liberty of London* (630 Fifth Ave.; phone: 391-2150) offers a sampling of popular textiles and notions from one of Britain's leading stores. *Paron* (60 W. 57th St.) specializes in discounted designer woolens, cottons, silks, and linen. Even better prices—up to 50% off—can be found on the second floor next door at *Paron*'s super-discount store (56 W. 57th St.; phone: 247-6451 for both). On the Lower East Side, *Interiors by Royale* (289 Grand St.; phone: 431-0170) features fine English linen, tapestries, and cotton prints imported from Italy, Spain, and France at discounts of up to 50%. And to add just the right finishing touch, visit *Tender Buttons* (143 E. 62nd St.; phone: 758-7004). The selection of antique and contemporary buttons here is extraordinary, if pricey. For less costly trim, there are dazzling displays at *G & P Buttons and Novelties* (247 W. 37th St.; phone: 719-5333).

FOOD In a city where one can dine out every night of the year at a different ethnic restaurant, it isn't surprising that delicacies and exotic foodstuffs are staples in a host of upscale grocery shops. Whether you're looking for a little something for a picnic, a snack for back at the hotel, a gift for your host, hostess, or the folks back home, or you merely want to take in a dazzling display of way-beyond-average comestibles, a visit to one of the following shops can be a most memorable part of your New York visit. *Zabar's* (2245 Broadway at W. 80th St.; phone: 787-2000) is a Manhattan institution—a huge, noisy emporium with a mock-Tudor exterior where thousands of New Yorkers and suburbanites stock up each day on pastrami, lox, fresh-roasted coffee beans, bread, pungent cheeses, luscious dried fruit, unusual condiments, and the very latest imported delicacies. *Balducci's* (424 Ave. of the Americas at W. Ninth St.; phone: 673-2600) and the flagship of *Dean & Deluca* (560 Broadway at Prince St.; phone: 431-1691; as well as six other locations) offer pricier fresh fruits and vegetables, plus wonderful imported foods and spices, fresh pasta, and great bread. Worth a visit on the Upper East Side are *Grace's Marketplace* (1237 Third Ave. at E. 71st St.; phone: 737-0600), for phenomenally fresh produce, imported coffees, spices, jams, and preserves, and *Fraser Morris Fine Foods* (1264 Third Ave. at E. 73rd St.; phone: 288-2727), which features items such as fresh caviar, salmon, and imported chocolates and pastries. For an intoxicating sampling of herbs, condiments, spices, and packaged goods from around the world, go to *Adriana's Bazaar* (2152 Broadway, between W. 75th and W. 76th Sts.; phone: 877-5757).

JEWELRY AND GEMS Diamonds are a girl's best friend, but so as not to limit ourselves, we'll include emeralds, rubies, sapphires, pearls, gold, silver, and other precious stones and metals. And so as not to discriminate, we'll include men too. Without a doubt, the most famous of all luxury emporiums is *Tiffany & Co.* (727 Fifth Ave. at E. 57th St.; phone: 755-8000). If you must have something from *Tiffany's* but can't afford a necklace or ring, purchase a novelty like a sterling silver key ring, bookmark, or toothpaste roller. Across the street, *Bulgari* dazzles in its prestigious corner boutique (730 Fifth Ave.; phone: 315-9000). *Cartier* (653 Fifth Ave. at E. 52nd St.; phone: 753-0111; and in *Trump Tower,* 725 Fifth Ave. at E. 56th St.; phone: 308-0840) is renowned for some of the world's finest jewelry and accessories. *Fortunoff* (681 Fifth Ave., between E. 53rd and E. 54th Sts.; phone: 758-6660) has a more moderately priced selection of fine gems, sterling, and gold. *Fred Leighton* (773 Madison Ave. at E. 66th St.; phone: 288-1872; and in *Trump Tower,* 725 Fifth Ave. at E. 56th St.; phone: 751-2330) is known for its exquisite antique and Art Deco designs. For pearls of quality in quantity, try *Mikimoto* (608 Fifth Ave., between W. 48th and W. 49th Sts.; phone: 586-7153). For watches, go to *Tourneau Corner* (500 Madison Ave. at E. 52nd St.; phone: 758-6098; and Madison Ave. and E. 59th St.; phone: 758-6688).

If your budget is limited, do your gem shopping along West 47th Street (the street sign here reads: "Diamond and Jewelry Way") between Fifth and Sixth Avenues. This is the heart of New York's wholesale jewelry district, whose vendors are largely Hasidic Jews of European background, and the best place to find sparkling stuff at mortal prices. If you're planning to get married (or even reaffirm your vows), *1873 Unusual Wedding Bands* (Booth 86 at the *National Jewelery Exchange,* 4 W. 47th St.; phone: 221-1873) is a good place to stop; it has the largest selection of wedding rings in the city.

KITCHEN EQUIPMENT At the *Bridge Co.* (214 E. 52nd St. at Third Ave.; phone: 688-4220), you'll find every possible domestic and imported item, from cherry pitters to copper fish poachers, on display on four floors. The *Broadway Panhandler* (520 Broadway at Spring St.; phone: 966-3434) has an enormous selection of cookware at affordable prices. *Williams-Sonoma* (110 Seventh Ave.; phone: 633-2203; 20 E. 60th St.; phone: 980-5155; and 1175 Madison Ave. at E. 86th St.; phone: 289-6832), of catalogue fame, carries first-rate cookware, and master chefs often do demonstrations on the premises. *Zabar's* (see *Food,* above) has a second floor stocked with a huge selection of kitchenware at competitive prices. In the Bowery, New York's kitchenware and lamp district, you'll find stores selling commercial products at reasonable prices.

LEATHER GOODS AND LUGGAGE You'll have no trouble finding a wide selection of both high- and low-priced leather goods and luggage in New York. *Hermès* (11 E. 57th St.; phone: 751-3181) is headquartered in Paris but known the world over for spectacular silk scarves and ties, as well as saddles and other fine leather goods in a variety of exotic skins, all at heart-stopping prices. *Prada Milan* (45 E. 57th St.; phone: 308-2332) has perhaps the best-quality leather goods and shoes from Italy. *Louis Vuitton* (51 E. 57th St.; phone: 371-6111) has a large selection of leather goods, many sporting the famous "LV" logo. If you prefer interlocking "G"s, visit *Gucci* (685 Fifth Ave. at E. 54th St.; phone: 826-2600). For elegant, high-quality merchandise that's only slightly less costly, try *Crouch & Fitzgerald* (400 Madison Ave. at E. 48th St.; phone: 755-5888) or *Mark Cross* (645 Fifth Ave., between E. 51st and E. 52nd Sts.; phone: 421-3000). Along less expensive lines, you will run into several leather goods and luggage stores during your strolls around the West Side, such as the *Westside Luggage Shop* (955 Eighth Ave.; phone: 757-3880) and *Rio Trading* (10 W. 46th St.; phone: 819-0304). The Lower East Side has countless stores offering suitcases at substantial savings, including *Altman Luggage* (135 Orchard St.; phone: 254-7275).

MALLS Indoor urban malls are a relatively recent phenomenon in New York City; they arrived a decade ago with the glitzy *Trump Tower* (725 Fifth Ave. at E. 56th St.). The vendors in the tower's six-story marble and mirrored atrium are among the world's most opulent (and most expensive): *Abercrombie & Fitch* (men's and women's sportswear and sporting goods); *Kenneth Jay Lane* (high-end costume jewelry); *Ferragamo* (top-quality Italian footwear; also see *Shoes,* below); *Asprey* (one of London's premier jewelers and silversmiths); *Buccellati* (silversmith); *Charles Jourdan* (men's and women's shoes); and *Harry Winston* (diamond jewelry; the main shop is at Fifth Ave. and W. 56th St.).

Close to *Macy's* is *A & S Plaza* (Ave. of the Americas from W. 32nd to W. 33rd St.; phone: 465-0500), a multilevel complex of shops and stores including *Ann Taylor, Oak Tree* (for menswear), and, of course, *A & S* (see *Department Stores,* above).

In lower Manhattan, *Pier 17* at the *South Street Seaport* is another shopper's magnet. For detailed information, see *Walk 1: Wall Street* in DIRECTIONS.

MENSWEAR Manhattan has fashions to fit every man's taste, from the astronomically glitzy at *Bijan* (by appointment only; 699 Fifth Ave., between E. 54th and E. 55th Sts.; phone: 758-7500) to westernwear at *Billy Martin*'s (812 Madison Ave. at E. 68th St.; phone: 861-3100). *Brooks Brothers* (346 Madison Ave. at E. 44th St.; phone: 682-8800; and 1 Liberty Plaza, downtown; phone: 267-2400); *Paul Stuart* (Madison Ave. and 45th St.; phone: 682-0320); and *F. R. Tripler* (366 Madison Ave. at E. 46th St.; phone: 922-1090) all offer expensive, high-quality, conservative business suits and classic furnishings. *St. Laurie* (895 Broadway at E. 20th St.; phone: 473-0100) carries similar merchandise with slightly lower price tags. *Barneys New York* (106 Seventh Ave., from W. 16th to W. 17th St.; phone: 929-9000; 225 Liberty St., in the *World Financial Center;* phone: 945-1600; and 660 Madison Ave. at 61st St.; phone: 826-8900) has an eclectic array of goods but includes top-drawer suits from the world's foremost designers. For Italian *alta moda* in SoHo, try *Di Mitri* (110 Greene St.; phone: 431-1090). *Beau Brummel* (four locations, including 1113 Madison Ave., between E. 83rd and E. 84th Sts.; phone: 737-4200) has everything for the fashion-conscious man. *Syms* (42 Trinity Pl.; phone: 797-1199) stocks fine discounted menswear on five floors. *Bergdorf Goodman Men* is a bastion of male chic (Fifth Ave. and E. 58th St.; phone: 753-7300). To top it all off, visit *Worth & Worth* (331 Madison Ave.; phone: 867-6058) for a large selection of hats.

MUSEUM GIFT SHOPS New York's outstanding art and cultural institutions-often have equally fine shops stocked with items related to their collections. Among the best are those at the *Fraunces Tavern Museum,* with books, reproductions of historic documents, and postcards; the *American Museum of Natural History,* with crafts and jewelry from North America, South America, and Asia, model dinosaurs, and prints of pre-Columbian art; and the *Solomon R. Guggenheim Museum,* with textiles, jewelry, posters, and toys. The *Metropolitan Museum of Art* has huge shops that sell fine-arts prints, jewelry, calendars, stationery, toys, and books, and there is also a more central branch in *Rockefeller Center* (15 W. 49th St.; phone: 332-1360). In addition to the bookstore (with posters, stationery, and other smaller gift items) in the *Museum of Modern Art,* there is the *MOMA Design Store* across the street (44 W. 53rd St.; phone: 767-1050), stocked with a large selection of contemporary home and office furnishings and jewelry. The gift shop next door to the *Whitney Museum of American Art* (943 Madison Ave. at E. 75th St.; phone: 606-0200) purveys toys, jewelry, crafts, and furniture. The *Cooper-Hewitt Museum,* part of the *Smithsonian Institution,* has a new shop in the museum's Louis XVI music room which sells books, tabletop items, and jewelry. (See *Special Places* and *Museums* for all addresses and phone numbers not listed above.)

POSTER AND PRINT SHOPS *The Old Print Shop* (150 Lexington Ave. at E. 29th St.; phone: 683-3950) has a huge collection of early American prints, watercolors, and paintings ranging in price from $10 to $20,000. For contemporary theater posters and some collector's items, try the *Triton Gallery* (323 W. 45th St., between Eighth and Ninth Aves.; phone: 765-2472). Rare movie posters are available at *Poster America* (138 W. 18th St.; phone: 206-0499). The *Gallery at Lincoln Center* (136 W. 65th St.; phone: 580-4673) has the largest collection of limited-edition paintings and photographs celebrating the performing arts—dance, theater, and opera—plus original silk-screen posters.

SHOES All of the top Italian designers of both men's and women's footwear are represented: *Gucci* (685 Fifth Ave.; phone: 826-2600); *Fratelli Rossetti* (601 Madison Ave.; phone: 888-5107); *Tanino Crisci* (660 Madison Ave.; phone: 535-1014); *Ferragamo* (for men, 730 Fifth Ave.; phone: 246-6211; for women, 717 Fifth Ave.; phone: 759-3822); and *Bruno Magli* (for men only, 677 Fifth Ave.; phone: 752-7900). Fine European shoes also are found at *Bally of Switzerland* (for men, 711 Fifth Ave.; phone: 751-9082; for women, 689 Madison Ave.; phone: 751-2163). For well-made men's boots and shoes, stop at *McCreedy & Schreiber* (37 W. 46th St.; phone: 719-1552; and 213 E. 59th St.; phone: 759-9241). *Susan Bennis/Warren Edwards* (22 W. 57th St.; phone: 755-4197) designs outré American shoes.

SPORTING GOODS The most elegant sporting goods store is *Abercrombie & Fitch* (*South Street Seaport;* phone: 809-9000; and *Trump Tower,* 725 Fifth Ave. at E. 56th St.; phone: 832-1001). *Herman's* (39 W. 34th St.; phone: 279-8900; and six other locations), New York's best-known sporting goods chain, has everything, but *Paragon* (867 Broadway at E. 18th St.; phone: 255-8036) says it has more—and at better prices. Serious joggers should stop in at the *Super Runners Shop* (416 Third Ave. at E. 29th St.; phone: 213-4560; and three other locations); tennis players will find good buys at *Mason's Tennis Mart* (911 Seventh Ave.; phone: 757-5374). *Gerry Cosby's* (3 Penn Plaza, above *Penn Station;* phone: 563-6464) outfits professional teams and offers top-of-the-line sporting goods and souvenirs. *Orvis* (355 Madison Ave.; phone: 697-3133) has fishing and hunting gear.

THRIFT SHOPS AND RETRO FASHION Most thrift shops carry a variety of merchandise, from men's and women's clothing to household items and appliances to battered furniture. And unfortunately, many of the secondhand clothes stores in New York carry the price tags of fine antiques stores. The best area for thrifting in New York is the East 80s along First, Second, and Third Avenues. Two interesting places to try are the *Stuyvesant Square Thrift Shop* (1704 Second Ave. at E. 96th St.; phone: 831-1830) and *Spence-Chapin Thrift Shop* (1430 Third Ave. at E. 81st St.; phone: 737-8448). Downtown the clothes get wilder and the prices lower. Go to *Screaming Mimi's* (382 Lafayette St. at E. Fourth St.; phone: 677-6464), *B-Flat* (125 E. Fourth St.; phone: 260-5220), or the *Antique Boutique* (712-714 Broadway; phone: 460-8830) for secondhand clothing from the 1920s through the 1960s. *Alice Underground*'s two shops (380 Columbus Ave. at W. 78th St.; phone: 724-6682; and 481 Broadway; phone: 431-9067) are other highly affordable havens for a changing collection of casual and dressier clothes. Hats and linen goods are sold as well in the uptown branch.

TOYS Once immersed in the enchanting world of toys and stuffed animals at *FAO Schwarz* (GM Bldg., Fifth Ave. and E. 58th St.; phone: 644-9400), adults have as difficult a time as children leaving empty-handed. It has every kind of plaything—from precious antiques and mechanical spaceships to simple construction sets and building blocks—but some items are very expensive. *Penny Whistle Toys* (448 Columbus Ave.; phone: 873-9090; and 1283 Madison Ave.; phone: 369-3868) offers everything from puppets and bubble machines to wooden blocks and educational toys. The *Enchanted Forest* (85 Mercer St.; phone: 925-6677) stocks fine toys and craft kits.

UNIQUELY NEW YORK Probably nowhere else on earth can you find everything from earplugs to fine silver under one roof. *Hammacher Schlemmer* (147 E. 57th St., between Third and Lexington Aves.; phone: 421-9000), the first store to offer the pop-up toaster and microwave oven, has it all. And what it doesn't have, it will try to order.

Century 21 (22 Cortlandt St., between Broadway and Church St.; phone: 227-9092) is the ultimate discount experience; it's a vast, crowded emporium of designer clothing and accessories, including Bally shoes, Gianni Versace tuxedos, and Carolina Herrera dresses at as much as 50% below retail price. It also stocks discounted linens.

47th St. Photo (67 W. 47th St., Second Floor) is a center for cameras, computers, and other electronic gear with excellent discounts and a huge selection (some 5,000 items in stock). The tiny headquarters and its branch (115 W. 45th St.; phone: 921-1287 for both locations) tend to be packed with customers and consequently chaotic. Know what you want before you go, because the brusque manner of the salesmen doesn't lend itself to extended dialogue; however, when they do answer a question, they know what they're talking about. Closed Friday afternoons and Saturdays.

Finally, travel 'round the world in a unique way via a trip to the *United Nations Gift Shop* (*UN Bldg.,* First Ave. and E. 46th St.; phone: 963-7702), featuring handicrafts, ethnic clothing, native jewelry, indigenous toys—lots of beautiful things from the member countries.

SPORTS AND FITNESS

New York is a sports-minded city, offering a great variety of spectator and participatory activities. It is the home of the *Yankees, Mets, Knicks,* and *Rangers.* The *Jets, Giants, Nets,* and *Devils* play about six miles from Manhattan in New Jersey, and the *Islanders* in suburban Nassau County on Long Island. There are racetracks, tennis and basketball courts, bridle and bike paths, pool halls, bowling alleys, skating rinks, running tracks, and swimming pools, to name but a few sporting spots.

BASEBALL The season, April through early October, features the *Mets (National League)* at *Shea Stadium* (Flushing, Queens; phone: 718-507-8499), and the *Yankees (American League)* at *Yankee Stadium* (the Bronx; phone: 718-293-6000). Take the *IRT* Flushing line (No. 7 train) to the Willets Point/Shea Stadium stop to the *Mets;* the *IRT* Lexington Avenue line (No. 4 train) or the *IND* line (C or D train) to the 161st Street stop for the *Yankees.* Tickets can be ordered through *Ticketmaster* for *Yankees* games only (phone: 307-7171).

BASKETBALL The *Knicks* play at *Madison Square Garden* (Seventh Ave. and W. 32rd St.; phone: 465-6741); and the *Nets* at the *Brendan Byrne Arena* in the *Meadowlands Sports Complex* in East Rutherford, New Jersey (phone: 201-935-8888), during the regular season from early November to late April. You can order *Nets* tickets through *Ticketmaster* (phone 307-7171). Buses to the *Meadowlands* leave from the *Port Authority Bus Terminal* (Eighth Ave. and W. 42nd St.; phone: 564-8484 or 564-1114 for ticket and schedule information).

BICYCLING There are over 50 miles of bike paths in the city, with *Central Park* in Manhattan and *Prospect Park* in Brooklyn the two most popular areas. Most roadways within the parks are closed to auto traffic from April through October, except during rush hours on weekdays; they are closed on weekends and holidays year-round.

Many of the parks listed below have bike rental concessions, although it's usually less expensive to rent a two-wheeler at one of the many cycling shops around the city. Check the yellow pages for the names of dealers convenient to you. More serious bikers should contact *Transportation Alternatives* (phone: 475-4600) for information on noncompetitive charity events such as bike-a-thons and weekend bicycling tours. For information on competitive cycling events and road races, call Len Preheim at the *Toga Bike Shop* (110 West End Ave.; phone: 799-9625).

BEST BIKE ROUTES

Central Park and Riverside Park The general sense of seclusion in *Central Park* increases on weekdays from 10 AM to 3 PM and from 7 PM to 10 PM), April through November, on holidays, and on weekends, when the park is closed to motor vehicles. Rentals are available next to the Loeb Boathouse (Fifth Ave. near E. 72nd St.; phone: 861-4137). Cyclists, who mostly use the central loop, must be on the lookout for roller-skaters, dog walkers, skateboarders, joggers, and other pedestrians. Because of all the bike racers who practice here, park police occasionally stop high-speeders. Another popular and less hectic biking path is through *Riverside Park,* which extends in one form or another from West 72nd Street to West 125th Street, over the *Amtrak* train tracks along the Hudson River.

Brooklyn Riders can traverse the *Coney Island* boardwalk from 5 AM to 10 AM daily from *Memorial Day* through *Labor Day,* from 5 AM to midnight the rest of the year. Other bicycle paths are located in *Prospect Park,* which is closed to motor vehicles at the same times as *Central Park* (see above). Another bicycle path stretches along the southbound lanes of Ocean Parkway from Church Avenue to Sea Breeze Avenue through a residential neighborhood of broad streets and stately homes. Continue south to the *New York Aquarium* (now the *Aquarium for Wildlife Conservation*) and the amusement area at *Coney Island.* Another route begins in *Owl's Head Park* in Bay Ridge and continues along Shore Parkway to Cropsey Avenue. Spectacular views of the harbor and the Verrazano-Narrows Bridge are there for the looking, and just past the bridge as you head east is historic *Fort Hamilton,* site of one of the largest battles of the Revolutionary War and still an active US Army post.

Bronx For a delightful sojourn through the Bronx, take the North Bronx Bikeway. The path begins at the junction of *Van Cortlandt Park South* and Mosholu Parkway, continues through *Bronx Park,* and ends at *Pelham Bay Park,* overlooking Long Island Sound. *Van Cortlandt Park* has many hills to challenge a cyclist's endurance, but the greenery is wonderfully distracting. The path exits *Bronx Park* and heads east along Pelham Parkway, a broad boulevard lined with an honor guard of trees that points straight to *Pelham Park.* A terrific way to end the trip is a visit to Orchard Beach for an invigorating dip.

Queens An 18-mile path extends from *Flushing Meadow Park,* just south of *Shea Stadium,* through *Kissena Park, Cunningham Park, Alley Pond Park,* and *Crocheron Park.* Rentals are available from *AAA Bike Rental* (phone: 718-699-9598) at the Passeralle Ramp at the Willets

Point station of the *IRT* Flushing line (No. 7 train) and at the Meadow Lake Boathouse in Flushing Meadow's *Corona Park*. Cyclists ride past structures such as the *Unisphere*, the *Hall of Science*, and the *Queens Museum*—all remnants of the *World's Fairs* of 1939–40 and 1964–65. Other sights include the *Historic Grove* in *Kissena Park*, a stand of rare Oriental trees planted in 1850, and the wildlife that abounds in *Alley Pond Park*, a noted environmental center and nature preserve.

Staten Island This is the most quiet and residential of all the boroughs, and bicycling here is sheer pleasure. One of the loveliest paths winds around Brooks Pond in *Clove Lake Park*. Another scenic route curves around the *Silver Lake Park* reservoir, and there also is cycling on the park road, which is closed to motorists on Sundays and holidays.

BILLIARDS AND BOWLING Extremely popular with many New Yorkers, pool halls and bowling alleys are plentiful throughout the city. Consult the yellow pages for the nearest location.

BOXING Major bouts are still fought at *Madison Square Garden* (see *Basketball*, above), and the *Daily News* continues to sponsor the *Golden Gloves* competition every winter (phone: 210-1952).

FITNESS CENTERS The *Poly Gym* (428 E. 75th St.; phone: 628-6969) offers one-on-one personal training 24 hours a day, seven days a week. The *Works* (29 W. 17th St.; phone: 627-3309) sponsors ongoing exercise classes for all ages. Open daily; hours vary. Newer and open 24 hours except on Sundays (when it's open from 8 AM to 10 PM) is the *World Gym*'s main location at *Lincoln Center* (1926 Broadway; phone: 874-0942). For information on the various Ys around the city, call 308-2899; 755-2410 after 5 PM.

FOOTBALL During the September–December season, the *Jets* and the *Giants* play at *Giants Stadium* in the *Meadowlands Sports Complex* (see *Basketball*, above). Tickets to *NFL* games are hard to get due to the great number of season subscribers. For *Giants* ticket information, call 201-935-8222; for *Jets* tickets, call 516-538-6600. *Columbia University* leads the local collegiate football scene; games are played at *Baker Field* (Broadway and W. 218th St.; phone: 567-0404).

GOLF While there are no public courses in Manhattan, golf enthusiasts can visit the city's outlying boroughs for an invigorating round—there are 13 courses in municipal parks operated by private concessionaires. Tee times and course information can be obtained by calling 718-225-GOLF. The *Department of Parks* public information office (phone: 800-834-3832) also can provide a complete list of public courses and how to get on them. For up-to-date information on tournaments, call the *Metropolitan Golf Association* (phone: 914-698-0390).

TOP TEE-OFF SPOTS

Brooklyn Near *Fort Hamilton*, the *Dyker Beach Golf Course* (Seventh Ave. and 86th St.; phone: 718-836-9722) has 6,500 yards of fairly flat, spotlessly maintained grounds, and while seasoned golfers may never use a long iron on its fairways, it still merits a favorable mention. Brooklyn's other venue is the *Marine Park Golf Course* (2880 Flatbush Ave., near the Belt Pkwy.; phone: 718-338-7113), which is part of the *Gateway National Recreation Area* on Jamaica Bay. This course has the advantage of refreshingly cool breezes, which can add a little comfort to your round.

Bronx Probably the easiest courses to reach from midtown are those in the west Bronx. The 6,050-yard *Van Cortlandt Park Golf Course* (Bailey Ave. and *Van Cortlandt Park South,* in the southwestern part of the park; phone: 718-543-4595) was the nation's first municipal course. Established in 1895, it still boasts rolling fairways and undulating greens. It is a favorite with collegiate teams who play competitive matches here in the spring, but even for more experienced golfers, *Van Cortlandt* is no picnic in the park. Farther east in *Van Cortlandt Park* is the shorter, flatter *Mosholu Golf Course* (Jerome Ave. and Holly La.; phone: 718-655-9164), with a nine-hole, 3,263-yard championship course and a 42-bay driving range nearby. The closest entrance is on Jerome Avenue at Bainbridge Avenue, within walking distance of the Woodlawn station on the *IRT* Lexington Avenue line No. 4 train.

Two of the loveliest courses in the area are in *Pelham Bay Park* near Long Island Sound: the *Pelham Park Golf Course* (Shore Rd., north of Bartow Circle; phone: 718-885-1258) and the *Split Rock Golf Course,* located west of the *Pelham Park* course (phone: 718-885-1258). The two links are separated by *Amtrak* railroad tracks and are bordered on the south by the *Thomas Pell Wildlife Refuge and Sanctuary.* The 6,405-yard *Pelham Park* course features broad fairways and gentle slopes, and is considered somewhat easier than the 6,492-yard *Split Rock* course, with its narrower fairways, deeper roughs, and dense woods surrounding the greens.

Queens The expansive *Clearview Golf Course* (202-12 Willets Point Blvd., near the Clearview Expwy.; phone: 718-229-2570) is highly favored by locals. Across the Cross Island Expressway from *Alley Pond Park* is the 5,482-yard *Douglaston Golf Course* (63-20 Marathon Pkwy. at Commonwealth Blvd; phone: 718-224-6566), which has a rolling layout with narrow fairways that require an excellent eye and careful swing. Fans of the *Forest Park Golf Course* (Forest Park Dr. and 80th St.; phone: 718-296-0999), which straddles the Glendale and Woodhaven sections of the borough, claim it is a fine test of skill. At 4,600 yards, the *Kissena Park Golf Course* (Booth Memorial Ave. and 164th St.; phone: 718-939-4594) is the shortest of the Queens courses. Still, the narrow fairways and surprising inclines offer a real challenge.

Staten Island *La Tourette Golf Course* (1001 Richmond Hill Rd.; phone: 718-351-1889), located in the center of the island, is a 6,600-yard beauty whose scenic fairways are long, wide, and simply glorious. Near Forest Avenue in the Grymes Hill section of the borough is the cozy *Silver Lake Golf Course* (915 Victory Blvd.; phone: 718-447-5686), which is accessible to the *Staten Island Ferry*. The hilly, 5,891-yard course, with its narrow fairways, makes gauging distances a formidable challenge. The *South Shore Golf Course* (200 Huguenot Ave.; phone: 718-984-0101) is pleasant, and the scenery is considered rural by New York standards.

HOCKEY Tickets are expensive and scarce during the early October to early April season, with the *Islanders* at the *Nassau Coliseum* on Long Island (phone: 516-794-4100), the *Rangers* at *Madison Square Garden,* and the *Devils* at the *Brendan Byrne Arena* (see *Basketball,* above, for the latter two).

HORSE RACING For a complete rundown, see *A Day at the Races* in DIVERSIONS.

HORSEBACK RIDING Horseback riding can be an exhilarating way to experience the city.

FOR URBAN EQUESTRIANS

Central Park Bridle Path A total of about six miles, including a trip around the reservoir, makes this is an unusually peaceful trek—given its proximity to the monumental traffic tangles just beyond the trees. The *Claremont Riding Academy* (175 W. 89th St.; phone: 724-5100), housed in a landmark building about a block and a half west of the park, is a vintage New York stable. (If you are serious about springing for this pricey pastime, you must reserve in advance.) Although the horses know the way, getting to the park necessitates navigation through traffic on horseback; you must obey all vehicular traffic regulations, including stopping at red lights. Once you enter the park, however, you are transported back into the 19th century; the rustling of the trees, the precise clip-clop of horses' hooves, and the verdant bridle path evoke a bygone era of riding corteges and elegant carriages. As you pass by the 86th Street transverse road, there's an abandoned barn and walking ring where the *New York Police Department*'s mounted troops once stabled their horses.

Bronx Rent a horse on an hourly basis from the *Van Cortlandt Riding Academy* (Broadway and 254th St.; phone: 718-543-4433), and meander through *Van Cortlandt Park,* with its wooded and open trails. The path over gentle hills passes outcroppings of local rock formations, and bird watchers can expect to spot woodpeckers and horned owls. The bridle paths in *Pelham Bay Park* stretch over 2,675 acres. Animal and bird life is abundant: everything from rabbits and raccoons to egrets and ospreys.

ICE SKATING You can show off your figure eights from October through April at the famous *Rockefeller Center* rink (phone: 757-5730); from November through March at the *Wollman Rink* in *Central Park* (phone: 517-4800); and from early November through February at the *Lasker Rink,* also in *Central Park* (phone: 986-1184). The small rink in front of the Rivergate Apartments (401 E. 34th St. at First Ave.; phone: 689-0035) is open from November through March. For information about skating conditions, call 397-3098 or 517-4800. Indoor skating year-round is possible at the Olympic-size *SkyRink* (450 W. 33rd St.; phone: 695-6556).

JOGGING This is undoubtedly the most popular sport in New York, with enthusiastic runners in all the city parks: on the paths at *Riverside Park* (near W. 97th St.); around the *Central Park* reservoir (from 86th to 95th St.); and along the East River promenade (from E. 84th to E. 90th St.). It is unsafe to run in *any* of these places after dark. The *New York Road Runners Club* (9 E. 89th St.; phone: 860-4455) offers guided runs on weekdays at 6:30 and 7:15 PM from their office and on Saturdays at 10 AM from Fifth Avenue and E. 90th Street; they take scenic routes, including a lap around the *Central Park* reservoir.

ROLLER-SKATING AND ROLLER-BLADING *Central Park* on spring and summer weekends is one huge skating rink, with rentals available from *Peck & Goodie* (917 Eighth Ave., between W. 54th and W. 55th Sts.; phone: 246-6123). Don't skate in the park after dark.

SWIMMING Several dozen indoor and outdoor pools are operated throughout the five boroughs by the *Parks Department.* Indoor pools are open most of the year, except Sundays and holidays, usually until 10 PM on weekdays. Call the *Parks Department*'s public information office (phone: 360-8141) for particulars. For information on the pools at the *Y*s, call 308-2899; 755-2410 after 5 PM.

Ocean swimming is a subway or bus ride away. Beaches within the city and maintained by it are Orchard Beach in the Bronx; Coney Island Beach and Manhattan Beach in Brooklyn; and *Riis Park* and Far Rockaway in Queens. *Jones Beach State Park* (Wantagh, Long Island, 30 miles east of the city) is Long Island's most popular public beach. It is a well-maintained, enormous stretch of sand offering surf bathing, swimming and wading pools, lockers, fishing, outdoor skating rinks, paddleball, swimming instruction, restaurants, and day and evening entertainment. It can be reached via the *Long Island Rail Road* from *Penn Station* (Seventh Ave. and W. 32nd St.; phone: 718-217-5477) and a connecting bus (the JB62 during the week and the JB24 on weekends; both run from *Memorial Day* through *Labor Day*). A note of advice: On summer weekends, although enormous, Jones Beach can be crowded as early as 10 AM.

TENNIS Courts maintained by the *Parks Department* require a season permit. Municipal facilities include 26 clay courts in *Central Park* (phone: 280-0205), 10 red-clay courts in *Riverside Park* (no phone), and seven clay and four hard-surface courts on Randall's Island (phone: 534-4845). In the Bronx there are 10 hard-surface courts at *Rice Stadium* in *Pelham Bay Park* and eight clay and four all-weather courts in *Van Cortlandt Park* (no phone for either). In Queens the *USTA National Tennis Center* in *Flushing Meadow Park* (phone: 718-592-8000), home of the *US Open,* has 26 outdoor and nine indoor courts. One of the larger privately owned clubs that will rent by the hour is the *Midtown Tennis Club* (341 Eighth Ave. at W. 27th St.; phone: 989-8572). Check the yellow pages for other locations.

THEATER

New York attracts the best and most accomplished talents in the world. However, there are devoted New York theatergoers who wouldn't dream of stepping inside a Broadway theater. They prefer instead the city's prolific off-Broadway and off-off-Broadway circuit, whose productions are less high-powered but no less professional than the splashiest shows on Broadway. On the other hand, there are theater mavens who've never seen a performance more than a few blocks from Times Square, and who can remember every detail of the opening night of *A Chorus Line* (the final curtain came down after 6,137 performances).

Broadway signifies an area—between West 42nd and West 53rd Streets both east and west and on Broadway—and a kind of production that strives to be the smash hit of the season and run forever. The glitter of the area has tarnished a bit since the halcyon days of the Great White Way, but hopes are that a general reconstruction and renovation of West 42nd Street will turn things around. In any case, the productions are getting more stellar (and pricier) than ever.

Off-Broadway and off-off-Broadway signify types of theater, in playhouses strewn from Greenwich Village to the Upper West Side. Off-Broadway productions are usually smaller in scale, with newer, lesser-known talent, than those on Broadway, and are likely to feature revivals of classics or more daring works. Off-off-Broadway is more experimental still: truly avant-garde productions in coffeehouses, lofts, or any appropriate makeshift arena. Off-Broadway tickets often cost nearly as much as those for a Broadway show, but the cost of a seat for an off-off-Broadway production is usually much less.

Take advantage of all three during a visit. The excitement of a Broadway show is incomparable, but the thrill of finding a tiny theater in SoHo or the West Village in which you are almost nose to nose with the actors is unforgettable. Planning your theater schedule is as easy as consulting any of the daily papers (they all list theaters and current offerings daily, with comprehensive listings on Fridays or Saturdays), the "Goings On About Town" section in *The New Yorker*, or "Theater Listings" in *New York* magazine, which lists current theater fare under headings of "Broadway," "Off-Broadway," and "Off-Off-Broadway."

Broadway tickets can be quite expensive (they average $30 to $65, with an occasional musical costing as much as $100, depending on seat and performance), but with a little patience, you can find cheaper tickets. The *TKTS* booths (Broadway and W. 47th St. in Times Square and in *2 World Trade Center* in lower Manhattan; phone: 768-1818) sell orchestra seats at half price, plus a service charge of $2.50 per ticket, for a wide range of Broadway and off-Broadway productions; tickets are sold only for the same day's performance. You must line up—there are no reservations—and payment must be made in cash or traveler's checks. *TKTS* booths are open as follows: On Broadway, sales for Monday through Saturday evening performances are from 3 to 8 PM; for Wednesday and Saturday matinees from 10 AM to 2 PM; and for Sunday matinees and evening performances from noon to 8 PM. At *2 World Trade Center* the booth is open weekdays from 11 AM to 5:30 PM and Saturdays from 11 AM to 3:30 PM; tickets for Wednesday, Saturday, and Sunday matinees are available the day *before* the performance. The *Broadway Show Line* (phone: 563-BWAY), sponsored by the *League of American Theaters and Producers,* gives recorded synopses and short reviews of Broadway and off-Broadway plays as well as ticket prices and schedules.

To help ease the post-theater cab crush, two taxi stands operate in the Broadway area. Line up on W. 45th Street, west of Broadway (near Shubert Alley), or on W. 44th St., east of Eighth Ave. (near the *St. James Theatre*).

THEATER COMPANIES One of New York's newer repertory companies is the *National Actors Theatre,* founded by actor Tony Randall, which presents revivals of classic plays, often featuring well-known artists, at the *Lyceum Theatre* (149 W. 45th St.; phone: 239-6200 for tickets). Others include the *Classic Stage Company (CSC),* which stages intriguing productions of classics of all centuries (126 E. 13th St., between Third and Fourth Aves.; phone: 677-4210); *Circle Rep* (99 Seventh Ave. S.; phone: 924-7100); *Hudson Guild Theater* (441 W. 26th St.; phone: 760-9810); *INTAR Theater* (420 W. 42nd St.; phone: 695-6134); *Irish Arts Center* (553 W. 51st St.; phone: 757-3318); *Jean Cocteau Repertory* (330 Bowery; phone: 677-0060); *Jewish Repertory Theater* (316 E. 96th St.; phone: 831-2000); *La Mama ETC* (74A E. Fourth St.; phone: 475-7710); *Manhattan Theatre Club* (*City Center,* 131 W. 55th St.; phone: 581-7907); *National Black Theatre* (2033

Fifth Ave., Second Floor; phone: 722-3800); *Pan Asian Repertory* (423 W. 46th St.; phone: 505-5655); *Playwrights Horizons Theater* (416 W. 42nd St.; phone: 279-4200); the *Joseph Papp Public Theater,* home of the *New York Shakespeare Festival* (425 Lafayette St.; phone: 598-7150); *Repertorio Español* (138 E. 27th St.; phone: 889-2850); *Charles Ludlum Theater* (1 Sheridan Sq.; phone: 691-2271); *Roundabout* (1530 Broadway; phone: 869-8400); the *Vivian Beaumont Theater* and the *Mitzi E. Newhouse Theater,* both at *Lincoln Center* (phone: 239-6200); and the *Westside Arts Theater* (407 W. 43rd St.; phone: 307-4100). All can provide a schedule of offerings and performance dates. Alternatively, call the *Theatre Development Fund's* hotline (phone: 587-1111; 800-STAGE-NY outside of New York State) or *New York* magazine's hotline, weekdays from 10:30 AM to 4:30 PM (phone: 880-0755).

For more information, see *New York Theater: On Broadway and Off* in DIVERSIONS.

MUSIC AND DANCE

New York is a world center for performing artists. It presents the best of classical and nonclassical works from all over the world, in a variety of halls and auditoriums filled with appreciative, knowledgeable audiences.

Lincoln Center for the Performing Arts (Columbus Ave. from W. 62nd to W. 66th St.; phone: 875-5400 for general information) represents the city's devotion to concerts, opera, and ballet. It consists of *Avery Fisher Hall,* home of the *New York Philharmonic* (phone: 875-5030); the *New York State Theater,* featuring the *New York City Ballet* and the *New York City Opera* (phone: 870-5570); the *Metropolitan Opera House* and the *American Ballet Theater* (phone: 362-6000); the *Damrosch Bandshell,* an open-air theater used for free concerts in the summertime; the *Juilliard School* for musicians, actors, and dancers (phone: 799-5000); *Alice Tully Hall,* home of the *Chamber Music Society* (phone: 875-5050); and the *Vivian Beaumont* and *Mitzi E. Newhouse Theaters* (see above). In addition, all the auditoriums in *Lincoln Center* present other musical events and recitals. While visiting the city, don't miss the *New York Public Library for the Performing Arts,* a unique repository and museum (phone: 870-1630). Guided tours of *Lincoln Center* are available daily (phone: 875-5000).

Other major venues are *Carnegie Hall,* which celebrated its centennial in 1991 (Seventh Ave. and W. 57th St.; phone: 247-7800), and its *Weill Recital Hall* (phone: 697-4188); *City Center* (131 W. 55th St.; phone: 581-7909); the *Grace Rainey Rogers Auditorium* (in the *Metropolitan Museum,* Fifth Ave. and E. 82nd St.; phone: 570-3949); the *Kaufmann Auditorium* (at the *92nd St. Y,* Lexington Ave. and E. 92nd St.; phone: 996-1100); *Symphony Space* (2537 Broadway at W. 95th St.; phone: 864-5400); and the *Brooklyn Academy of Music* (30 Lafayette Ave., Brooklyn; phone: 718-636-4100). Also check music and dance listings in the newspapers, *New York* magazine, and *The New Yorker.*

The *TKTS* booth in Times Square, which sells discount theater tickets, has a counterpart on the West 42nd Street side of *Bryant Park* (behind the *New York Public Library,* just east of the Ave. of the Americas; phone: 382-2323) for those interested in buying half-price tickets to music and dance events on the day of the performance (very occasionally, they also have tickets for opera and operetta performed by smaller companies). The booth is open Tuesdays through Sundays from noon to 2 PM and 3 to 7 PM. Full-price tickets for future performances also are available here. For more information on New York's performing arts scene, see *New York Theater: On Broadway and Off* in DIVERSIONS.

Many pop, rock, rhythm-and-blues, and country artists perform at *Madison Square Garden* (Seventh Ave. and W. 32nd St.; phone: 465-6741) and at several clubs around the city (see below). The *Nassau Coliseum* (Hempstead Tpke., Uniondale; phone: 516-794-9300) holds large concerts on Long Island. The downtown weekly *The Village Voice* plus *The New Yorker* and *New York* magazine offer good listings of current and upcoming events.

NIGHTCLUBS AND NIGHTLIFE

The scope of nightlife in New York is as vast as the scope of daily life. Cultural trends strongly affect the kinds of clubs that are "in" at any given time, and their popularity has a tendency to peak, then plunge rather quickly. Old jazz and neighborhood clubs, on the other hand, usually remain intact, catering to a regular clientele. They offer various kinds of entertainment, and many stay open until the wee hours of the morning, serving drinks and food. It's a good idea to call clubs in advance to find out when they are open and what performers or acts are appearing; or, consult the "Nightlife Directory" in *New York* magazine. Many of the city's nightclubs with live entertainment and/or dancing have cover charges of $10 and up; most accept major credit cards.

The current focus of the trendy crowd is on clubs that offer a kind of relaxed gentility. This sophisticated atmosphere may include the coveted (or cursed, as the case may be) velvet rope across the entrance, alluring interiors by top designers, elegant cocktails, and ultrachic denizens of the night. One of the swankiest places in town is *Nell's* (246 W. 14th St., between Seventh and Eighth Aves.; phone: 675-1567), a Victorian-style nightclub immortalized by *People* magazine but less exclusive than in its early days. *Tatou* (151 E. 50th St.; phone: 753-1144), another posh spot, is a cozy supper club with live jazz during dinner; it metamorphoses into a disco later in the evening. Among the city's newer nightspots are *Webster Hall* (125 E. 11th St., between Third and Fourth Aves.; phone: 353-1600), a multitiered dance hall with a lot of Art Deco touches, including antique furniture from local flea markets, and *USA* (218 W. 47th St., between Broadway and Eighth Ave.; phone: 869-6001), a cavernous club with a deliberately debauched and decadent atmosphere, replete with blown-up cartoon characters as part of the decor; it's loud, too, except for the upstairs lounge, which is sometimes used for private parties. Another multilevel club is *Le Bar Bat* (311 W. 57th St.; phone: 307-7228), where you can hear live blues Wednesdays through Saturdays. The quiet nights, Mondays and Tuesdays, have recorded music.

POP AND ROCK The Big Apple's top rock 'n' roll clubs generally feature lavish sound systems, videos, live bands, several bars, and lots of room for dancing. Try *Limelight* (47 W. 20th St. at the Ave. of the Americas; phone: 807-7850), a late-night favorite for denizens of the downtown scene, and that dance palace *extraordinaire,* the *Palladium* (126 E. 14th St.; phone: 473-7171), with a cavernous interior that attracts an MTV-generation crowd. The *Big City Diner* (572 11th Ave. at W. 43rd St.; phone: 244-6033), open 24 hours, is a trendy place serving American fare with a dance club bisecting it. The ultra-funky *CBGB & OMFUG* (315 Bowery at Bleecker St.; phone: 982-4052) continues to give fringe groups their moment in the spotlight.

For the younger set, the ubiquitous *Hard Rock Café* (221 W. 57th St.; phone: 489-6565) is a monument to rock 'n' roll sporting all manner of memorabilia, a 45-foot guitar-shape bar, and a 1959 Cadillac jutting out from the second floor over the entrance. At *Planet Hollywood* (40 W. 57th St.; phone: 333-7827), owned (but not operated) by Arnold Schwarzenegger, Sylvester Stallone, and other Hollywood superstars, you can watch trailers for upcoming movies while you munch on burgers and pizza. And at press time, the young and the restless were heading for the reopened *Tunnel* (220 12th Ave.; phone: 695-7292), in Manhattan's seamy meat-packing district.

BLUES AND JAZZ Among popular nightspots that feature live music are *Honeysuckle West* (170 Amsterdam Ave. at W. 68th St.; phone: 873-4100) and *Dan Lynch* (221 Second Ave., between 13th and 14th Sts.; phone: 677-0911), a barebones bar with live bands. The *Bitter End* (149 Bleecker St.; phone: 673-7030) and the *Bottom Line* (15 W. Fourth St.; phone: 228-7880) often feature blues, folk, and jazz groups. The *Village Vanguard* (178 Seventh Ave. S.; phone: 255-4037), the *Village Gate* (160 Bleecker St.; phone: 475-5120), *Sweet Basil* (88 Seventh Ave. S.; phone: 242-1785), and the *Blue Note* (131 W. Third St.; phone: 475-8592) also spotlight top jazz artists.

Casual jazz clubs with reasonable prices and a relaxed atmosphere include *Arthur's Tavern* (57 Grove St.; phone: 675-6879) and *Bradley's* (70 University Place; phone: 228-6440). For nostalgic, traditional jazz try downstairs at *Fat Tuesday's* (190 Third Ave.; phone: 533-7900) or *Michael's Pub* (211 E. 55th St.; phone: 758-2272), where Woody Allen often plays his clarinet on Monday nights.

Birdland (2745 Broadway at 105th St.; phone: 749-2228) serves up dinner and jazz combos nightly. For big band sounds try *Red Blazer Too* (349 W. 36th St.; phone: 262-3112). Order up some gumbo and jambalaya with the Dixieland jazz featured nightly at *Cajun* (129 Eighth Ave. at 16th St.;

phone: 691-6174). For down-and-dirty Chicago blues head to *Manny's Car Wash* (1558 Third Ave. near 87th St.; phone: 369-2583).

COUNTRY AND INTERNATIONAL Country and rockabilly sounds headline at the *Lone Star Café Roadhouse* (240 W. 52nd St.; phone: 245-2950). The *Eagle Tavern* (355 W. 14th St., between Eighth and Ninth Aves.; phone: 924-0275) is good for country, bluegrass, and Irish music. For dancing to a Latin beat, try the *Sounds of Brazil (S.O.B.)* supper club (204 Varick St.; phone: 243-4940) or *Boca Chica* (13 First Ave. at First St.; phone: 473-0108), where salsa and other rhythms throb until 4 AM. For avant-garde sounds head for the *Knitting Factory* (47 E. Houston St., near Mulberry St.; phone: 219-3055).

SUPPER CLUBS AND CABARETS For a low-key, elegant evening of dancing to live music, a good show, and dinner, try one of New York's supper clubs. Among the city's small, intimate spots with good food and quality entertainment, the *Café Carlyle,* in the hotel of the same name, leads the pack when pianist Bobby Short, a New York institution himself, plays Cole Porter tunes, and Harry Connick Jr. made his New York debut tickling the ivories at the *Oak Room* in the *Algonquin* (see *Checking In* for both). *Au Bar* offers all the lofty but cozy accoutrements of London's Belgravia (41 E. 58th St.; phone: 308-9455). The *Rainbow Room* (30 Rockefeller Plaza; phone: 632-5100), restored to the splendor of its 1930s heyday, has good cheek-to-cheek dance music and dazzling views of the city from the 65th floor of the GE Building. The adjacent *Rainbow Promenade* is a less expensive café for midnight snacks, and *Rainbow and Stars* showcases cabaret acts (phone: 632-5100 for all three).

Although it doubles as a *tapas* bar and restaurant, the *Ballroom* (see *Eating Out*) has a regular program of international cabaret stars, including an occasional drag queen. A supper club presentation of popular musical revues is featured at *Steve McGraw*'s (158 W. 72nd St.; phone: 595-7400). For traditional ballroom fun with American and Latin live dance music, trip the light fantastic at the famous *Roseland* (239 W. 52nd St.; phone: 247-0200)—it holds up to 4,000 dancers. *Laura Belle* (120 W. 43rd St.; phone: 819-1000), an intimate eatery with a nostalgic 1940s atmosphere, features fine swing and jazz combos.

SINGLES BARS AND COMEDY CLUBS The largest concentration of singles bars in New York can be found on First, Second, and Third Avenues between East 61st and East 86th Streets. Walk along any one of these thoroughfares to find a place that suits your fancy. The low-key *Beach Café* (1326 Second Ave.; phone: 988-7299), with its handsome wood bar, is a popular hangout for a beer and burger. Oversize margaritas are the draw for the youngish bar crowd at *Juanita's* (1309 Third Ave.; phone: 517-3800). The bar at *Jim McMullen's* (1341 Third Ave.; phone: 861-4700), whose owner is a former fashion model, attracts the beautiful people from the top agencies.

The West Side has its strips of bars and restaurants along Broadway, Amsterdam, and Columbus Avenues between West 50th and West 86th Streets. If you're into the urban cowboy scene, try the *Yellow Rose Café* (450 Amsterdam Ave.; phone: 595-8760), also great for the fried chicken. Check out the upstairs jazz room at *B. Smith's* (771 Eighth Ave. at W. 47th St.; phone: 247-2222) or the ever-crowded *Whiskey* bar in the *Paramount* hotel (see *Checking In*), where waitresses wear gray leotards.

Lively "showcase" clubs, where comedians, singers, and musicians try out their acts, include *Caroline's* (1626 Broadway, between W. 49th and W. 50th Sts.; phone: 757-4100); *Improvisation* (433 W. 34th St.; phone: 279-3446); *Catch a Rising Star* (1487 First Ave.; phone: 794-1906); and *Dangerfield's* (1118 First Ave.; phone: 593-1650).

Best in Town

CHECKING IN

Host to more visitors than any other city in the world, New York can be one of the hardest places to find an empty hotel room from Sunday through Thursday nights, even though a rash of new properties has opened. However, don't expect this increased supply to offset inflation's upward push on room rates in the foreseeable future. Do expect to pay $250 or more—often *lots* more—per night for a very expensive room for two in Manhattan; $175 to $250 for an expensive one; $125 to $175 for a moderately priced room; and less than $125 for an inexpensive one. These prices do not include any meals nor the hefty hotel tax (see "Sales Tax" in the *Sources and Resources* section earlier in this chapter for current rates). *Note:* Many hotels offer relatively low-priced weekend packages which also may include a variety of amenities, such as breakfast and/or dinner, champagne, theater tickets, and parking. Reservations always are necessary, so write or call in advance.

Visitors who yearn to be in the thick of New York's theater district will find a variety of options. Choices include the *Macklowe, Holiday Inn Crowne Plaza, Paramount, Embassy Suites, New York Renaissance, Sheraton Manhattan,* and *Sheraton New York* hotels (see below for all).

An alternative to a standard hotel room is to try bed and breakfast accommodations in private homes or in an apartment. This option includes continental breakfast and costs from $60 to $125 per night for a double room. Unhosted, fully furnished apartments also are available, starting at $75 per night for a small studio. Weekly and monthly rates are offered by both B&Bs and apartments. For information, contact *Urban Ventures* (PO Box 426, New York, NY 10024; phone: 594-5650; fax: 947-9320); *At Home in New York* (PO Box 407, New York, NY 10185; phone: 956-3125; fax: 247-3294); the *Bed and Breakfast Network of New York* (134 W. 32nd St.; phone: 645-8134); *Bed and Breakfast and Books* (35 W. 92nd St., New York, NY 10025; phone: 865-8740 or 800-900-8134); *City Lights B&B* (P.O. Box

20355, New York, NY 10028; phone: 737-7049; fax: 535-2755), or *Abode B&B* (P.O. Box 20222, New York, NY 10028; phone: 472-2000 or 800-835-8880). Other options: Double rooms at many of the coed *Y*s throughout the city run about $45 a night, and the *New York Student Center* (895 Amsterdam Ave., between W. 103rd and W. 104th Sts.; phone: 666-3619; fax: 666-5012), in cooperation with *American Youth Hostels,* offers students and budget travelers accommodations priced as low as $20 per night.

To reserve a suite in one of nine different all-suite hotels around Manhattan, call the *Manhattan East Suite* hotel (phone: 800-637-8483). These accommodations are located in areas that range from the commercial (the *Southgate Tower* at Seventh Ave. and W. 31st St.) to the posh (the *Surrey* at Madison Ave. and E. 76th St.); this service represents a total of 1,633 suites around the city.

Most of New York's major hotels have complete facilities for the business traveler. Those listed below as having "business services" usually offer such conveniences as meeting rooms, photocopiers, computers, translation services, and express checkout, among others. Call the individual hotel for additional information. All telephone numbers are in the 212 area code unless otherwise indicated. Twenty-four-hour room service and CNN (Cable News Network) are available in all hotels unless otherwise noted.

For an unforgettable New York City experience, we begin with our favorites, followed by our recommendations of cost and quality choices, listed by price category.

GRAND HOTELS

Carlyle A marvel of understated elegance and gentility whose sleek black-and-white entranceway conceals a world of extraordinary style and beauty. To many frequent visitors (such as the late President and Mrs. Kennedy) this is the *only* place in town. The 180 guestrooms—affording expansive views of the Upper East Side and *Central Park*—are decorated with comfortable, overstuffed chairs, tasteful antiques, and heavy, flowered drapes; some suites boast pianos for those who like to tickle the ivories. Downstairs the Turkish-inspired *Gallery,* with large, burgundy banquettes and hand-painted screens, is a great place to have tea and people watch.

Ludwig Bemelmans, author and illustrator of the *Madeleine* books (an engaging children's series), painted the walls of the bar (that now bears his name) with fanciful New York scenes inhabited by genteel rabbits languidly sipping martinis and ice-skating elephants. Other delights are the *Café Carlyle* (see *Nightclubs and Nightlife*) and the restaurant, whose velvet-covered walls and English hunting prints are complemented by the subtle yet excellent menu. And for guests who are athletically inclined, there is a deluxe for-guests-only spa and a skylit fitness center on the third floor. Business services are available. 35 E. 76th St. (phone: 744-1600 or 800-227-5737; fax: 717-4682).

Drake Swissôtel Established in 1926, this hotel has been part of the Swissôtel group since 1981. Inside the grand stone and brick building, rooms are high on comfort; most are decorated in minty greens and ivory hues, with extra touches such as phones in the marble bathrooms, hair dryers, and full-length mirrors; some have terraces. About 10% of the 615 rooms are suites, some with wood-burning fireplaces. This institution on Park Avenue has embarked on a multimillion-dollar improvement program that is bringing guests totally refurbished rooms and highly sophisticated business services, including personal computers, fax machines, and modem hookups. The *Drake Bar* has its own entrance on Park Avenue, and the *Café Suisse* is popular for breakfast and lunch. The staff is multilingual. There is a fitness center, and business services are available (including a center with six computer work stations). 440 Park Ave. at E. 56th St. (phone: 421-0900 or 800-DRAKE-NY; fax: 371-4190).

Lowell One step through the revolving doors of this Art Deco delight—with 65 mostly one- and two-bedroom suites—and you are transported to a cosmopolitan European townhouse where staff members, impeccably clad in morning coats, await your bidding. Details such as the small library behind the concierge's desk, filled with tooled-leather volumes, add to the sense of luxury. Other creature comforts include the wood-burning fireplaces that grace most guestrooms, 18th- and 19th-century prints, Chinese porcelains, and plump down comforters. Elegant bath toiletries, in-room kitchens whose refrigerators are stocked with pâté, fine cheeses, and champagne, as well as a set of bone china and crystal stemware from which to feast, are considered basic necessities. There is even a one-bedroom suite complete with Nautilus weight-lifting equipment. Others can use the new patrons-only gym on the second floor.

Anything from cheeseburgers to caviar is served in the *Pembroke Room,* a re-created 18th-century English tearoom, and room service is available until midnight. At afternoon tea, as guests settle back into Louis XVI striped silk chairs, all seems right with the world—reason enough for this property to be the only Manhattan member of the prestigious Relais & Châteaux group. Business services are available. 28 E. 63rd St. (phone: 838-1400 or 800-221-4444; fax: 319-4230).

Mark This graceful hostelry, whose house motto proclaims, "Your demands, our obsession," offers service with a capital S. A mixture of 18th-century English and Italian-influenced art and architecture creates a pleasingly uncluttered look; Piranesi prints, marble, and delicate floral patterns repeated in the wallpaper and fabrics harmonize beautifully. The 120 rooms and 80 suites feature overstuffed chairs, credenzas, and sofas, all in a neoclassical Italian motif; cable TV; two-line phones; pantries with refrigerator, sink, and stove; and luxurious bathrooms with heated towel bars and heating lamps, separate glass shower stalls, tub, bidet, and vanity. Suites are large, with a library, wet bar, large terrace, and separate living, dining, and bedroom areas (try to book one of the five suites that open out onto terraces with truly dazzling views). Those in the mood for serious pampering should consider the Presidential Suite, with its immense circular foyer and substantial columns. The hotel's continental *Mark's* restaurant has become an Upper East Side favorite. Business services are available. 25 E. 77th St. (phone: 744-4300 or 800-THE-MARK; fax: 744-2749).

Mayfair Hotel Baglioni Diplomats, socialites, and royalty probably would be more vocal in their approval of this polished, European-style beauty (formerly the *Mayfair Regent*) if they weren't fearful that their coveted hideaway would become wildly overcrowded. General Manager Dario Mariotti orchestrates the inner workings of this pleasure palace, and he is always on hand to discuss a guest's special preferences or share an anecdote.

The 80 regally furnished rooms and 120 suites (28 with woodburning fireplaces) are adorned with antiques as well as excellent reproductions. Tea here is considered de rigueur among the social set. The hotel's restaurant, *Le Cirque,* is considered one of the city's best (see *Eating Out*). Business services are available. 610 Park Ave at 65th St. (phone: 288-0800 or 800-223-0542; fax: 737-0538).

Peninsula Nothing short of "top drawer" will do to describe this sumptuous, 242-room wonder, a turn-of-the-century landmark (originally the *Gotham*) that has undergone multiple reincarnations in style. Its current owners, the Peninsula Group, have transformed the property into an Americanized version of their legendary flagship, the *Peninsula* in Hong Kong, whose reputation among travelers is unparalleled. Art Nouveau guestrooms are ample and attractive, subtly decorated in shades of rose and celadon green, and a few even overlook *St. Patrick's Cathedral.* The hotel's pièce de résistance is the Presidential Suite, available for $3,000 per night.

If sightseeing pressures prove overwhelming, unwind in the *Pen Top Bar* on the roof or the *Gotham Lounge*. Exercise mavens may want to visit the elaborate two-story fitness center and spa, where they can aerobicize until they are just exhausted enough to stagger to the massage rooms for a muscle-soothing session. Grab a tasty snack or light meal at *Le Bistro d'Adrienne,* or wait until dinnertime to sample the excellent Swiss and Oriental-influenced fare at the *Adrienne* restaurant. Business services are available. 700 Fifth Ave. at W. 55th St. (phone: 247-2200 or 800-262-9467; fax: 903-3974).

Pierre Built in 1930, this respectable grande dame, currently owned by the nonpareil Four Seasons Group of Canada, has preserved its pristine reputation and exquisite ambience. The staff still caters to its guests with the expertise of family retainers. The 206 guestrooms are furnished with Chippendale pieces and fabrics in subdued tones, and some have *Central Park* views. Elevators are still operated by attendants, and the entrance areas were refurbished in 1993. There also is a new gym exclusively for hotel guests. Good news for animal lovers: This is one of the few hotels in New York City where small pets are allowed.

The *Café Pierre* has all the elegance of a French château, with its low marble balconies, tall candelabra, and gray velvet chairs; the fare is first-rate. The *Rotunda Room* boasts playful cherubim and demigods looking down from immense murals, a white marble staircase, and a high-domed ceiling; try the delectable sandwiches and scones that accompany afternoon tea. For the ultimate indulgence, order breakfast in bed—a morning feast served on a white wicker tray with a copy of your favorite newspaper tucked in the side; choices include Yorkshire popovers filled with wild mushrooms and scrambled eggs, and raisin and cinnamon French toast with orange syrup. Business services are available. Fifth Ave. and E. 61 St. (phone: 838-8000 or 800-PIERRE4; fax: 826-0319).

Plaza Athénée Set discreetly on a quiet residential street between Park and Madison Avenues, this elegant establishment, built in 1927, was purchased in 1981 by the Forte hotel chain and re-created in the image of the century-old *Plaza Athénée* in Paris. Small and sumptuous, this stateside version of that landmark has earned a reputation for excellence, and rivals the French original in both ambience and service.

The 17-story structure has 153 guestrooms, including 36 suites, all of which meld a European aura with American attention to detail and convenience. The bedrooms are decorated with paisley fabrics and velvet headboards, and include such modern amenities as VCRs and dehumidifiers. The marble bathrooms are luxurious, adorned with fresh flowers and equipped with every necessity. Most of the rooms and suites have pantries with a refrigerator and small stove; the 10 deluxe suites have dining rooms and/or terraces and solariums. Other highlights include *Le Régence* restaurant, which serves French fare in grand surroundings, and the cozy lounge, with nightly piano music. The guests-only gym is equipped with rowing, Nautilus, and stair machines plus free weights. Business services are available. 37 E. 64th St. (phone: 734-9100 or 800-447-8800; fax: 772-0958).

Regency This Loews landmark is prized by businesspeople, society matrons, and rock and movie stars for its exclusivity and privacy, and a 1990 basement-to-roof restoration and 1993 refurbishing have only added to its luster. The 374 guestrooms are decorated in mauve, green, and salmon, with tasteful antique reproductions adding to the sense of coziness. Downstairs is a state-of-the-art fitness center; on request stationary bicycles can also be whisked up to your room.

In the *540 Lounge* trilingual young men debate the state of the world as a pianist plays background music. Arise early on a weekday morning and join the elite crowd in the sober *540 Park Avenue* restaurant, where the term "power breakfast" originated. Business services are available. 540 Park Ave. at E. 61st St. (phone: 759-4100 or 800-23LOEWS; fax: 688-2898).

St. Regis Built in 1904 by John Jacob Astor and now under the Sheraton banner, this completely renovated (1991), elaborate, 20-story Beaux Arts landmark, with its prestigious Fifth Avenue address, offers all the sophisticated grandeur of turn-of-the-century Manhattan. Many of the hotel's best-known features have been carefully preserved, including the famous *St. Regis Roof* (the only hotel rooftop ballroom in New York City), with its crystal chandeliers, elaborate floral wall panels, and sky-blue ceiling painted with puffy clouds. The equally renowned *King Cole* bar also has been faithfully re-created, with its Maxfield Parrish *King Cole* mural returned to its rightful place over the bar. Also on the premises are *Lespinasse,* an elegant dining room serving French fare (see *Eating Out*), and *Astor Court,* a handsome first-floor salon for afternoon tea, drinks, and light snacks.

The 313 rooms, including 91 palatial suites, are decorated in soft grays, whites, and blues with antique Louis XV furnishings and Oriental rugs, and are equipped with fax machines and special two-line telephones that can deliver messages and information in five languages, operate the TV set and radio, and adjust the room temperature. The gray marble bathrooms feature double sinks, separate showers and baths, hair dryers, scales, and other special touches. Other guest-pampering features are a private butler on each floor and a concierge. Business services are available. Fifth Ave. and E. 55th St. (phone: 753-4500 or 800-759-7550; fax: 787-3447).

Waldorf Towers With a private entrance that leads into a rarified world, this *très soigné* landmark is an adjunct of the fabled *Waldorf-Astoria* (see below). From floors of tricolored marble to acanthus moldings, the interiors are reminiscent of another, more gracious age.

The *Towers* has played host to such international leaders as Queen Elizabeth II and Prince Philip, Winston Churchill, and Anwar Sadat. Others, like Cole Porter, the Duke and Duchess of Windsor, and the Douglas MacArthurs, set up permanent residence here. And every US president from Herbert Hoover to Bill Clinton has used the Presidential Suite as a home base while in New York. The 92 guestrooms, 106 suites, and a number of residential apartments are individually—and exquisitely—decorated: from the ornate carved reliefs to the solid Queen Anne chairs to the richly patterned wallpapers. A crackerjack staff practically jumps to respond to guests' needs. 100 E. 50th St. at Park Ave. (phone: 355-3000 or 800-HILTONS; fax: 758-9209 or 872-4799).

VERY EXPENSIVE

Beekman Tower Small and pleasantly old-fashioned, this 171-suite establishment (convenient to the *United Nations*) has a cocktail lounge boasting splendid skyline views, the *Zephyr* restaurant on the ground floor, and a health club. Business services are available. 3 Mitchell Pl., at First Ave. and E. 49th St. (phone: 355-7300 or 800-ME-SUITE; fax: 753-9366).

Essex House Overlooking *Central Park,* this 40-story landmark (now owned by Nikko Hotels International) recaptured its original 1931 grandeur after a $70 million restoration completed in 1991. Its 595 large guestrooms are tastefully decorated in French and English country styles, although the public areas have a 1920s flavor. In addition to its chi-chi restaurant, *Les Célébrités* (which features primarily French fare with Oriental accents), there is the less formal *Café Botanica,* with a pleasant continental/California menu. Business services are available. 160 Central Park S. at Seventh Ave. (phone: 247-0300 or 800-NIKKO-US; fax: 315-1839).

Four Seasons New York This executive-oriented property opened in 1993 on one of the city's most sought-after shopping streets, just steps from Fifth Avenue. The 52-story French limestone building was designed in a clean, Art Deco–influenced style by eminent American architect I. M. Pei. With a lofty marble lobby whose onyx ceiling arches 30 feet overhead, tall, elegant windows, and skyscraper tower, the hotel harkens back to the grand hotels of the 1920s and 1930s. The 307 exceptionally spacious rooms and 60 one- and two-bedroom suites feature refrigerators, cable TV and VCRs, modems for personal computer hookup, and large, luxuriously equipped marble bathrooms. There are two restaurants (*5757* and the *Lobby Lounge*), a 24-hour concierge, a spa, and a health club. Business services are available. 57 E. 57th St., between Madison and Park Aves. (phone: 758-5700 or 800-332-3442; fax: 758-5711).

Michelangelo The former *Parc Fifty One* provides luxury lodgings in a part of town not traditionally associated with deluxe digs. The 178 large guestrooms come with such amenities as multi-line phones, two TV sets, and computer and fax hookups. There are valets to pack and unpack for you and even an electronic paging service. The hotel's lobby bar is a far more quiet and soothing place to have a drink than the popular *Bellini by Cipriani* restaurant that holds court on the ground floor. The hotel is part of the Italian Star chain, which explains the large number of Italian guests, the stylish Italian ambience, and, of course, the name. Business services, including free limousines to Wall Street, also are available. 152 W. 51st St. at Seventh Ave. (phone: 765-1900; 800-237-0990 outside New York State; fax: 541-6604).

New York Palace This midtown property combines the landmark Henry Villard house with a 51-story high-rise as its backdrop. The historic areas of the building boast elegant public rooms decorated in marble, crystal, and gold. The 963 guestrooms are fine, though not special. There are three entrances: one less hectic on East 50th Street, one on East 51st Street, and the third through wrought-iron gates on Madison Avenue. At press time this former Helmsley property was in the process of being bought by the Sultan of Brunei, who owns the *Dorchester* in London. Business services are available. 455 Madison Ave., from E. 50th to E. 51st St. (phone: 888-7000 or 800-697-2522; fax: 303-6000).

Omni Berkshire Place This property will undergo an extensive, $50-million renovation that is not expected to be complete before the autumn. Visitors interested in staying here should call for updated information. 21 E. 52nd St. (phone: 753-5800 or 800-THE-OMNI; fax: 355-7646).

Parker Meridien Billing itself as New York's "first French hotel," this establishment offers 648 tasteful rooms, several bars, and the new *Shin's,* serving Japanese-American cuisine. The hotel completed renovations last year with the opening of a new lounge, the *Bar Montparnasse,* in the former formal dining room; the food includes *tapas* and seafood, and there is live music at night. The sports-minded will enjoy *Club Raquette,* for racquetball, handball, and squash, and the rooftop running track that encircles an enclosed pool—from which the views of *Central Park* are lovely; there's a health club too. Business services are available. 118 W. 57th St. (phone: 245-5000; fax: 307-1776).

Plaza The only New York City hotel designated a historic landmark, this erratic, but mostly elegant hostelry, with over 800 rooms, affords most guests lovely views of *Central Park*. Hansom cabs can be hired right outside the entrance. Now a Donald Trump property, the hotel has long been renowned for (pricey) tea in the *Palm Court* and drinks in the *Oak Room,* not to mention dinner in the *Oyster Bar* or *Edwardian Room*. Business services are available. Fifth Ave. from W. 58th to W. 59th St. (phone: 546-5493 or 800-228-3000; fax: 759-3167).

Rihga Royal New York's tallest hotel (54 stories high) is also the most luxurious of the all-suite properties, catering to the corporate traveler. Each of the 500 one- and two-bedroom suites is equipped with two TV sets, a VCR, a kitchen, three telephones, and computer hookups. Business services are available. 151 W. 54th St. (phone: 307-5000 or 800-937-5454; fax: 765-6530).

Ritz-Carlton A number of the 174 rooms and 40 suites at this classic property offer wonderful views of *Central Park* and the city skyline. Some of the suites have small terraces, and nonsmoking rooms and handicapped access are available. Amenities include twice-daily maid service, terry-cloth robes in the rooms, two-line telephones, and personal valet service. Facilities include a fitness center with park views and the *Fantino* restaurant, which came about as part of renovations completed last year; the bar is a popular meeting place for both guests and New Yorkers. Business services, including complimentary limousines to Wall Street, also are available. 112 Central Park S. (phone: 757-1900 or 800-241-3333; fax: 757-9620).

Royalton The management of ultra-hip *Morgans* (see below) impressed New York once again, this time with a 167-room property not far from Times Square. The block-long lobby, with areas specifically designed for reading, conversation, and board games, is a popular gathering spot (and the restrooms have to be seen to be believed). Many of the guestrooms, designed by architect André Putman, come with a wood-burning fireplace in the living area, which also includes a VCR and stereo cassette deck. The bar/restaurant *44* fills up with fashionable types from the nearby Condé Nast Building on Madison Avenue. Business services are available. 44 W. 44th St. (phone: 869-4400 or 800-635-9013; fax: 869-8965).

Sherry-Netherland Though a little less renowned than the *Plaza* and the *Pierre* (its immediate neighbors), it is no less luxurious, especially since a full restoration was completed in 1993. Keep in mind that reservations can sometimes be a problem, because this establishment is largely residential, with only about 60 rooms available for visitors. The *Harry Cipriani* restaurant features a northern Italian menu. 781 Fifth Ave. at E. 59th St. (phone: 355-2800; 800-223-0522 outside New York State; fax: 319-4306).

Stanhope This posh, upper Fifth Avenue place has 141 rooms, most of them one- or two-bedroom suites with views of *Central Park* or Manhattan's spectacular skyline. Guests meet and relax in the opulent public rooms and enjoy a wide range of dining options, including an outdoor café in summer and afternoon tea in the sitting room. There is a fitness club, and complimentary limousine service is provided to midtown weekday mornings and to *Lincoln Center, Carnegie Hall,* and the theater district in the evenings. Business services are available. Across from the *Metropolitan Museum of Art* at 995 Fifth Ave. (phone: 288-5800; 800-828-1123 outside New York City; fax: 517-0088).

UN Plaza Park Hyatt In addition to its beautifully integrated modern design, from the sleek, green-tinted glass exterior through the dark green marble reception area to the top 10 floors, this property also offers 428 rooms with magnificent city views. Managed by Hyatt International, it has both a truly international staff and exceptional facilities—including a tennis court, heated pool, and exercise room. Its restaurant is the aptly named *Ambassador Grill,* for the hotel faces the *UN.* Business services are available. First Ave. and E. 44th St. (phone: 355-3400 or 800-228-9000; fax: 702-5051).

Westbury The tapestries at the entrance are Belgian, the soft pink carpeting in the marble lobby, Irish—as befits this tranquil, European-style hotel (part of the Forte group) with its large international clientele. There are 231 handsome rooms, and the *Polo* restaurant serves fine continental fare. Business services are available. 15 E. 69th St. at Madison Ave. (phone: 535-2000 or 800-225-5843; fax: 535-5058).

EXPENSIVE

Algonquin Long a favorite among literary types, this 165-room hotel's reputation is most closely connected with the days of the literary "Round Table" in the *Oak Room,* its famous piano bar and cabaret restaurant. Convenient to both midtown and the theater district. Business services are available. 59 W. 44th St., between Fifth and Sixth Aves. (phone: 840-6800 or 800-548-0345; fax: 944-1419).

Box Tree Eccentric, unusual, and housed in two East Side brownstones, this place is for those who appreciate detail-oriented luxury. Each of the 13 rooms is individually designed with different European furnishings. The restaurant serves very good French fare with an English accent. Photocopiers are available. 250 E. 49th St. (phone: 758-8320; fax: 308-3899).

Doral Tuscany In the middle of attractive Murray Hill (between 34th and 40th Sts. on the East Side), this 121-room hotel is not widely known outside the city, but guests who know it well treasure the high level of service and discreet atmosphere. There's a restaurant, and guests have free access to a fitness center a block away. Business services are available. 120 E. 39th St. (phone: 686-1600 or 800-22-DORAL; fax: 779-7822).

Embassy Suites This 460-suite property has an elegant lobby, well-appointed rooms, and an instantly attentive staff. All suites, some of which look out over Times Square, come equipped with a wet bar, microwave oven, and refrigerator. Business services are available. 1568 Broadway (phone: 719-1600 or 800-EMBASSY; fax: 921-5212).

Grand Hyatt Originally, this was Donald Trump's idea of how a glitzy New York City hotel should look: mirrored exterior glass and lots of shiny chrome. Now managed by Hyatt, one of its prime attractions is the lobby's upper-level *Sungarden,* a glass-enclosed bar, cocktail lounge, and restaurant that overhangs the hotel's entrance and the busy East 42nd Street traffic. There are 1,400 smallish rooms dressed in rich, earthy tones. Business services are available. 109 E. 42nd St. at Park Ave. (phone: 883-1234, 800-233-1234, or 800-228-9000; fax: 697-3772).

Holiday Inn Crowne Plaza This razzle-dazzle, 46-story glass tower in the Times Square area offers 770 guestrooms, six Crowne Plaza Club floors (VIP floors with special services), the 15th floor *New York Health Club* (which has a 50-foot pool under a domed skylight), and the popular *Broadway Grill,* featuring California-style fare. Business services are available. 1605 Broadway at W. 49th St. (phone: 977-4000 or 800-HOLIDAY; fax: 333-7393).

Inter-Continental New York Formerly the *Barclay,* this large, distinguished property with 692 smallish guestrooms on a busy East Side corner is one block south of the *Waldorf.* The well-appointed suites have two-line phones with speaker capabilities. Amenities include a health club and the oak-paneled *Barclay* restaurant. Business services are available. 111 E. 48th St. at Lexington Ave. (phone: 755-5900 or 800-327-0200; fax: 644-0079).

Loews New York This 726-room midtowner, convenient for businesspeople and conventioneers with East Side interests, offers a reliably good restaurant, the *Lexington Avenue Grill,* the Club 51 floor with a private lounge and concierge, and a fully staffed fitness center. Business services are available. Lexington Ave. at E. 51st St. (phone: 752-7000 or 800-23-LOEWS; fax: 758-6311).

Macklowe With 638 starkly chic guestrooms by well-known designer Bill Durham, this 52-story tower in the Times Square area features a fitness center as well as a 100,000-square-foot conference center, all built around an existing theater (the *Hudson*). Business services are available. 145 W. 44th St. (phone: 768-4400; fax: 789-7688).

Marriott East Side Formerly the *Halloran House,* this historic 665-room hotel was built in the 1920s by A. L. Harmon, who designed the *Empire State Building;* it is a mix of Gothic, Byzantine, and Italian architectural styles. The informal *Champions* and more formal *Shelton Grille* are both enjoyable dining options; the 16th-floor *Fountain Room and Terrace* is the hotel's private meeting room. There also are nonsmoking and Concierge Club floors.

Room service is available until 11:30 PM. Business services also are available. 525 Lexington Ave., between E. 48th and E. 49th Sts. (phone: 755-4000 or 800-228-9290; fax: 751-3440).

Morgans Without so much as a sign out front, this 112-room treasure by Ian Shrager, of *Paramount* and *Royalton* fame, is named for the nearby *Pierpont Morgan Library*. Some unusual standards include continental breakfast (at no extra charge) each morning, and, in guestrooms, a stereo cassette player and TV with stereo sound (VCRs and videotapes are available). Bathrooms are pure high-tech, and artwork is by the late avant-garde photographer Robert Mapplethorpe. The suites are reasonably priced. Business services are available. 237 Madison Ave. at E. 37th St. (phone: 686-0300 or 800-334-3408; fax: 779-8352).

New York Helmsley A shining glass skyscraper on East 42nd Street, this executive-oriented, 788-room facility has special services for the business traveler—secretaries, fax machines, photocopying, a concierge desk, express checkout, and seven meeting rooms among them. For dining there's *Mindy*'s, a continental restaurant, and for drinks and piano music try *Harry's New York Bar*. Room service can be called upon until 1 AM. 212 E. 42nd St. (phone: 490-8900 or 800-221-4982; fax: 986-4792).

New York Hilton An enormous modern structure near *Rockefeller Center*, this is one of New York's largest properties, and it's about as efficiently run as any hotel with more than 2,000 rooms can be. The well-equipped health club has saunas and even a videocassette player for your own workout tape. Small pets (under 20 pounds) are allowed. Business services are available. 1335 Ave. of the Americas, between W. 53rd and W. 54th Sts. (phone: 586-7000 or 800-HILTONS; fax: 315-1374).

New York Renaissance Built in 1992 as the *Ramada Renaissance Times Square*, this 25-story black tower overlooking the theater district has 305 rooms and 10 suites furnished in Art Deco style. In addition to sybaritic marble baths, there is a fax machine and three telephones in every guestroom, and an exercise room is on the premises. The public rooms include a restaurant, a bar, and a lounge featuring nightly entertainment. Business services are available. 714 Seventh Ave. at W. 47th St. (phone: 765-7676 or 800-228-9898; fax: 765-1962).

Sheraton Manhattan Formerly the *Sheraton City Squire*, this property underwent an enormous renovation in 1992. The façade now features Art Deco grillwork, tinted windows, and an elegant canopy; the lobby and reception area have been expanded and decorated with contemporary furniture and richly textured carpets and upholstery. In addition, the pool has been refurbished, and there is a fitness club. The 659 comfortable, modern rooms offer such amenities as in-room office supplies, computer and fax connections, coffee makers, cable TV, and express video checkout. Business services are also available. 790 Seventh Ave. at W. 51st St. (phone: 581-3300 or 800-325-3535; fax: 315-4265).

Sheraton New York Part of the same mega-renovation as its *Sheraton* neighbor (above), this 50-story modern monolith, previously the *Sheraton Centre,* is always busy. The 1,752 rooms are quite comfortable, and it's only a short walk to the theater district or the *Museum of Modern Art.* The top five floors, called the *Sheraton Towers,* are for more exclusive "business class" clients. (Business services are available for non-*Towers* guests as well.) There is a fitness center too. 811 Seventh Ave. at W. 53rd St. (phone: 581-1000 or 800-325-3535; fax: 315-4265).

Sheraton Park Avenue Formerly the *Russell,* this is one of those "secret" hotels that regulars love to keep to themselves. The 150-room property is convenient to *Grand Central Station* and the garment center, and the comfortable guestrooms boast high ceilings, walk-in closets, three phones, and separate work areas. *Russell's* is a fine dining restaurant, and the *Judge's Chamber* serves buffet lunch in a book-lined club setting. Business services are available. 45 Park Ave. at E. 37th St. (phone: 685-7676 or 800-325-3535; fax: 889-3193).

Tudor Located in New York's historic *Tudor City* district, steps away from the *United Nations* and directly across town from major theaters, this 1931 property, with a unique façade combining Art Deco design with Tudor touches, offers 300 comfortable guestrooms. Each has a mini-bar, two-line telephones, outlets for computers and fax machines, and a marble bathroom with towel heaters; some of the suites have Jacuzzis and private terraces. An innovative touch is the addition of six Circadian rooms, whose special features, including the lighting, help jet-lagged travelers adjust. *Cecil's* serves fine American/English fare; there's also *The Regency* lounge, where afternoon tea is served. The fitness center is fully equipped with massage rooms. Business services are available. 304 E. 42nd St. (phone: 986-8800 or 800-TRY-TUDOR; fax: 986-1758).

Waldorf-Astoria The degree of comfort delivered in this 1,212-room legend has contributed to its good reputation; it is also a popular convention property. *Peacock Alley* is both a lively cocktail rendezvous and elegant French restaurant; the clock in the middle of the lobby may be New York's favorite meeting place; and the *Plus One* fitness center features a wide variety of exercise equipment, health treatments, and consultations and escorted jogs with licensed trainers. *Kenneth's,* run by the legendary hairdresser himself, is on site. Business services are available. See also the *Waldorf Towers* in "Grand Hotels," above. 301 Park Ave., from E. 49th to E. 50th St. (phone: 355-3000 or 800-HILTONS; fax: 872-6380).

MODERATE

Barbizon This East Side establishment offers 345 rooms, a comfortable café, and an obliging concierge desk. Business services are available. 140 E. 63rd St. (phone: 838-5700 or 800-223-1020; fax: 223-3287).

Gorham The variety of room-and-bed combinations possible in this recently restored hotel, and the fact that all 120 units have a kitchenette, dining table, and color TV set, make this a great boon to families traveling with children. Business services are available. 136 W. 55th St. (phone: 245-1800 or 800-735-0710; fax: 582-8332).

Holiday Inn Downtown Chinatown's first hotel, this 223-room property (formerly the *Maria*) is reminiscent of Hong Kong: Exotic flowers fill the lobby, and Chinese screens and marble and rosewood furnishings grace the public areas. Although the rooms are not large, many offer fine views of Chinatown and the Hudson River. The *Pacifica Lounge* serves afternoon tea, and the *Pacifica* restaurant features authentic Cantonese cooking as well as continental cuisine. Additional amenities include a concierge on each floor, nightly turn-down service, and valet parking. Business services are available. 138 Lafayette St. (phone: 966-8898 or 800-HOLIDAY; fax: 966-3933).

Journey's End This 29-story property is noteworthy for its excellent location (just east of Fifth Avenue, across from the *New York Public Library*) and reasonable rates—well below the city's standard. All 187 guestrooms are equipped with a work area and cable TV set, and guests receive complimentary morning coffee (plus complimentary pastries on weekends) and a copy of *USA Today*. Business services are available. 3 E. 40th St. (phone: 447-1500 or 800-221-2222; fax: 685-5214 for reservations, 213-0972 for guests).

Mayflower This establishment is a favorite with ballet, opera, and concert buffs (it's close to *Lincoln Center*), as well as celebrities from the arts world. Guests enjoy a relaxed atmosphere and 377 large, comfortable rooms with pantries. Room service delivers until midnight. Business services are available. 15 Central Park W., between W. 61st and W. 62nd Sts. (phone: 265-0060 or 800-223-4164; fax: 265-5098).

New York Hotel Pennsylvania Once the *Statler,* more recently the *Ramada Madison Square Garden,* this 1,700-room Stanford White landmark building across from *Penn Station* offers both comfort and class. It is now part of the Best Western chain. Business services are available. 401 Seventh Ave. at W. 33rd St. (phone: 736-5000 or 800-223-8585; fax: 212-502-8798).

Paramount Another Ian Schrager dazzler, designed by Philippe Starck, this trendy hotel in the middle of the theater district has 610 tiny guestrooms filled with oddly shaped furniture. There's a theatrical, dual-level lobby for socializing, the *Whiskey* bar, and even a playroom for kids. Business services are available. 235 W. 46th St. (phone: 764-5500 or 800-225-7474; fax: 354-5237).

Radisson Empire The 375 rooms in this Metromedia property all offer compact disc players, VCRs, and heated towel racks. The *Empire Grill* is the hotel's restaurant. Business services are available. 44 W. 63rd St. (phone: 265-7400 or 800-333-3333; fax: 315-0349).

Salisbury Owned by the Calvary Baptist Church (thus, no alcohol is permitted on the premises), it has a small, welcoming lobby and 320 nice-size, pastel-decorated rooms (all with refrigerators and pantries but no stoves). It's a favorite with musicians who like the location near *Carnegie Hall*. Business services are available. 123 W. 57th St. (phone: 246-1300 or 800-223-0680; fax: 977-7752).

Shoreham On a fashionable block off Fifth Avenue and fresh from a stylish restoration, this place has 47 contemporary, good-size rooms and 37 suites, all with modern bathrooms and cable TV. The hotel has a new lounge (for guests only) where breakfast and specialty coffees are served; another addition is the glassed-in roof deck. Each guestroom has a small refrigerator. 33 W. 55th St. (phone: 247-6700 or 800-553-3347; fax: 765-9741).

Wales Comfortable, recently restored, and reasonably priced, this hotel is in a very appealing residential neighborhood, close to *Central Park* and the *Metropolitan* and *Guggenheim Museums*. It offers more than 90 individually decorated rooms and suites, some with kitchenettes or four-poster beds, all with cable TV. One of the city's best breakfasts can be had in the lobby's *Sarabeth's* restaurant. 1295 Madison Ave. at E. 92nd St. (phone: 876-6000 or 800-428-5252; fax: 860-7000).

Wyndham This extremely well-located, 125-room property has been fondly described as being like a posh country inn; a fine, small London hotel; and a private club. It takes a certain self-sufficiency to enjoy its special appeal; there's no room service, and the hotel restaurant is closed on weekends. 42 W. 58th St., between Fifth and Sixth Aves. (phone: 753-3500 or 800-257-1111; fax: 754-5638).

INEXPENSIVE

Broadway American This Upper West Side establishment is a good bet for the budget-minded. Only 10% of its 430 rooms have private bathrooms; other baths are shared. Each room has a refrigerator, and there are kitchenettes on every other floor in lieu of room service. Broadway and W. 77th St. (phone: 362-1100; fax: 787-9521).

Chelsea At this architectural and historic landmark, Dylan Thomas, Arthur Miller, Lenny Bruce, Diego Rivera, Martha Graham, and others once found their New York home. The down-at-the-heels atmosphere in this 19th-century structure with local art in the lobby is distinctly unmodern, unhomogenized, and unsterilized; it is not for those who want to feel pampered. There is a large permanent occupancy in about 200 of the rooms, with 100 rooms available for shorter-term guests; almost all of these have private baths. Some rooms have a kitchen, a fireplace, and a bathroom; others have none of the above. Service is quirky, and the management is not overly generous with amenities like washcloths and bath mats. For the adventurous only; make reservations well in advance. 222 W. 23rd St. (phone: 243-3700; fax: 243-3700).

Herald Square With no frills (no room service or restaurant) but neat, clean, and well located, this budget hotel is in a century-old building that served as the original home of *Life* magazine. The 120 rooms are modestly decorated, and a few of the bathrooms have only showers, not tubs. The lobby is purely functional. 19 W. 31st St. (phone: 279-4017 or 800-727-1888; fax: 643-4208).

Olcott Comfortable and adequate, this typical New York residential hotel offers some 100 rooms as transient accommodations. Spacious facilities and a homey atmosphere are its advantages. Most rooms are suites, with a living room, bedroom, kitchen, and bathroom. Reservations should be made several weeks in advance. 27 W. 72nd St., only a block from *Central Park* (phone: 877-4200; fax: 580-0511).

Roosevelt Long established, this traditional favorite with 1,008 rooms is quaint, clean—and a little tattered looking these days. For some guests, however, the low price may make up for the worn carpets and wallpaper, and the location is still prime, as evidenced by the hotel's busy meetings schedule. Room service is on call until 11 PM. Business services are available. Madison Ave. at E. 45th St. (phone: 661-9600; 800-223-1870 outside New York State; fax: 687-5064).

EATING OUT

New York City is, plain and simply, the culinary capital of the world. There may be more good French restaurants in Paris or more fine Chinese eating places in Hong Kong, but no other city can offer the gastronomic diversity available in New York; it is not unusual for dedicated eaters to make several pilgrimages to New York each year simply to satisfy their sophisticated palates.

Regrettably, New York's tastiest dishes do not come cheap, though there are places to dine around the city where you need not pay the check in 30-, 60-, or 90-day notes. Currently, a new breed of American bistros is cropping up and challenging the reputation of New York restaurants for being uniformly overpriced and intimidating. Their simple approach toward both food and atmosphere is helping to redefine the way New Yorkers dine out. Although prices have leveled off and even dropped in recent years in response to the recession, you can expect to pay top dollar for top establishments here. For the restaurants we list as very expensive, the tab for two for a three-course dinner will come to $135 or more; at restaurants in the expensive category, $90 to $135; at a moderate restaurant, $60 and $90; and in an inexpensive establishment, $30 to $60. These price ranges do *not* include drinks, wine, tip, or tax. All telephone numbers are in the 212 area code unless otherwise indicated.

> **NOTE**
>
> Unless otherwise mentioned, restaurants are open for lunch and dinner, and reservations are *always necessary;* for the higher priced and more popular places, reservations may be necessary several weeks in advance. In addition, men are required to wear a jacket and tie at many of the more expensive restaurants. And major credit cards are accepted unless otherwise indicated.

New York's finest restaurants offer far more than food and drink; dining out in the city's better establishments is often a gala event, rather than a simple meal. With that in mind, we begin with our favorite dining spots, which are guaranteed to pique your curiosity and delight your palate, followed by our recommendations of cost and quality choices, listed by price category.

BEST BITES OF THE BIG APPLE

Bouley Behind the handsome, carved wooden door is a perfect venue for fine French (and American) fare—a shimmering mirage of lace curtains, Impressionist paintings, and meticulously prepared dishes—all under the stewardship of owner David Bouley. The spectacular selections—based on what's most fresh at the market—are served without fuss. Cream-less butternut soup topped with roasted chestnuts, hot foie gras salad, and roast monkfish accompanied by savoy cabbage and a tomato-coriander sauce are instant hits. Jacket and tie required. Closed Saturdays for lunch and Sundays. Reservations are necessary at least three to four weeks in advance for Friday and Saturday nights. 165 Duane St. (phone: 608-3852).

Café des Artistes From the frolicking wood nymphs of Howard Chandler Christy's rather risqué murals to the leaded-glass windows, this elegant dining place exudes romance. One drawback is that tables practically abut one another, which discourages spontaneous wedding proposals. Owner George Lang periodically tours the dining room and encourages his guests to sample such country French dishes as sweetbread headcheese with cucumber vinaigrette, pot au feu, and the illustrious Ilona torte, a flour-less chocolate cake that contains 10 (ah, cholesterol!) eggs. Come here on weekends for the most beautiful brunch in town. Jacket (no tie) required. Open daily. 1 W. 67th St. (phone: 877-3500).

Daniel Two years ago, after an illustrious six-year reign at the celebrated *Le Cirque,* Daniel Boulud of Lyon decided it was time to strike out on his own. Set in an airy, sedate dining room, this dining place offers culinary memories that will stay with you. Begin with the nine-herb ravioli, sauced with a *coulis* (purée) of tomato, sage, wild mushrooms, and pine nuts, then move on to the grilled pepper tuna prepared in a red wine sauce. Leave room for the warm chocolate soufflé with pistachio ice cream—divine taste experiences like this don't come along every day. Jackets required, ties requested. Closed Sundays and briefly after *New Year's.* Reservations necessary one month in advance for weekend dining; otherwise, two weeks is recommended. 20 E. 76th St., between Fifth and Madison Aves. (phone: 288-0033).

Four Seasons A dining establishment that reaffirms one's faith in an expertly prepared meal, gracefully presented in perfect surroundings. Patrons can choose to dine in either the more intimate Grill Room or the coolly elegant Pool Room. The menu changes with the seasons, and highlights might include the delectable chicken liver terrine with black truffles; soft-shell crabs with lemon butter, fiddlehead ferns, and aiole; or *côte de boeuf* with bone marrow and bordelaise. Weight-conscious diners can sample superbly prepared spa dishes, which include veal paillard with peppers and pineapple, and poached sea bass with yucca and hearts of palm. In addition to a reasonably priced prix-fixe menu, there is also a pre- and après-theater menu, as well as a "Grill at Night" choice. For dessert order one of the delicate soufflés at the beginning of the meal so that it will arrive in a state of puffed perfection by the time coffee is served. Closed Sundays. 99 E. 52nd St., between Park and Lexington Aves. (phone: 754-9494). See also *Quintessential New York* in DIVERSIONS.

Lutèce The beloved child (actually over 30 years old) of proprietor André Soltner, this extraordinary place prides itself on its unflaggingly fine service and soul-satisfying culinary achievements. Located in a townhouse on the East Side, it is a perfect rendezvous to linger over dinner and then sip a licorice-flavored Pernod at the tiny, zinc-covered bar. Soft light filters down from the high ceiling of the main dining room, which resembles a beautifully cultivated garden.

A curving staircase leads up to the more formal, crystal-chandeliered dining rooms, one wall of which is adorned by a fine

Gobelin tapestry. Menu highlights range from simple sole meunière to rack of lamb caramelized in honey. To sample the combination of classic selections, innovative nouvelle creations, and Alsatian specialties, order the *menu de dégustation,* a tasting of six or seven small courses, or the reasonably priced prix-fixe menu. Delectable desserts, such as chocolate mousse with rum, and flambéed Alsatian crêpes, have inspired many to inquire if *Lutèce* would mind setting up a permanent guestroom in the back. Jacket and tie required. Closed Sundays. Make reservations (required) a month in advance. 249 E. 50th St. (phone: 752-2225).

Oyster Bar Deep in the cavernous underground of *Grand Central Station* lies this landmark place where the sound of lobster claws being cracked open mingles with the far-off voice of a stationmaster announcing departures. The *Oyster Bar* packs in the commuter crowd, and it's not unusual for a regular to devour half a dozen bluepoint oysters before catching the evening train. The atmosphere is not exactly genteel. It's noisy, it lacks air conditioning, and there is an ever-present cloud of cigar smoke. Furthermore, the presentation and service can be unpredictable, but to dine here is to be a part of New York.

Those dining at the long, S-shaped counter opt for chiloé oysters from Chile, New Zealand coromandels, Alaskan sourdoughs, or Virginian mobjacks. The rest of the seafood on the menu is less consistently amazing, but the littleneck and cherrystone clams, Maine lobsters, Dutch herring, Dover sole, and Maryland softshell crabs are delicious—especially when accompanied by a glass or two from the excellent wine cellar. Closed weekends, and open only until 9:30 PM weekdays. Reservations unnecessary. *Grand Central Station* (lower level), E. 42nd St., between Vanderbilt and Lexington Aves. (phone: 490-6650).

Peter Luger New Yorkers who have said fie to their cholesterol counts consider this 1887 Brooklyn steakhouse a godsend. An upscale yet totally relaxed place, it features exposed wooden beams, brass chandeliers, and very low lighting that encourage conversation even from table to table; a dull roar is the quietest level it ever reaches.

In addition to all this congeniality, the food is heartbreakingly good. No menus are handed out; the presumption is that you've come here for one reason: aged porterhouse steak that many swear is the best in town. Accept the premise that you're in good hands, and you'll get along perfectly with the brusque staff. Steaks traditionally arrive accompanied by spinach creamed within an inch of its life and excellent home-fried potatoes (evenings only).

Open daily. Reservations for weekends should be made six weeks in advance; only on Mondays or Tuesdays can you get seated without a reservation. No credit cards accepted. 178 Broadway, Brooklyn (phone: 718-387-7400).

VERY EXPENSIVE

Aquavit In a landmark Rockefeller townhouse, this Scandinavian dining place is actually two dining spots: a formal dining room set around an atrium and waterfall, with prix-fixe and pre-theater menus, and a more casual, less expensive room upstairs featuring simpler fare from a choice of menus. There are many varieties of salmon and game, such as Arctic venison (reindeer) and snow grouse. Try the smorgasbord, caviar bank, and "aquavit chiller," consisting of eight flavored vodkas. Jacket required in the dining room; the upstairs café calls for casual but neat attire. Closed Saturdays for lunch and Sundays. 13 W. 54th St. (phone: 307-7311).

Le Bernardin Gilbert and Maguy Le Coze moved their headquarters from Paris to the Big Apple, where they occupy subtly elegant premises. The menu is fiercely seafood-oriented, and no one prepares the products of the world's oceans more imaginatively or deliciously. Since the doors opened here in 1986, such unusual specialties as tuna tartare and sea urchin soup have become staples of the New York restaurant scene, and it's worth a visit just to see what new wonders are swimming out of the kitchen. A prix-fixe menu is available at dinner. Closed Saturdays for lunch and Sundays. 155 W. 51st St. (phone: 489-1515).

Chanterelle This SoHo eatery, seriously committed to elegant dining, features an excellent prix-fixe meal and a tasting menu, plus a relatively reasonably priced lunch. Begin with seafood sausage, then choose from such entrées as salmon en papillote, rack of lamb, duck in sherry vinegar, or sautéed soft-shell crabs. A cheese board is offered, and dessert might be chocolate pavé, a dense, rich, mousse-like cake. Jacket and tie required. Closed Sundays and Mondays. Make reservations about one month in advance. 2 Harrison St. at Hudson St. (phone: 966-6960).

Le Cirque The tables are too close together, the noise level can be deafening, and reservations must be made many weeks and sometimes months in advance. Still, the remarkable continental fare is enough to make legions of dedicated diners put up with the less-than-ideal atmosphere. Everything on the menu is special and prepared perfectly, but the main reason for dining here is to taste the sublime *crème brûlée* for dessert; nowhere in the world is it better. Jacket and tie required. Closed Sundays. 58 E. 65th St. (phone: 794-9292).

La Grenouille Soft green walls and glorious floral arrangements provide a romantic setting in which to sample such house masterpieces as frogs' legs, thin, sautéed calf's liver, and roast duck. Be prepared, however, for a very haughty, condescending attitude if you're not known to the staff. Closed Sundays and Mondays. 3 E. 52nd St. (phone: 752-1495).

"21" Club The legendary atmosphere and lingering cachet are what lure most visitors, but longtime favorites from the menu, such as the *"21"* burger and chicken hash, are a treat as well. If you're not a regular or a celebrity, the welcome sometimes isn't quite so warm, but to some, just being here is a true New York experience. The elegant upstairs dining room is open on weekdays for lunch only. Jacket and tie required. Closed Sundays. 21 W. 52nd St. (phone: 582-7200).

EXPENSIVE

Alison on Dominick Street This romantic spot on the western fringe of SoHo serves wonderful French-Mediterranean peasant fare. Try the rabbit stew with white-bean ravioli or chef Tom Valenti's signature dish—crusty braised lamb shank. Jacket suggested. Open daily for dinner only. Reservations advised. 38 Dominick St. (phone: 727-1188).

An American Place Celebrated chef-owner Larry Forgione is regarded as one of the spearheads of the New American food preparation movement; sample his American/continental specialties and you'll discover why. Gastronomic delights include grilled free-range chicken with Jerusalem artichokes in a cream sauce, and pan-roasted lamb with black pepper and cumin. Closed Sundays. 2 Park Ave. at E. 32nd St. (phone: 684-2122).

Il Cantinori A beamed ceiling, terra cotta floor, and chairs of wood and straw create the charming ambience at this Tuscan eatery, located on one of the city's loveliest blocks. Begin with *risotto nero* (a rice delicacy in squid ink) or *ravioli alla fiorentina* (dumplings filled with spinach and ricotta cheese) before an entrée of excellent fish or game. For dessert try the chef's version of the popular Italian confection *tiramisù*, espresso-soaked ladyfingers and sweet mascarpone cheese. Closed for lunch on weekends. 32 E. 10th St. (phone: 673-6044).

La Caravelle A traditional bastion of classic French cuisine with all of the attendant hauteur, this is often the choice of New York's smartest set. Menus are consistently interesting, and the kitchen is not merely competent but innovative. The pre-theater menu is a relative bargain. Jacket and tie required. Closed Sundays. 33 W. 55th St. (phone: 586-4252).

Cesarina Pricey but good northern Italian fare, including risotto, pasta, and regional specialties prepared with fresh seafood, and pleasant service are the lures here. If osso buco is on the winter menu, go for it. Very popular at lunch with the elite executive crowd and a nice choice for pre-theater dinner, it is owned by Italy's renowned and elegant *Villa d'Este* hotel. Closed weekends. Reservations advised for lunch. 36 W. 52nd St. (phone: 582-6900).

Gotham Bar & Grill The space here is cavernous (it was originally a warehouse), but an award-winning bilevel design and lofty decor bring the space down to *grand café* scale. Chef Alfred Portale's creations continue to amaze. Sample such dazzlers as grilled Muscovy duck breast with Szechuan peppercorns, apricots, and turnips; grilled salmon; and artichokes *à la grecque*. Open daily. 12 E. 12 St., between Fifth Ave. and University Pl. (phone: 620-4020).

Grotta Azzurra More friendships than can be counted have begun in the lines of people waiting on the steep staircase leading down to this star attraction in the very heart of Little Italy. Everyone agrees: It's well worth the wait. Though the decor is hardly sumptuous, the food is incredible. Since 1908 four generations of the Davino family have re-created Neapolitan specialties that leave customers pleading for recipes. The lobster *fra diavolo* is out of this world, and the garlic bread is so stuffed with crunchy, toasted cloves that it's more like eating a little bread with your garlic. (Sadly, the slices are not available on Saturday evenings.) Other favorites include veal scaloppine à la marsala and sautéed calf's liver. On many evenings an energetic guitar player entices guests to join in a sing-along. Closed Mondays. No reservations. No credit cards accepted. 387 Broome St. (phone: 925-8775).

Jo Jo This East Side bistro is another feather in the toque of former *Lafayette* chef Jean-Georges Vongerichten. Currently a New York hot spot, low fat is the rule here, but don't be fooled: Flavor and innovation are at the top of the list. There might be shrimp with a Thai-accented carrot broth; goat cheese and potato terrine with arugula juice; or rabbit, Swiss chard, and tomato oil enveloped in thin pasta. The desserts are the stuff of dreams. Ask to have coffee served around the fireplace upstairs. Closed Sundays. 160 E. 64th St. (phone: 223-5656).

Lespinasse This serene, formal dining salon in the *St. Regis* hotel gleams with polished marble and gold-leaf trim. Gray Kunz, formerly the chef at *Adrienne* in the *Peninsula,* uses his Hong Kong–influenced artistry to produce such dishes as black bass poached in a delicate broth flavored with Asian spices, and gingered chicken with a soy vinegar dressing. The wine list is surprisingly affordable. Closed Sundays. 2 E. 55th St. (phone: 339-6719).

Manhattan Ocean Club Both the lower-level and upstairs dining rooms of this fine seafood house have original Picasso ceramic plates and prints displayed behind glass on their white walls, set off by a few Greek columns. Although you may find it crowded, this restaurant's appeal is its fresh, delicious fish and shellfish—the Hawaiian wahoo and melt-in-your-mouth *kumomoto* oysters are particularly good. The *pâtissier* is winning awards with such sumptuous treats as calvados ice cream on apple tarts, and the service is attentive. Open daily. 57 W. 58th St. (phone: 371-7777).

Montrachet The cooking is best described as nouvelle French, with an emphasis on traditional flavors. Favorite dishes include duck in red wine sauce with mission figs or fresh ginger, and roast chicken with garlic and potato purée. In addition to an extensive à la carte menu, there are three excellent prix-fixe menus. Jackets requested. Closed Sundays. American Express accepted. 239 West Broadway, between Walker and White Sts. (phone: 219-2777).

Il Nido A superb menu of northern Italian specialties and the highest standards of service are the hallmarks of Adi Giovannetti's attractive, if somewhat cramped, East Side establishment, which is popular for business lunches. *Crostini di polenta* with a mushroom and chicken liver sauce is the perfect starter, to be followed by mixed fried fish, shellfish in marinara sauce, or any of a host of other specialties. Closed Sundays. 251 E. 53rd St. (phone: 753-8450).

Palio Here is an elegant entry in New York's abundant inventory of fine Italian eateries. The street-level bar is surrounded by artist Sandro Chia's mural of Siena's exciting medieval horse race that gives this place its name; the upstairs dining room is spacious, elegant, and perfect for a pre-theater meal. Closed Saturdays for lunch and Sundays. 151 W. 51st St., in the Equitable Center (phone: 245-4850).

Palm Good sirloin steaks are served in an atmosphere so unassuming that the draw has got to be the food. Sawdust covers the floor, tables and chairs are refugees from a thrift shop, but the beef is first-rate. The largest (and most expensive) lobsters in New York also are served here. *Palm, Too,* directly across the street at 840 Second Ave. (phone: 697-5198), offers identical food and is open for Sunday lunch. Reservations advised for lunch; for dinner, they are accepted only for parties of four or more. Closed Sundays for lunch. 837 Second Ave., between E. 44th and E. 45th Sts. (phone: 687-2953).

Parioli Romanissimo This classy restaurant in an attractive East Side townhouse is especially popular with executive diners who come to feast on the pricey but delicious Italian specialties. Opt for a meaty main course like veal chop *giardiniera,* then splurge on the chocolate torte for dessert. Service is notoriously chilly, and even when reservations are in hand, expect a wait. Closed Sundays. 24 E. 81st St. (phone: 288-2391).

Raphael Situated on the ground floor of a townhouse, this classic French dining spot is a series of interconnecting rooms that range from rustic (brick walls and rough plaster) to princely (trompe l'oeil gardens). There's also a real trellised garden where meals are served in summer. The menu offers very good peasant food: Try the loin of rabbit, lentils with garlic sausage, or onion tart. Closed Saturdays for lunch and Sundays. 33 W. 54th St. (phone: 582-8993).

Remi Beneath a wraparound mural of Venice, diners indulge in such northern Italian fantasies as cuttlefish in its own ink over polenta, smoked prosciutto with greens and truffled olive oil, and ravioli Marco Polo with fresh tuna and ginger. A dessert favorite is the three-nut tart (pine, pecan, and walnut) with homemade ice cream. And if you've still got the heart and room, there are 45 different kinds of grappa to follow the meal. Open daily. 145 W. 53rd St., between Sixth and Seventh Aves. (phone: 581-4242).

River Café Set on a barge on the Brooklyn shore of the East River, with spectacular views of the lower Manhattan skyline, this is one of the top American restaurants, with an especially good weekend brunch menu featuring lobster baked in horseradish oil with oyster risotto, poached eggs on smoked salmon waffles, and duck *confit* with roasted garlic and white beans. Jackets required; ties optional. Open daily. Reservations necessary two weeks ahead. 1 Water St., Brooklyn (phone: 718-522-5200).

Russian Tea Room With enough *blinis* to float diners down the Volga, this festive place (always decked out with *Christmas* ornaments) is an almost obligatory stop for any visitor who plans to attend a concert at adjacent *Carnegie Hall*. Try the borscht or chicken Kiev, abide by the waiter's suggestions, or let your Slavic instincts have free rein. There is now a cabaret on some Sunday nights. Jacket and tie requested. Open daily. 150 W. 57th St. (phone: 265-0947).

Tavern on the Green The food is less famous than the decor and location (just inside *Central Park*) at this, one of New York's most beautiful dining establishments. In winter the snow-covered trees trimmed with tiny white lights outside the Crystal Room make a dazzling display (and reservations are a must a month in advance). Summer is only slightly less spectacular, when diners can sit in the outdoor garden. The *Tavern Store* (phone: 873-7720) offers souvenirs with the restaurant's logo plus a variety of ornaments, toys, and china. Open daily. Central Park W. and W. 67th St. (phone: 873-3200).

Tribeca Grill Stargazers come here in hopes of seeing one of the co-owners: Robert De Niro, Sean Penn, Mikhail Baryshnikov, or Bill Murray. Serious diners flock to sample such temptations as duck *confit* with crisp greens, and *cavatelli* with plum tomatoes, basil, and pecorino cheese. Open daily. Reservations necessary three weeks in advance for weekends. 375 Greenwich St. at Franklin St. (phone: 941-3900).

Union Square Café The menu at this informal, perenially popular eatery changes with the seasons, but classic American dishes prepared with a hint of old Italy are always featured. Appetizers may include *bruschetta* (grilled garlic bread with tomatoes), polenta, or a dish of creamed turnips; filet of tuna, fine hamburgers, and calamari often appear as options for the main course. The atmosphere is airy and pleasant, with Italian-style furnishings and oil paintings. Closed for lunch on Sundays. 21 E. 16th St. (phone: 243-4020).

Water Club The decor at this restaurant/barge in the East River is nautical, but with restraint, since the view is decorative enough: river traffic and the twinkling lights of the Manhattan and Queens skylines. The menu, too, is nautical, with similar restraint. Appetizers range from oysters and smoked salmon to beluga caviar, entrées from Maryland crab cakes to Dover sole and lobster—but diners also can order pâté or filet mignon. Jacket requested. Open daily. It's tricky to get here, so take a cab. East River at E. 30th St., on the northbound service road of the FDR Dr. (phone: 683-3333).

MODERATE

American Festival Café This place is cheery, very American, and right on the famous ice skating rink in *Rockefeller Center*. The reasonably priced and varied menu includes prime ribs, steaks, roast chicken, and warm and cold seafood. It's also noted for its desserts, including Mississippi mud pie, New York cheesecake, and Key lime pie. The atmosphere is best from November to April, when the rink is open. Open daily. 20 W. 50th St. (phone: 246-6699).

Arqua This stylish TriBeCa spot specializes in the food of the Veneto, but chef-owner Leo Pulito (from the town of Arqua, near Venice) has as fine a touch with grilled salmon and rack of lamb as with artichoke lasagne and game prepared Italian-style. Look into the reasonable prix-fixe menu for either lunch or dinner. Closed for lunch on weekends. American Express accepted. 281 Church St. at White St. (phone: 334-1888).

Azzurro This Upper East Side bastion of Sicilian specialties attracts hordes of fans with its grilled fish, fine pasta specials, and delectable *vino santo*. Most members of the staff are related, and Mama Sindoni is in the kitchen. Open daily. 245 E. 84th St. (phone: 517-7068).

Ballroom When it opened in 1983, this very pretty bistro introduced a new twist to Manhattan dining—the *tapas* bar. A changing, varied menu of *tapas* (Spanish for "appetizers") is spread along a lengthy bar, and patrons either nibble their way through dinner there or head for the dining room, where waiters circulate with trays of the same. There's also a less tempting menu of main courses, a reasonable and tasty buffet lunch, and a dessert table that's as much a feast for the eyes as for the taste buds. Cabaret-type entertainment on Tuesdays through Saturdays is another reason to go here. Closed Mondays. 253 W. 28th St. (phone: 244-3005).

Bice Excellent northern Italian dishes and a warm, informal atmosphere have made this bistro one of the most popular dining places in the city. Homemade pasta is the mainstay of the ever-changing menu; chef Giacomo Galena's specialties on any given day might include *tagliolini* (thin noodles) with white truffles or grilled tuna with black peppercorns. Open daily. 7 E. 54th St. (phone: 688-1999).

Black Sheep The place has an utterly romantic country French atmosphere, enhanced by a fireplace. The regional farmhouse specialties, primarily from Provence and Burgundy, include duckling braised over an open fire with armagnac, prunes, and apricots; loin rack of lamb Tuscan-style; and subtly flavored seafood. Vegetarian dishes are imaginative and tasty (try the artichokes with potatoes). There is an extensive wine list. Open daily. American Express accepted. 344 W. 11th St. (phone: 242-1010).

Il Bocconcino The celebrity photographs in the window date back to *La Dolce Vita* days, when Gilberto was a paparazzo in Rome. Now he and co-owner Giorgio run this modest but congenial Greenwich Village spot, with lace curtains, white tablecloths, and some murals of Italianate architecture to remind them of home. Sample the *bruschetta* (grilled bread with tomatoes), then follow with pasta, chicken, veal, seafood, or pizza. Sidewalk tables are set outside in summer. Open daily. 168 Sullivan St. (phone: 982-0329).

Café Luxembourg The interior here is Art Deco in style, brightly lit, and noisy, with everyone appearing to be looking around for someone famous. Not far from *Lincoln Center,* it is especially popular with concertgoers. The fare is nouvelle, though the specials tend to be uneven. For the best look at the chic crowd, come after 8 PM. There's also a Sunday brunch featuring *boudin blanc,* a white pork sausage. Open daily. Reservations advised. 200 W. 70th St. (phone: 873-7411).

Café Un Deux Trois In this very lively theater district bistro, whose name is its address, patrons draw on the paper tablecloths with crayons while waiting to sample carefully prepared daily specialties that include fresh sea trout, steaks with *pommes frites,* and couscous with chicken, lamb, and chick-peas. Theatergoers should plan to dine very early to be sure to make curtain time. Open daily. Reservations accepted for parties of five or more. 123 W. 44th St. (phone: 354-4148).

Cent' Anni A Little Italy gem, it serves down-to-earth northern Italian fare in an unpretentious storefront setting. There are only 60 seats, so evenings tend to be both crowded and convivial as diners enjoy classic pasta. The name comes from the traditional toast "May you live 100 years!" Open daily. American Express accepted. 50 Carmine St., between Bleecker and Bedford Sts. (phone: 989-9494).

Chin Chin This stylish Chinese eatery is somewhat formal at lunchtime, but the atmosphere relaxes in the evening. The three dining rooms are paneled with maple wood, and skylights lend a cheerful brightness. Excellent dishes include Peking duck, Grand Marnier prawns, and cold noodles with sesame sauce. Closed for lunch on weekends. 216 E. 49th St. (phone: 888-4555).

Jean Lafitte As accurate an evocation of a cozy and unpretentious Parisian neighborhood bistro as exists in New York. Go for the excellent tripe, the authentic *choucroute* (on specials only), or steak *au poivre*. Superb soups, which change daily, are a special treat during a cold New York winter. Convenient to *Carnegie Hall*. Closed for lunch on weekends. 68 W. 58th St. (phone: 751-2323).

Le Madri Delicacies such as fresh prawns stuffed with wild mushrooms and ricotta cheese, antipasto with caramelized onions, and osso buco are fabulous at this stylish Italian dining spot. The menu changes seasonally, and there is a weekend brunch menu. For dessert try the apple tart with cinnamon ice cream. Open daily. 168 W. 18th St. (phone: 727-8022).

Mesa Grill The sassy Southwestern fare here, served up by young up-and-coming chef Bobby Flay, surpasses anything of its kind in New York. And the sizzling, noisy social scene adds nearly as much heat as the chilies he uses so liberally. Try the *posole* (a Mexican fish stew made with hominy), the moist, blue corn–encrusted fried chicken, or the grilled swordfish with cilantro pesto. Open daily. 102 Fifth Ave. (phone: 807-7400).

Moreno The leafy Gramercy Park neighborhood of Manhattan is the home of this gracious but relaxed Italian restaurant with outdoor tables. Its Milanese owner, Moreno Maltagliati, has created a warm ambience by painting the walls ochre and having waiters serve complimentary hors d'oeuvres shortly after patrons are seated. Featured dishes include starters of grilled vegetables and a gorgonzola, apple, and walnut salad, and main courses such as fresh ravioli and grilled tuna and salmon. Some desserts are Italian, such as the *tiramisù,* but seasonable fresh fruit also appears on the menu. In addition, delicate lace cookies are offered gratis. Prix fixe meals are served Sundays. Closed Saturday lunch. Reservations advised for groups of four or more. 65 Irving Pl. at E. 18th St. (phone: 673-3939).

Odéon In a gray cast-iron building, this high-style, refurbished cafeteria is in the midst of TriBeCa. Casual touches such as an orange neon "Cafeteria" sign set off the simple but elegant Art Deco–influenced decor. One of the first trendsetting restaurants to open in this neighborhood, it remains a popular magnet until well after midnight. Look for entrées such as squab with shiitake mushrooms and wild rice, and roast loin of lamb with white peppercorns. A dessert worth trying is crêpes with praline butter and apricot liqueur. Open daily. 145 West Broadway (phone: 233-0507).

Park Bistro This fashionable French eatery features classic presentations of seafood, chicken, and meat. The menu changes frequently, but shellfish soup, warm potato salad with goat cheese and herb dressing, roast monkfish, and leg of lamb are among the succulent possibilities. Closed for lunch on weekends. 414 Park Ave. S. (phone: 689-1360).

Periyali In this cool Aegean oasis, patrons enjoy traditional Greek fare prepared with an exceptionally light touch. Specialties include lima bean salad with *skordalia*, a tangy potato-based purée; baked sea bass with garlic, tomato, and white wine; and moussaka with grilled zucchini. For dessert, don't miss the luscious custard-filled *galaktoboreko*. Closed Sundays. 35 W. 20th St. (phone: 463-7890).

Pierre au Tunnel Onion soup, mussels, frogs' legs, and grilled steaks typify the French provincial dishes featured in this theater district bistro since 1950. Try the loin of veal sautéed with fresh mushrooms and shallots or tripe cooked with white wine and calvados. Closed Sundays. Reservations necessary for pre-theater dinner. Major credit cards accepted. 250 W. 47th St. (phone: 575-1220).

Provence At this perfect French dining spot in the Village, the spices and tomato-based sauces of southeastern France are nowhere better utilized, and the roast chicken with garlic gives a whole new meaning to the serving of fowl. A huge vat of aging brandy adorns the bar and provides an excellent digestive at the conclusion of a meal. In summer the back patio is an idyllic dining spot. Open daily. American Express accepted. 38 MacDougal St. (phone: 475-7500).

Sammy's Roumanian Steak House At this last survivor of a long Lower East Side tradition of ethnic meat restaurants, Eastern European favorites are featured, as is Old Country music of a sort you're not likely to hear in any other establishment. The makings for egg creams (milk, seltzer, and chocolate syrup) are set right on the table—an experience you don't usually find anymore in New York. Open daily. Major credit cards accepted. 157 Chrystie St. (phone: 673-5526 or 673-0330).

Santa Fe Unlike many other Mexican eateries that have sprung up around the city, there are no hanging plants, no neon signs, no ear-splitting noise levels here. Instead, crisp linen and salmon-colored walls hung with Mexican tapestries provide a serene setting for nicely tart margaritas and well-prepared Southwestern dishes. Closed for lunch on weekends. 72 W. 69th St., just a few blocks from *Lincoln Center* (phone: 724-0822).

Shun Lee Palace The late T. T. Wang was one of New York City's most talented Chinese cooks, and the menu here still includes some of his most exciting temptations. If you can round up a group of 10 to dine together, you might order Wang's special Chinese feast. Jacket required. Open daily. 155 E. 55th St. (phone: 371-8844).

Shun Lee West More sophisticated both in palette and palate than its older East Side cousin above, this establishment features flavorful Szechuan and Mandarin dishes. Try the giant prawns with black bean sauce, grilled scallops, and jellyfish (for courageous souls only). Choice entrées include crisp Peking duck marinated in five spices; *chan-do* chicken, which is sautéed in hot pepper, scallions, garlic, and ginger; and salmon with Szechuan sauce. This dining spot's proximity to *Lincoln Center* makes it the perfect place for a pre- or post-performance feast. For those looking for lighter fare, the adjoining *Shun Lee Café* serves dim sum—Chinese hors d'oeuvres. Jacket required. Open daily. Reservations advised for pre-theater or pre-concert meals. 43 W. 65th St. (phone: 595-8895).

Tropica The setting is an amalgam of just about every island in the Caribbean, and the menu is similarly inspired—saucy and piquant, with an emphasis on freshly caught seafood. Its location on the lobby level of the Met-Life Building (formerly the Pan Am Building), in the middle of the traffic path to and from *Grand Central Station*, attracts crowds of expense-account types at lunch; it can be noisy at dinner too. Closed weekends. Met-Life Building, Vanderbilt Ave. and E. 45th St. (phone: 867-6767).

Zarela Among the city's better Mexican eateries, this festive East Sider flourishes under the direction of its high-profile owner, Zarela Martínez. Menu selections range from the familiar to such eclectic dishes as roast duck with tomato and red chili sauce, and shrimp with tomato *poblano* salsa. There are spice levels for every palate, so the cautious needn't fear, and there are great tangy margaritas to shore up everyone's courage. Closed for lunch on weekends. American Express and Diners Club accepted. 953 Second Ave. near E. 50th St. (phone: 644-6740).

INEXPENSIVE

Mocca Close your eyes and you're dining in downtown Budapest. Start with the gutsy goulash soup, go on to the stuffed cabbage heaped with sauerkraut, then try *palacsintas* (crêpes with jam) for dessert. A bargain at thrice the price. Open daily. Reservations advised for dinner. No credit cards accepted. 1588 Second Ave. at E. 82nd St. (phone: 734-6470).

Carmine's This eatery lures the hungry hordes to its two locations with oversize portions of home-style food at reasonable prices. There's nothing "nouvelle" about the menu of Italian favorites like fried calamari, spaghetti with meatballs, and chicken Contadina (with sausage, peppers, and lots of garlic). Waiters are friendly and forthright—they won't hesitate to tell you that you're ordering too much (portions here are huge and meant to be shared). Open daily. Reservations are accepted only for parties of six or more; otherwise, be prepared to wait in a long line. American Express accepted. 2450 Broadway, between W. 90th and W. 91st Sts. (phone: 362-2200), and 200 W. 44th St. (phone: 221-3800).

Carnegie Delicatessen At this, the quintessential New York deli, the sandwiches are enormous, seemingly too big to put in a normal human mouth, and corned beef and pastrami are king. There are communal tables and no atmosphere, except the frantic Seventh Avenue scene, but waiters provide entertaining banter. Save room for the velvety cheesecake. Open daily from

6:30 AM to 3:30 AM. No reservations or credit cards accepted. 854 Seventh Ave., near, of course, *Carnegie Hall* (phone: 757-2245).

Dock's Oyster Bar There are two of these huge seafood palaces, and each is packed at lunch- and dinnertime. The sprawling raw bar attracts social nibblers, while others head for the crisply nautical dining area to tackle a lengthy menu that often includes seared and gingered tuna, tangy chowders, and a catch-of-the-day selection, which regulars order with a side dish of sweet potato fries. Open daily. 2427 Broadway, between W. 89th and W. 90th Sts. (phone: 724-5588), and 633 Third Ave. at E. 40th St. (phone: 986-8080).

Florent This classic 1940s diner in the wholesale meat district, converted into a hip French restaurant, is the last word in trendy New York style. With so much to look at, one almost forgets to eat! Open 24 hours daily. No credit cards accepted. 69 Gansevoort St., between Washington and Greenwich Sts. (phone: 989-5779).

Fourteen There are two of these attractive, convivial bistros where diners may eat either at the marble-topped bar or in the dining room with an oak floor, white linen-draped tables, and a wall of red velvet banquettes. Try the chicory and bacon salad drenched in a hot vinaigrette dressing, then the grilled salmon in choron sauce (a purée of tomato béarnaise) or the grilled chicken. At press time the majority of the main courses came with an easy-to-remember price tag—$14. Choose the crispy, warm, thin-crusted apple tart for dessert. The short wine list includes some interesting, reasonably priced offerings. Formerly called *Quatorze*. Open daily. 240 W. 14th St. (phone: 206-7006) and 323 E. 79th St. (phone: 535-1414).

Gage & Tollner Holding forth at this stand since 1879, the renowned seafood house is worth a visit, not only for the food but also for the sight of the gaslight glowing over the canopy in the evening. Renowned Southern chef Edna Lewis's specialties include lobster Newburg, crabmeat Virginia, and 15 different styles of potatoes. Open daily. 372 Fulton St. at Jay St., Brooklyn (phone: 718-875-5181).

Golden Unicorn The dim sum in this Chinatown eatery (served from 8 AM to 4 PM—but try to get here by 10:30 on a Sunday morning) are arguably the city's best. This stylish spot also specializes in Cantonese dishes such as scallops and bean curd in black bean sauce and shrimp with walnuts served with a mayonnaise dressing. If you're unfamiliar with Chinese food, rely on the advice of the courteous and attentive staff. For a special taste treat, try the shark's fin dumpling in its own soup. Open daily. 18 East Broadway (phone: 941-0911).

Hatsuhana Still winning kudos from some of New York's toughest restaurant critics, this Japanese eatery serves some of the best sushi, sashimi, and tempura in town. Closed Sundays. Reservations necessary for dinner only. 17 E. 48th St. (phone: 355-3345).

Hunan House Among Chinatown's best, this pleasant place specializes in the subtly spiced food of the Hunan province. Start off with fried dumplings or hot and sour soup, then have Hunan lamb with scallions; Changsha beef, done in a hot sauce with broccoli; or Confucius prawns with cashews. Open daily. No reservations. American Express and Diners Club accepted. 45 Mott St. (phone: 962-0010).

Louisiana Community Bar & Grill The city's best Cajun and creole specialties, along with extraordinarily friendly and welcoming service, are the attractions at this informal eatery. Try the blackened prime ribs with mashed potatoes, crawfish *étouffée* with rice, and, whenever available, chocolate mocha cake for dessert. Open daily for dinner only. 622 Broadway, between Bleecker and Houston Sts. (phone: 460-9633).

Pamir Small and family-run, this spot specializes in Afghan (much like Indian) cooking. The delicately seasoned lamb dishes are very good. Open daily. MasterCard and Visa accepted. 1437 Second Ave. (phone: 734-3791). A larger, more comfortable second location is on the corner of First Ave. and E. 58th St. and also accepts American Express (phone: 644-9258).

Serendipity 3 Definitely not for kids only, this East Side classic has been packing them in for as long as most of us can remember. The front room resembles an old-fashioned general store (but the merchandise is cutting-edge chic and trendy); the rear dining room is a cozy jumble of antique oak tables, Tiffany-style lamps, and old-time tin signs. Chocoholics delight in the bathtub-size hot fudge sundaes; other favorites are the foot-long hot dogs and frozen hot chocolate. It's a great place to rest up after a *Bloomingdale's* binge. Open daily. 225 E. 60th St., between Second and Third Aves. (phone: 838-3531).

A TASTE OF HISTORY

New York has been around for quite some time—and so have some of its most famous restaurants. If you'd like a taste of America's past with your meal, there are lots of choices. *Fraunces Tavern* (54 Pearl St. at Broad St., near Wall St.; phone: 269-0144), built in 1719, is the oldest structure in Manhattan, and George Washington really did eat here. *Gage & Tollner* (see main entry, above) opened in 1879 and specializes in seafood and Virginian victuals. Lillie Langtry, turn-of-the-century British music-hall star and paramour of England's Edward VII, was wont to flout the men-only policy at *Keen's Chophouse* (72 W. 36th St.; phone: 947-3636). The *Old Homestead* (56 Ninth Ave.; phone: 242-9040) has been serving steaks to famous and not-so-famous New Yorkers since 1868. *Sardi's* (234 W. 44th St.; phone: 221-8440), opened in 1921, is the traditional place for theater folks to go to wait for the reviews of their latest Broadway show. (Check out the almost floor-to-ceiling celebrity caricatures.) And Brooklyn's famed

Peter Luger steakhouse (see full description, above) is more than a century old and a mecca for beef mavens.

SUNDAY BRUNCH

This is a cherished tradition among New Yorkers. Some popular spots—a few of which have long lines waiting to get in—are *Sarabeth's Kitchen* (423 Amsterdam Ave.; phone: 496-6280; and 1295 Madison Ave.; phone: 410-7335); *Man Ray Bistro* (169 Eighth Ave.; phone: 627-4220); the *Brasserie* (100 E. 53rd St.; phone: 751-4840); and *Florent,* the *River Café,* the *Water Club, Odéon,* and *Provence* (see above for all five). One of the few places that take brunch reservations is *Zoë* (90 Prince St.; phone: 966-6722). Hotel dining rooms with copious—and more costly—brunch buffets are the *Café Pierre* at the *Pierre;* the *Ambassador Grill* at the *UN Plaza Park Hyatt; Peacock Alley* at the *Waldorf-Astoria;* and the *Palm Court* at the *Plaza* (see *Checking In* for all four).

On board one of *World Yacht*'s five restaurant/yachts, you can enjoy Sunday brunch ($40 per person at press time) while cruising the Hudson River and New York Harbor past the glittering Manhattan skyline. There are luncheon and dinner cruises as well. Jacket required (no tie). Open daily. Advance reservations and tickets are necessary. Major credit cards accepted. Sailings are from Pier 81 on the Hudson River at W. 41st St. (phone: 630-8100).

TAKING TEA

New Yorkers have become quite fond of the British tradition of afternoon tea, and a number of the city's most posh hotels have jumped on the bandwagon. The *Carlyle*'s *Gallery,* the *Mayfair Hotel Baglioni,* the *Lowell,* the *Plaza*'s *Palm Court,* the *Rotunda Room* at the *Pierre,* the *New York Palace,* and the *Stanhope* (see *Checking In* for all) offer superlative service and a variety of teas, scones, sandwiches, and condiments. Taking tea is a great way to experience the ambience of these elegant hostelries without having to stay the night. Tea for two usually costs $40 to $50; à la carte service is also available at some hotels. Reservations are usually necessary.

For those who prefer cappuccino to a cup of tea, *Caffè Roma* (385 Broome St.; phone: 226-8413), in the heart of Little Italy, is one of the few remaining old-style coffeehouses still operating. Everything from espresso to egg creams and Italian cookies and pastries are served daily from 8 AM to midnight.

Diversions

Exceptional Pleasures and Treasures

Quintessential New York

Whether browsing through antiques shops for an 18th-century armoire, bicycling along a secluded wooded path, watching an ambitious juggler's skilled street performance, or sipping a double espresso at 2 AM, it's impossible not to be impressed (and occasionally overwhelmed) by the Big Apple. From the unbelievable traffic jams to the inner sanctums of the city's museums, New York is the kind of town whose virtues and foibles are ever apparent. Seedy sidewalk stands and elegant boutiques alternately repel and delight the eye, yet each contributes to the incredible diversity that weaves the city together. If there is anything at all quintessential about New York, it is that there is always another surprise just around the corner.

DINING AT THE FOUR SEASONS For those who dream of dining in a superb New York restaurant as the height of sophistication, it's a regrettable truth that expectations often outdistance reality. Too often maître d's, captains, and waiters at overly pretentious establishments try to achieve an elegant atmosphere by treating patrons as though they were not quite worthy of being on the premises. However, at the *Four Seasons* (99 E. 52nd St.; phone: 212-754-9494), in the *Seagram Building* on Park Avenue (Mies van der Rohe's high-rise masterpiece), the ambience, friendliness, and remarkable food are nonpareil—albeit at a high price.

The Pool Room, with its extraordinary glittering metal curtains, was designed by Philip Johnson and is one of the rare interior spaces to have been declared a landmark. The real stunner is the marble pool in the center. The Grill Room, with its burnished rosewood walls and astrodome ceiling, is where the captains of publishing and industry gravitate regularly to fine-tune business deals over lunch. The surroundings are understated, and Richard Lippold's glass rod sculpture adds panache. *Le Tricorne,* a large Picasso tapestry, brightens the corridor between the two rooms.

The *Four Seasons*' á la carte menu changes quarterly, along with the decor, to herald spring, summer, autumn, and winter. A reasonably priced prix-fixe lunch and pre- and après-theater menus are also offered. No other dining establishment in New York promises such excellence and delivers it so impeccably.

TASTES OF NEW YORK In this city of almost eight million residents and what seems like almost as many restaurants, fast-food outlets, delicatessens, Korean markets, and sidewalk stands hawking everything from hot dogs to souvlaki, it's not surprising that New York lays claim to many culinary signatures. What follows are a few favorite Gotham goodies.

The egg cream is an old-time New York libation that has neither egg nor cream, but is made of syrup (usually chocolate), milk, and seltzer and is a close cousin to the ice cream soda. It used to be available at every drugstore counter but now is rarely found. To sample the authentic recipe, stop in at the *Gem Spa* (131 Second Ave. at St. Mark's Pl.; phone: 212-529-1146); most will be converted in less than two sips.

To try another of New York's incredible edibles—bagels and lox (smoked salmon)—try the *Second Avenue Deli* (156 Second Ave. at E. 10th St.; phone: 212-677-0606), where thin layers of fish (Nova Scotia is less salty, but belly lox is better) are heaped atop a cream cheese–laden bagel.

Sink your teeth into a four-inch-thick (honest!) sandwich at the legendary *Carnegie Deli,* grab a cab to Brooklyn for one of *Peter Luger'*s legendary porterhouse steaks, or try the pungent grilled garlic bread at *Grotta Azzurra*—but be warned that on busy Saturday nights, it may be hard to come by. (See *Eating Out* in THE CITY for more on all three.)

Even if the hot dog didn't originate at *Nathan's Famous,* it should have. On the Boardwalk in Coney Island since 1916 (1310 Surf Ave., Brooklyn; phone: 718-946-2202), *Nathan's* has been serving generations of New Yorkers who come for its all-beef franks and thickly cut French fries. *Nathan's* also has three locations in Manhattan, at 401 Avenue of the Americas (phone: 212-947-1259), 325 Fifth Avenue (phone: 212-447-1240), and 115 E. 23rd Street (phone: 212-777-7361). *Katz's Deli* (205 E. Houston St.; phone: 212-254-2466) serves wonderful wieners that rival those of its Coney Island competitor, and it still slices sandwich ingredients by hand (all-important to purists).

A traditional ethnic taste (Jewish in origin) of New York's Lower East Side is the knish, dough stuffed with a filling and baked or fried. In all its myriad varieties, it is best evaluated at *Yonah Schimmel* (137 E. Houston St.; phone: 212-477-2858), the oldest knish kitchen in New York. We recommend potato or kasha (buckwheat), although nontraditionalists may opt for sweet potato, sauerkraut, cabbage, cheese, or even cherry or blueberry.

And no visit to Manhattan should be without a trip to Chinatown for dim sum, which roughly translates as "tidbits" or "snacks." It's a wonderful way to become acquainted with different Chinese dishes without having to commit to an entire entrée. At *HSF* (46 Bowery; phone: 212-374-1319), Sunday dim sum is the equivalent of a noonday picnic in Beijing and has become a Manhattan ritual. Waiters wheel carts of delectable dishes, many of which are stuffed dumplings, by your table; just point to the ones you'd like to taste. The cost of the meal is determined by counting the number of empty dishes stacked on your table.

SHAKESPEARE IN THE PARK Unrequited love, lyrical soliloquies, and murderous deeds come to the outdoor stage summer evenings at the *Delacorte Theater* in *Central Park* (access from the W. 81st St. or E. 79th St. park entrances; phone: 212-871-PAPP from mid-June through early September for schedules and recommendations of what time to begin queuing on performance days). There are two productions each summer; performances begin in July, and each play runs about three weeks, with a two-week break in between. This theater marathon, which goes on despite the sometimes hellish summer temperatures, was the pet project of late New York theater impresario Joseph Papp. Recent casts have included such luminaries as Gregory Hines, Raul Julia, Blair Underwood, and Tracey Ullman. Also, the repertoire is not limited to the Bard. Kevin Kline, for example, starred in the Gilbert and Sullivan musical *The Pirates of Penzance;* and *The Mystery of Edwin Drood,* a musical version of a Charles Dickens story that later moved to Broadway, was first produced in the park.

Tickets are free, however, on the day of the performance, those seeking entry must join a line. Tickets are distributed at 1 PM for that evening's 8 PM performance at the *Delacorte* and at *The Public Theater* downtown (425 Lafayette St.; phone: 598-7150); each individual can get a maximum of two tickets.

AN EVENING AT A BROADWAY MUSICAL Gone are the days when women in shimmering gowns and 16-button gloves were accompanied by men in white tie and tails to the "Great White Way." However, although no one raises a lorgnette to scan the crowd these days, there is plenty of whispered commentary and avid people watching. Before the performance, a sense of excitement permeates the theater as the murmurings of the audience mingle with the discordant notes floating up from the orchestra pit. As the lights are lowered and the last coughs echo to the rafters, hearts pound a little in childlike anticipation. Suddenly, the strains of the overture resound through the darkened theater.

Though many Broadway theaters present extravaganzas where the caliber of the script, score, and performers is secondary to the exotic scenery and over-mechanized props, there *are* shows that still adhere to the grand old traditions of the genre. Few experiences are as mesmerizing as an expertly choreographed dance number or a sultry siren belting out the blues in three octaves. For more information, see "Theater" in *Sources and Resources,* THE CITY.

CHRISTMAS IN NEW YORK As nippy December breezes whip color into New Yorkers' cheeks, a mood of gentility and geniality seems to envelop Manhattan. Verdant wreaths and crimson ribbons adorn doorways, and sidewalk trees are dressed in whorls of glowing lights. Neighbors and strangers alike actually smile at one another (really!).

The lighting of the *Christmas* tree in *Rockefeller Center* is a particularly joyous event. This tradition began in 1931, when a small tree decorated with a few streamers stood amid the rubbish of ongoing construction. Today a sky-high tree and brilliantly white angel sculptures lining the facing *Channel Gardens* are visions that dazzle even the most jaded passerby. It's best to visit at night, when the enormous fir is aglow with tens of thousands of colored lights. On the ice rink below Paul Manship's graceful golden statue of Prometheus watches over the skaters whirling in circles.

The decorated department store windows at *Lord & Taylor* (424 Fifth Ave., from W. 38th to W. 39th St.) and *Saks Fifth Avenue* (611 Fifth Ave., from E. 49th to E. 50th St.) both draw long lines of people waiting to get a glimpse of the delightful holiday vignettes based around mechanized dolls. *Barneys New York* (Seventh Ave. from W. 16th to W. 17th St.) has strictly *un*traditional windows, whose themes vary wildly from year to year.

Fine dining establishments around the city also celebrate the season with panache. In fact, *Christmas* is so beloved at the *Russian Tea Room* (150 W. 57th St.; phone: 212-265-0947) that the restaurant is decorated year-round with tinsel. *Tavern on the Green* (Central Park W. and W. 67th St., in *Central Park;* phone: 212-873-3200), however, surpasses them all. Diners can sit in the *Christmas* tree–bedecked Crystal Room, overlooking a terrace framed by trees electrified with thousands of tiny lights.

PARADES As with almost everything they do, New Yorkers go all out with parades. Elaborate preparations worthy of a New Orleans *Mardi Gras* involve hundreds of volunteers who, along with police officers, politicians, and city planners, do everything from inflating balloons to shredding ticker tape.

New Yorkers find a reason to march at almost any time of the year. As the last traces of autumn leave the city, *Macy's Thanksgiving Day Parade* is a joyous celebration. On the night before the parade, a fleet of trucks carrying a limp Mickey Mouse, Superman, and Garfield and huge supplies of helium invade Central Park West at 77th Street (the starting point of the parade). The next day each balloon is inflated and anchored by volunteer *Macy's* employees; these larger-than-blimp cartoon characters, many of which span nearly a city block, are greeted with loud cheers from the delighted children who line the parade route down Broadway. Santa himself is the grand finale, ushering in the *Christmas* season.

The *Easter Parade* is fanciful in quite a different manner, with nary a float in sight. Since the 19th century city folk have strolled down Fifth Avenue on *Easter Sunday* decked out in their holiday finery, the crowning glory of which was once the ubiquitous bonnet. (Remember Judy Garland and Fred Astaire in *Easter Parade*?) These days top hats and broad-brimmed chapeaux festooned with ribbons have been replaced by more outlandish headdresses, as New Yorkers strut down the avenue sporting everything from Carmen Miranda turbans piled high with fake fruit to large, furry bunny ears.

Perhaps the most boisterous procession is the *St. Patrick's Day Parade,* populated by many who travel yearly from Ireland just to march alongside their fellow expatriated countrymen. This high-spirited (and spirits-filled) occasion gives everyone an excuse to proclaim his or her Gaelic ancestry—or at least pretend to have a drop of Irish blood somewhere in the family tree. The parade route travels up Fifth Avenue, painted with a green center stripe, past *St. Patrick's Cathedral.*

ELLIS ISLAND AND THE STATUE OF LIBERTY If the United States is a melting pot, then New York is its overheated crucible. This blend of a thousand races, creeds, and cultures is frequently explosive, but it has also produced the most vital urban culture on the planet. Gotham's claim to the title as the first city of contemporary life certainly is supported by the astonishing variety of languages, styles of dress, and cuisines encountered in a 10-minute stroll along many Manhattan streets. Two landmarks connected with this rich ethnic mix are Ellis Island, once the gateway for millions of refugees from faraway lands, and the *Statue of Liberty,* their symbol of welcome.

Liberty Enlightening the World, as she is more properly named, stands valiantly in New York Harbor, her uplifted right hand holding the torch of freedom, her left arm cradling a tablet inscribed with the date of American independence, July 4, 1776. French sculptor Frédéric Auguste Bartholdi designed the massive structure as a gift from France to the US on its first centennial, giving the statue a kindly face modeled after his mother's. At the end of long, miserable ocean voyages, it was the immigrants' sign that they really had arrived in America. Today visitors can climb to the crown of the statue for a breathtaking view of the city (or just take the elevator up to the top of the pedestal). In 1976 the statue was given a major facelift, and a museum was added to its base. Improved lighting makes the statue more dazzling than ever after dark.

Between 1892 and 1924, when the immigration center closed, more than 17 million disembarked at Ellis Island, desperately hoping to be admitted to the US. There was both joy and heartbreak following the physical and mental examinations they underwent to determine if they could stay; the less fortunate were forced to return home on the next ship, and many families were divided. Now run by the *National Park Service,* the *Ellis Island Immigration Museum* has films, artifacts, oral histories, and period photographs dramatically recounting the immigrants' stories. For more on the *Statue of Liberty* and *Ellis Island,* see *Special Places* in THE CITY.

VIEWS Those who venture to Brooklyn will find that the Promenade along the Brooklyn Heights riverfront offers a magnificent panorama of Lower Manhattan, including its tallest buildings and three famed late-19th/early-20th-century suspension bridges across the East River: From north to south, they are the Williamsburg, Manhattan, and Brooklyn. In warm weather residents from the five boroughs favor this esplanade for its cool breezes and relative serenity. Those preferring an aerial view may wish to join the camera-toting crowds at the *Empire State Building* or the *World Trade Center* (see *Special Places* in THE CITY for details on both). The latter offers a breathtaking view of outlying historical points of interest, such as Ellis Island and the *Statue of Liberty,* from its observation deck on the 107th floor. From the four corners of the outdoor, 86th-story observation deck at the *Empire State Building,* you can trace a map of the city. To the north you can see past the beveled Art Deco crown of the *Chrysler Building* all the way over *Central Park* to the Bronx; to the west, the Hudson River and New Jersey's smokestack-crowded meadowlands; to the south, Lower Manhattan; and to the east, the *United Nations* and, across the East River, the teeming boroughs of Queens and Brooklyn. For a nighttime glimpse of midtown—or a wonderful daytime view of *Central Park*—sophisticates may opt to mingle with the stars and dine at the legendary *Rainbow Room* in *Rockefeller Center* (see *Nightclubs and Nightlife* in THE CITY).

A Few of Our Favorite Things

New York's world class hotels and restaurants play a large part in making this city an urban planet unto itself. What follows are some of our top picks—those places that offer the best supping and sleeping in the Big Apple. Follow our lead; we promise you won't be disappointed.

Each place listed below is described in greater detail in THE CITY chapter.

GRAND HOTELS

The following are our accommodations favorites. Complete information can be found on pages 92 to 105 in THE CITY.

Carlyle
Drake Swissôtel
Lowell
Mark
Mayfair Hotel Baglioni
Peninsula
Pierre
Plaza Athénée
Regency
St. Regis
Waldorf Towers

BEST BITES OF THE BIG APPLE

Not surprisingly, there are myriad dining possibilities in New York. The places listed below get our vote for providing a peak dining experience—fine service, a rich atmosphere, and, of course, fantastic food. Complete information about our choices can be found on pages 105 to 121 in THE CITY.

Bouley
Café des Artistes

Daniel
Four Seasons
Lutèce
Oyster Bar
Peter Luger

New York Discount Shopping Spree

Admittedly, there is some hyperbole to the New Yorker's frequent boast, "I never buy retail." For most savvy shoppers, buying items wholesale—or at least at a considerable discount—is a personal triumph. Almost any native can reveal the whereabouts of a small mother lode of mode in some unassuming building where incredible discounts are always available. If you don't have a personal pipeline to the fashion industry, however, here are a few places where you can find a bargain. (For a complete roundup of shopping in New York City, see *Shopping* in THE CITY.)

LOEHMANN'S Many a New York City woman equates the first stirrings of her adolescence with a foray to this venerable discount institution. Even the gentlest of souls manages to discard some of her politesse and elbow with the best of them through the racks filled with designer clothes—with the labels removed, so you have to be a savvy shopper. The unflattering lighting and truly unattractive linoleum floors will never win an interior design award, and the dressing rooms are communal, but canny bargain hunters can come away with a Bill Blass, Ralph Lauren, or Calvin Klein creation at less than half its retail price. Information: *Loehmann's,* 5740 Broadway, Riverdale, the Bronx (phone: 718-543-6420), and other locations.

DAFFY'S At this relative newcomer to the discount world, shoppers pursue fashion with a passion. Each floor is crammed with extraordinary clothes: Outrageous Italian dresses snuggle up against poor polyester imitations. Togs of a more classic cut are hidden somewhere in between—all it takes to find the frock of your dreams is patience. The price tags are exceptionally reasonable; the store is a veritable battleground during sales on cashmere sweaters. Although women's apparel is the primary stock in trade, there are good finds in men's and children's clothing, as well as accessories, shoes, jewelry, and leather goods. Information: *Daffy's,* 335 Madison Ave. at E. 44th St. (phone: 212-557-4422) and 111 Fifth Ave. at E. 18th St. (phone: 212-529-4477).

S & W This is the place where orphaned outerwear for women finds a temporary home. Last season's finest wool and cashmere coats from Perry Ellis, Ellen Tracy, and Calvin Klein are eagerly snapped up, and those that remain unclaimed after a few months are transferred to the clearance room upstairs, where they are sold for one-fifth of the original retail price. For those with one too many coats in the closet, there are top-of-the-line dresses, handbags, and shoes practically begging to be bought. As in most discount outlets, the fluorescent lights may give the complexion a sickly cast, but they really do show the clothes (and any ripped seams, holes, or lipstick marks) to their best advantage. Information: *S & W,* 287 Seventh Ave. at W. 26th St. (phone: 212-741-1069).

BOLTON'S AND LABELS FOR LESS Although haute couture rarely makes an appearance at either of these chain stores, many businesswomen swear by the drastically marked down Harvé Benard blazers and Albert Nippon dresses. Admittedly, there are always some unappetizing articles in puce polyester, but the wise shopper will prevail and find that gem of a silk blouse or pair of linen trousers. There are frequent promotional sales on new arrivals. *Bolton's* also has a decent collection of rainwear, gloves, pantyhose, and scarves; *Labels for Less* occasionally sells separates at super-reduced prices. Information: *Bolton's,* 685 Third Ave. at E. 43rd St. (phone: 212-682-5661), and other locations; *Labels for Less,* 551 Madison Ave. at E. 55th St. (phone: 212-888-8390), and other locations.

MOE GINSBURG Lest the gentlemen feel neglected, Mr. Ginsburg stocks an enormous supply of fine menswear. Over 30,000 cashmere, wool, and linen suits, as well as an immense selection of coats, shirts, and ties, are displayed on the four floors of this vast store. Customers who prefer a European cut to their clothes will find much from which to choose. On the seventh floor the lively banter of the fitters as they make expert slashes with their chalk is an integral part of the scene. Information: *Moe Ginsburg,* 162 Fifth Ave. at W. 21st St. (phone: 212-242-3482).

ROTHMAN'S Harry Rothman's brainchild has always had a faithful following of businessmen, many of whom still return to be catered to by owner (and Rothman's grandson) Ken Giddon. Discounts of up to 40% on top-quality menswear such as Hickey Freeman and Perry Ellis are available on suits, outerwear, and furnishings. Information: *Rothman's,* 200 Park Ave. S. at E. 17th St. (phone: 212-777-7400).

CENTURY 21 Shopping may not be on your mind when you head to Lower Manhattan to see the *World Trade Center,* but perhaps it should be. Residents come from all over for the discounted designer clothes here (labels intact), amid other low-priced stock. Renovated and expanded in the early 1990s to give it a bit more polish, this store sells clothes for men, women, and children in addition to bags and shoes, bed and bath linens, cosmetics, and over-the-counter pharmaceuticals. Information: *Century 21,* 22 Cortlandt St., between Broadway and Church Sts. (phone: 212-227-9092).

FILENE'S BASEMENT This Boston-based institution insinuated itself on the Upper West Side in late 1993. Although lacking the character of the flagship store's lower level, its bargain-basement prices challenge New York's Lower East

Side, and it is somewhat less chaotic than other such outlets. Large and unpredictably stocked with middle to top designer names, it offers an almost department store–sized selection of clothing, shoes, and accessories for men, women, and children. Information: *Filene's Basement,* 2226 Broadway at W. 79th St. (phone: 873-8000).

LOWER EAST SIDE The area of Manhattan along Orchard, Delancey, and the adjacent side streets is for some a sprawling market for all manner of clothing and housewares. Finding the bargains can be only half the battle, for then the good-natured haggling begins. The merchant says something along the lines of, "I couldn't give you this for a penny less than $12," to which you respond that it's not worth more than 50¢, and usually you come to terms. A lot of the selling is done in a mixture of Yiddish, English, Russian, and Spanish, and if you know any or all four, you'll do better than wholesale. Most stores are closed Saturdays but open Sundays, the busiest day; they also close early on Fridays, the evening before major Jewish holidays, and all day on the holidays.

Both classic clothes and more daring designs, some made of sumptuous fabrics, find their way down to the cramped little shops of Orchard Street. Casual fashions and a wide range of eveningwear are available at *Forman's,* which has separate shops for petite, misses, and larger women's sizes (78, 82, and 94 Orchard St., respectively; phone: 212-228-2500 for all three). *Shulie's* (175 Orchard St.; phone: 212-473-2480) sells Tahari clothes at impressive discounts, and *Fine and Klein* (119 Orchard St.; phone: 212-674-6720) carries an immense selection of handbags by top designers. See *Special Places* in THE CITY for more on the Lower East Side.

Antiques: New York's Best Hunting Grounds

Whether it's a fascination with the past or an appreciation for the quality of workmanship that is rarely duplicated these days, antiquing is a favorite pastime of millions of Americans. They may be investment-minded bargain hunters or lovers of beautiful things who are willing to pay whatever it costs for that object of desire. In New York every taste and pocketbook is likely to be satisfied. Handsomely displayed, museum-quality pieces can be found in elegant shops along Madison Avenue in the East 60s, 70s, and 80s and along East 57th Street. The wholesale outlets along East 11th and 12th Streets between University Place and Broadway tend to be more cluttered and generally open only to the trade, but a note or business card from a local architect or decorator may gain you entrance. You might also explore the array of loft shops near the intersection of Lafayette and West Houston Streets, which specialize in 20th-century designs. Here are a few places to begin browsing.

ANNEX ANTIQUES FAIR AND FLEA MARKET Acquisitive shoppers and casual strollers love to haunt this open-air hodgepodge of stands. Hundreds of dealers bring a potpourri of silver, china, jewelry, furniture, and other random collectibles here each week. Despite the flea market atmosphere, the dealers know the value of their goods, so walking away with a "steal" is unlikely, but not impossible. Still, put on your best negotiating cap, and feel free to haggle. Among the unusual finds offered here lately are Civil War memorabilia and wooden duck decoys. Open weekends only, year-round. Information: *Annex Antiques Fair and Flea Market,* Avenue of the Americas between W. 24th and W. 26th Sts. (phone: 212-243-5343).

CHELSEA ANTIQUES BUILDING If you are not totally overwhelmed by the *Annex* (above), drop by this slim, 12-story building housing more than 150 vendors. This is not for serious museum-quality collectors, but a discerning eye can ferret out some exquisite pieces from an extensive collection that includes jewelry, decorative objects, and furniture. Information: *Chelsea Antiques Building,* 110 W. 25th St. (phone: 212-929-0909).

INDOOR ANTIQUES FAIR This year-round, weekends-only hunting ground presents an unpredictable selection of middle- to upper-range goods. Information: *Indoor Antiques Fair,* 122 W. 26th St. (phone: 212-627-4700).

MANHATTAN ART & ANTIQUES CENTER A collection of superb, timeless pieces and utter monstrosities cram more than a hundred shops in this three-floor concourse. An exquisite Chippendale armoire may be juxtaposed against an absolutely horrid desk, but that's half the fun of antiquing. Everything from Judaica to Cartier is on the selling block, with items such as Lalique and Baccarat perfume bottles eliciting the most audible cries of delight. Patchwork quilts from the 19th and early 20th centuries, Hung and Tang pottery, and Russian samovars and lacquer boxes are among the finer articles here. Information: *Manhattan Art & Antiques Center,* 1050 Second Ave. at E. 55th St. (phone: 212-355-4400).

EAST 60TH STREET The block of East 60th between Second and Third Avenues is once again (as it was until the 1960s) home to a charming colony of quality antiques dealers. Just a stone's throw from *Bloomingdale's,* and with some restful sidewalk cafés nestled between, the shops here offer merchandise many classes above flea market fare; although not of museum quality, the decorative pieces and furniture are in fine shape. A few places to investigate, especially if you are after 18th- and 19th-century French or English antiques, are *Antiques on 60* (207 E. 60th St.; phone: 212-754-4810); *Objets Trouvés Antiques* (217 E. 60th St.; phone: 212-753-0221); and *Victor Antiques* (223 E. 60th St.; phone: 212-752-4188).

STAIR & CO. On the north side of a distinguished English Renaissance–style building, a charming courtyard forms the entryway to this very British shop.

Inside is a remarkably decorated "home" filled with some of the loveliest 18th- and early 19th-century English furniture in the country. Another attraction is that there's actually enough space between pieces to walk around them, to consider how they'd look in *your* home. Only the best inlaid mahogany, fruitwood tea caddies, and Chinese porcelain are sold here; the shop also boasts an unusual collection of antique mirrors. Don't forget to take a turn in the galleries on the second and third floors, which are carefully arrayed in period style. Information: *Stair & Co.,* 942 Madison Ave. at E. 74th St. (phone: 212-517-4400).

HYDE PARK ANTIQUES This showroom may well have the world's largest inventory of genuine period furniture. Floor upon floor of beautiful English mirrors, paintings, vases, desks, and chests compose the vintage collection. Anglophiles in need of a Regency desk or a William and Mary side table are certain to find something on which to rest their treasured volume of Alfred Lord Tennyson or Virginia Woolf. Information: *Hyde Park Antiques,* 836 Broadway (phone: 212-477-0033).

URBAN ARCHAEOLOGY Wanderers through Manhattan often admire a filigree molding or sly-faced stone gargoyle, and wish that they could take it home with them. This fantasy is not altogether absurd, for captivating cornices and other decorative accoutrements populate the four floors of this eccentric shop. All the offerings here are authentic, right down to the claw-foot marble bathtubs, wooden Indians, 19th-century cast-iron urns, Victorian floor tiles, turn-of-the-century brass shower fittings, and early-20th-century street lamps. There are even showrooms that re-create a barber's shop, complete with shaving brushes and porcelain basins, and an old-fashioned general store. Information: *Urban Archaeology,* 285 Lafayette St. (phone: 212-431-6969).

ISRAEL SACK This longtime antiques dealer (established in 1905) is synonymous with excellence. Eighteenth-century American furniture and folk art are the specialties, and all the merchandise is presented as if it had taken up residence in the *American Wing* at the *Metropolitan Museum of Art.* Typical pieces come from the workrooms of such master craftsmen as New Englander John Goddard and cabinetmaker Benjamin Rudolph of Philadelphia. Information: *Israel Sack,* 730 Fifth Ave. (phone: 212-399-6562).

LEO KAPLAN For decades this Madison Avenue purveyor of fine antiques has enjoyed a brisk business. Zero in on the antique and modern paperweights, but don't let the 18th-century English pottery and porcelain go unnoticed. Also keep an eye out for Art Nouveau glass and Russian artwork. Information: *Leo Kaplan Ltd.,* 967 Madison Ave. (phone: 212-249-6766).

Other fine shops include *Howard Kaplan Antiques* (827 Broadway; phone: 212-674-1000) for Belle Epoque items; *Reymer-Jourdan Antiques* (43 E. 10th St.; phone: 212-674-4470), which has a fine collection of 18th- and

19th-century European furniture; and *Classic Toys* (69 Thompson St.; phone: 212-941-9129), for toy soldiers and miniatures.

RULES OF THE ROAD FOR AN ODYSSEY OF THE OLD

Buy for sheer pleasure, not for investment. Forget about the carrot of supposed retail values that dealers habitually dangle in front of amateur clients. If you love something, it will probably grace your home long after the *Statue of Liberty* lowers her torch.

Buy the finest example you can afford of any item, in as close to mint condition as possible. Chipped or broken "bargains" will haunt you later with their shabbiness. They also don't increase in value the way mint-condition pieces do.

Train your eye in museums and/or collections for things that interest you. These are the best schools for the acquisitive senses, particularly as you begin to develop special passions.

Get advice from specialists when contemplating major acquisitions. Much antique and collectible furniture and many paintings have been restored several times. If you want to be absolutely certain that what you're buying is what you've been told it is, stick with the larger dealers. Some auction houses and even small museums have an evaluation office whose experts will make appraisals for a fee.

Don't be afraid to haggle—a little. Most dealers don't have fixed prices, so sharpen your negotiating skills, and make an offer they can't refuse. A word of warning: While most larger dealers take credit cards, smaller shops do not.

When pricing an object, don't forget to figure the cost of shipping. Shipping a large piece and insuring it can add considerable cost. Be sure to figure this in when calculating your purchase spending limits.

Auction Houses: Best Bids

The auction world was always something of a private club, where dealers stocked up in order to mark up, and amateurs dared not tread. But during the inflation-ridden 1970s and 1980s, the art market caught the public eye. Although recessionary times have come, auction action persists.

Salerooms are wonderful places to learn about the art of the auction—and auction makes great theater. The bidding has a seductive rhythm, and the tension has a way of catching you up, even if you're not vying for the lot on the block. The auctioneer—now more often a distinguished purveyor in pinstripes than a fast-talking spieler—becomes a pied piper, with the bidders winking, blinking, and nodding in time to his or her music.

Although you can no longer expect to make a killing at an auction, there are some good values still to be found. Sales held when the weather is unspeakably foul may keep down the crowds—and the prices. Similarly, there are sometimes a few bargains at the beginning of a sale, before most of the potential buyers have arrived and the bidding has warmed up. In any event, you can sometimes buy an item on the block for about 30% off its price in a store—providing you know how to go about it.

The most important rule, according to seasoned auctiongoers, is to view the exhibition of merchandise that takes place on the few days preceding a sale. Only there will you have the chance to examine the lots at close range, to inspect them for nicks, cracks, and other flaws that can affect their value. Caveat emptor is the order of the day, and disclaimers are made by the score by nearly every house in the business. (One *Christie's* catalogue warned: "Each lot is sold by the Seller thereof, and with all faults and defects therein and with all errors of description, and is to be taken and paid for whether genuine and authentic or not, and no compensation shall be paid for same.") Consequently, it behooves you to make a pest of yourself: Have paintings moved to eye level, have objects under lock and key removed from their cases. If you anticipate buying furniture for your home, remember your measuring tape. If you're contemplating a substantial purchase, get an expert to accompany you.

Reputable houses make every effort to help their customers avoid mistakes, publishing lists of prices they estimate the lots will fetch. Also, they frequently produce illustrated catalogues with carefully worded descriptions that can give you a great deal of information about the house's opinion of a lot's age and authenticity. (Here, too, there are disclaimers—that, for instance, the "origin, date, age, attribution, genuineness, provenance, or condition of any lot is a statement of opinion, and is not to be relied upon as a statement or representation of fact." But catalogue descriptions are usually accurate, and in some cases regulated by law.)

An elaborate lexicography prevails, and a phrase in a catalogue like "style of the 18th dynasty" in a sale of Egyptian statues denotes a fake, whereas a simple "18th dynasty" identifies the real McCoy. "Signed" means that the house believes that the signature on a painting is the artist's own, while "bears signature" indicates only the possibility. "Dated" means that the lot bears a date, and that the date may be accurate. Even the typography of the catalogue can help you out. Descriptions that begin with capital letters refer to items the house considers particularly valuable—but not as valuable as those allotted a whole page. Provenance is also a clue to an item's value; previous ownership by well-known collectors increases the likelihood of value. Once you've digested the catalogue and looked over the goods, you're ready for the auction. Based on your inspection, decide on your top bid (remembering to figure in the house's commission, up to 20%), and don't allow yourself to be pushed beyond it. It *can* happen that in their excitement, people bid out of their price range. In such an emergency, you can rescind by *immediately* calling out "withdrawn!"

A visit to one or more of the city's leading auction houses will give you a good idea of the going rates for various high-quality antiques and should prove enjoyable even if you aren't tempted to bid. The following are three of the city's best.

SOTHEBY'S In 1972, when *Parke Bernet,* New York's preeminent auction house, merged with *Sotheby's,* London's oldest, a sort of multinational corporation of art was born. Well-heeled private investors and dealers bid with a liberal hand and unconcernedly wrote checks with endless zeros. This is a true aristocrat among the many auction houses, whose staff is extremely knowledgeable and earnest about its work, and very receptive to answering the questions of novices. *Sotheby's* is *the* place to find top-of-the-line merchandise, such as a Louis-Philippe armoire or a fabulous Fabergé egg. Among its more publicized sale items have been Vincent van Gogh's *Irises,* which commanded $53.9 million in 1987, and Andy Warhol's eccentric estate collection. More affordable art and antiques are sold at the *Sotheby Arcade* in the same building. Information: *Sotheby's,* 1334 York Ave. at E. 72nd St. (phone: 212-606-7000).

CHRISTIE'S Like *Sotheby's,* this famed house of British origin has a sterling reputation that matches its top-drawer antiques. Most of its offerings are snatched up by dealers, but if you can beat them to the block, you may be able to acquire the Louis XIV settee of your dreams. Items here include jewelry, furniture, stamps, wine, and movie memorabilia. Excellent Impressionist artworks also habitually show up for sale. *Christie's East* (219 E. 67th St.; phone: 212-606-0400) is a bit more downscale and handles pieces at slightly lower costs. Information: *Christie's,* 502 Park Ave. at E. 59th St. (phone: 212-546-1000).

WILLIAM DOYLE GALLERIES The largest American-owned auction house, *Doyle* specializes in estate sales and does the highest volume of trading in New York City. Decorative arts, ranging from the 16th to the 20th centuries, are sold on alternate Wednesdays throughout the year. Among its other treasures are books, jewelry, and furniture. The action tends to be livelier here than at *Christie's* or *Sotheby's.* Information: *William Doyle Galleries,* 175 E. 87th St. (phone: 212-427-2730).

New York Theater: On Broadway and Off

Ever since the days when *Oedipus Rex* was the hit of the Greek theater circuit, dramatic presentations have had mass appeal. Relatively few experiences on earth are as exciting as an opening night on Broadway, long known as "The Great White Way" for its dazzle of nighttime lights: A cavalcade of celebrities pours from limousines to fill the audience, and the tension that infuses the house before the overture begins or curtain rises can be cut with a knife. New York is the venue for the most brilliant talent in the United States—the very best in music, dance, drama, and performance art.

New Yorkers are dedicated theatergoers; therefore, for a visitor, getting last-minute tickets to performances can be a scramble. Before you shell out premium price for theater seats, stop by the *Times Square Ticket Centers (TKTS)* booth at either Broadway and West 47th Street or *2 World Trade Center;* a third booth on the Avenue of the Americas and West 42nd Street, behind the *New York Public Library,* handles tickets to music and dance events. All three sell tickets at half price for same-day performances, but you'll have to arrive early to beat the crowds. For more details, see *Theater* in THE CITY. Below, the best on the boards.

CARNEGIE HALL When confronted with the out-of-towner's query, "How do you get to *Carnegie Hall?*" even the most humorless New Yorker knows the answer: "Practice, practice!" This corny joke underscores the deep affection city dwellers still hold for sometime musical impresario Andrew Carnegie. The Scottish industrialist erected this august, Italian Renaissance building in 1891 to house the *Oratorio Society.* Although its façade may strike some as severe, there is magic beyond the threshold. Inside breathes the spirit of Euterpe, the patron muse of music, to whom countless contraltos and tenors, cellists and drummers, pay homage every evening. These prayers must please the gods, for the concerts here are rarely less than superb. Among the legendary men who have conducted performances are Toscanini, Stokowski, Bernstein, and Solti; during the hall's opening week, Tchaikovsky was the guest conductor. Contemporary performers have included Luciano Pavarotti, Frank Sinatra, and Ella Fitzgerald.

Midway through the 20th century, this musical landmark appeared to be headed for the wrecker's ball, but thanks to a preservationist group headed by world class violinist Isaac Stern, the great hall was saved and given a face-lift in time for its centennial celebrations in 1991.

Ensconced within *Carnegie Hall* is a much more intimate venue, the *Weill Recital Hall,* which features an array of not only established artists and up-and-comers in the classical music field, but also cabaret and musical theater. A small but interesting museum opened here in 1993, a tribute to the concert house's first century of music. Information: *Carnegie Hall,* 154 W. 57th St. at Seventh Ave. (phone: 212-247-7800).

CITY CENTER Skilled craftsmanship of the *Ancient and Accepted Order of the Mystic Shrine* (otherwise known as the *Masons)* created this opulent showplace, which has been refurbished to reveal the original stained glass windows and gilt trim. In 1943 Mayor Fiorello La Guardia's administration saved this finely wrought, arabesque building from demolition and transformed it into a 2,000-seat theater. Today preeminence in dance is its trademark. Classical and modern troupes such as the *Paul Taylor Dance Company,* the *Joffrey Ballet,* the *Merce Cunningham Dance Company,* and the late Martha

Graham's *School of Contemporary Dance* have strutted, fretted, and pirouetted across its stage. Downstairs the *Manhattan Theater Club* has taken up residence with an eclectic program of new plays as well as revivals. Information: *City Center,* 131 W. 55th St. (phone: 212-581-7907; mailing address: 130 W. 56th St., New York, NY 10019-3818).

BROOKLYN ACADEMY OF MUSIC A veritable volcano of genius, its acronym, *"BAM,"* pithily describes the mind-shattering effect of some of its more cosmic performances. The white Renaissance Revival structure was built in 1908 and houses a 2,100-seat opera house, a main playhouse, and a third area that is used as a symphony and chamber music hall. Erudite performance artists routinely air their intellectual laundry, avant-garde musicians play phantasmagoric compositions, and playwrights strain their imaginative faculties each fall during the always provocative *Next Wave Festival.* Stellar performers such as Laurie Anderson, Philip Glass, John Adams, Meredith Monk, and Mark Morris frequently present multimedia productions that combine music, dance, and dramatic theater, as well as video images. Information: *Brooklyn Academy of Music,* 30 Lafayette St., Brooklyn (phone: 718-636-4100).

LINCOLN CENTER FOR THE PERFORMING ARTS A 14-acre complex of six austere, white marble buildings centered around a fountain and set off by huge works of art by Marc Chagall, Henry Moore, and Alexander Calder, *Lincoln Center* is home to the *Metropolitan* and *New York City Operas,* the *New York City Ballet* and *American Ballet Theater,* the *New York Philharmonic,* the *Juilliard School of Music,* the *New York Film Festival,* the *Chamber Music Society of Lincoln Center,* and the *Lincoln Center Theater.* Here incomparable works of opera, drama, dance, music, and film are performed by resident artists as well as by top performers from around the world. Protestations of woe, promises of retribution, and murderous declarations hold court at the *Metropolitan Opera,* the edifice at the complex's center and the most eye-catching of the buildings at night, when the deep reds of Chagall's murals glow from its multitiered lobby. On any given evening audiences might be taking in the passionate arias of Marilyn Horne or Placido Domingo, while the neighboring auditoriums will be focused on the lofty leaps of the *Bolshoi Ballet* or dulcet sounds of the *New York Philharmonic.*

The *Met* is also the home of the *American Ballet Theater.* To its south lies the *New York State Theater,* home of the *New York City Ballet* and the *New York City Opera.* Here you can see December performances of *The Nutcracker,* and in the fall and spring ballet fans flock to *NYCB* performances of *The Sleeping Beauty.* Concerts of the *Mostly Mozart Festival* (in the summer) and the *New York Philharmonic* (in the fall and winter) are held at *Avery Fisher Hall,* just north of the *Met.* Behind and to the right of the *Met* is a reflecting pool with a Henry Moore sculpture; adjacent is the *New York Public Library for the Performing Arts* (with its own *Bruno Walter Auditorium,* offering free concerts), and the *Vivian Beaumont* and *Mitzi E.*

Newhouse theaters. Here plays and musicals are presented by stellar up-and-comers as well as by established box-office draws. Meanwhile, the performing arts conservatory, *Juilliard,* showcases its talent—orchestras, dance troupes, and theater groups—at the *Juilliard Theater*. The *Chamber Music Society of Lincoln Center* performs in *Alice Tully Hall,* which also offers films, music recitals, and small theater productions. The *New York Film Festival* usually starts in late September or early October, when for two and a half weeks it shows its committee's selections of new cinema from around the world. It also is held in *Alice Tully Hall* (phone: 212-875-5610 for festival information) except for opening and closing nights, which are at *Avery Fisher Hall.* The newest building in the complex is the *Walter Reade Theatre,* where classic, new, and non-Hollywood films are presented in a state-of-the-art facility. Information: *Lincoln Center for the Performing Arts,* Columbus Ave. from W. 62nd to W. 66th St. (phone: 212-875-5400).

JOSEPH PAPP PUBLIC THEATER Built in 1854 by John Jacob Astor to house the city's first public library, this handsome, Italian Renaissance–style building is now home to five different stages and the headquarters of the *New York Shakespeare Festival.* Long directed by the late Joseph Papp, and now under the direction of producer George C. Wolfe, Shakespeare's works are staged in addition to contemporary interpretations of other classics. The *Public* also presents plays by promising new writers, foreign films, and musical events. Half-price tickets are sold in the lobby on the day of performance. The *Public* also produces *Shakespeare in the Park* each summer at the open-air *Delacorte Theater* in *Central Park* (see *Quintessential New York,* above). Information: *Public Theater,* 425 Lafayette St. (phone: 212-598-7150; fax: 212-598-7127).

RADIO CITY MUSIC HALL Although many believe that the halcyon days of theater vanished with Flo Ziegfeld's spats, this Art Deco palace of the 1930s is still going strong. Aside from the legendary *Rockettes,* much of this landmark's cachet lies in its colossal interior, with grand lobby staircases that sweep visitors up to the balconies. The sheer immensity of the place—it seats 6,200—is redoubtable; the effect is heightened by the 60-foot foyer, two-ton crystal chandeliers, and a Wurlitzer organ with Herculean lungs. (Even the restrooms are decorative.) Long, snaking queues that reach almost to Fifth Avenue are a regular occurrence around *Christmas* and *Easter,* when holiday extravaganzas attract out-of-town visitors and even the most jaded New Yorkers. *Radio City* also hosts special awards events such as the *Grammies,* and pop and jazz musicians and singers hold concerts here. Information: *Radio City Music Hall,* Ave. of the Americas and W. 50th St. (phone: 212-247-4777).

THEATER ROW While it is unlikely that the lights along Broadway will ever dim, there are many pint-size theaters with first-rate actors performing equally first-rate plays that are often overlooked in favor of their neon-lit neighbors. In recent years, the south side of West 42nd Street west of Ninth Avenue has become an important adjunct to Broadway. For adventurous theatergoers, houses such as the *Samuel Beckett, John Houseman, Douglas Fairbanks, Harold Clurman,* and *Playwrights Horizon* offer exciting new works and intelligent revivals. Check the local papers for current offerings.

CIRCLE IN THE SQUARE UPTOWN Theater in the round began as an experimental concept in universities in the 1930s in an attempt to involve audiences more intimately in the play. At this theater, 650 seats surround the stage, forming a circle around a square; the design has resulted in some inventive staging for revivals of distinguished plays and premieres of new works. Among the stars who have trod its boards are James Earl Jones, Joanne Woodward, George C. Scott, and Al Pacino. Information: *Circle in the Square Uptown,* 1633 Broadway (phone: 212-307-2700).

CORT Indisputably one of the city's most beautiful theaters, the *Cort*'s elegant façade of Corinthian columns and classic terra cotta ornamentation is reminiscent of the *Petit Trianon* outside Paris. Its opening night in 1912 starred Laurette Taylor in *Peg o' My Heart,* which became an immediate hit, and in 1949 a then-unknown beauty named Grace Kelly impressed the critics in a small role in Strindberg's *The Father.* Lillian Gish, Laurence Olivier, Katharine Cornell, and Ethel Barrymore are among the other greats who performed here. Information: *Cort Theatre,* 138 W. 48th St. (*Telecharge* phone: 212-239-6200).

SHUBERT When the three Shubert brothers arrived in Manhattan at the turn of the century in search of their American dream, they probably never thought their initial purchase of a small theater would lead to a theatrical empire. The Shubert organization developed a monopolistic control over the booking and presentation of shows in the city until the 1950s, when an antitrust action by the federal government forced the group to sell 12 of its theaters. But since its opening in 1913, the 1,400-seat *Shubert Theatre* has maintained an impressive track record: Barbra Streisand made her Broadway debut here in *I Can Get It for You Wholesale,* and *A Chorus Line* had its record-breaking run on this stage from 1976 to 1990. Information: *Shubert Theatre,* 225 W. 44th St. (*Telecharge* phone: 212-239-6200).

BOOTH This diminutive, 800-seat gem was designed as a companion piece to the *Shubert.* Housed in a Venetian Renaissance–style building, the two theaters are connected by an interlocking façade of brick and terra cotta. Named for Edwin Booth, the theater has presented such Broadway hits as Noël Coward's *Blithe Spirit,* William Inge's *Come Back, Little Sheba,* and Harold Pinter's *The Birthday Party.* Henry Fonda and Anne Bancroft played opposite each other in *Two for the Seesaw* here, and Dorothy McGuire starred in *Claudia.* Information: *Booth Theatre,* 222 W. 45th St. (*Telecharge* phone: 212-239-6200).

PALACE Once the world's foremost vaudeville house, this was where stars such as Fanny Brice, the Marx Brothers, Judy Garland, W. C. Fields, Houdini, and Sarah Bernhardt electrified audiences almost every night of the week. When the appeal of slapstick faded, the *Palace* became a movie theater. Then, in 1965, James Nederlander restored its original crimson velvet and gold trimmings, rehung the crystal chandeliers, and announced that it was once again open for legitimate business. Among the roster of rousing musicals that have played here are *Sweet Charity, Applause, La Cage aux Folles, The Will Rogers Follies,* and, as of press time, *Beauty and the Beast.* Information: *Palace Theatre,* 1564 Broadway at W. 47th St. (phone: 212-307-4100).

Historic Churches and Synagogues

Base rumors have always abounded that this wicked city harbors none save reprobates. And while most New Yorkers who hear the rantings of street proselytizers automatically cringe and turn away, a substantial number of people have returned to their religious communities. These institutions in turn help contribute to the culture and history of the city, and provide peaceful havens for believers and nonbelievers alike with their lucid architectural beauty.

ABYSSINIAN BAPTIST CHURCH A neo-Gothic beauty, this house of worship is blessed with one of the largest and most enthusiastic Baptist congregations in the country. Founded in lower Manhattan in 1808, the church resettled uptown in 1923 and became one of the first religious institutions in Harlem. One of the charismatic individuals who preached from this pulpit was the late Adam Clayton Powell Jr., the controversial preacher, civil rights leader, and US congressman. A side room contains photographs and other memorabilia of his career. Sunday services are conducted with the spirit and energy of an old-time revival meeting, and the gospel choir sings with unbridled zeal. Information: *Abyssinian Baptist Church,* 132 W. 138th St. (phone: 212-862-7474).

CATHEDRAL OF ST. JOHN THE DIVINE Since 1892 generations of stonecutters have labored with painstaking diligence on this vast Gothic masterpiece, employing medieval European techniques to carve an architectural fantasy of Romanesque columns and Gothic spires. An enormous edifice (it encompasses over 121,000 square feet), it will become the largest Christian house of worship in the world when construction on it is finished, probably near the end of the 21st century. A broad flight of steps leads up to massive bronze central doors which complement its majestically ornamented façade, with recessed niches containing statues of the saints. Inside, a long corridor of pews surrounded by veined stone arches gradually leads to an imposing altar. An extraordinary pipe organ envelops the entire nave and apse with soulful melodies. Many works of art adorn the cavernous interior, among them the 17th-century Barberini tapestries displayed in its vaulted crossing and the liturgical medallions commemorating famous religious scenes that line the floor of the nave. Another wonder is the delicately beautiful rose window, which measures 40 feet in diameter and contains over 10,000 pieces of glass. The seven chapels that open out from the ambulatory are called the Chapels of Tongues, because each represents a different nationality. There is also a gift shop with an interesting array of stone carvings (including some great gargoyles), jewelry, and garden ornaments.

A community church dedicated to the impoverished, *St. John the Divine*'s homeless shelter and soup kitchen are funded by private contributions and fund-raising events. Two highlights are the *Procession of St. Francis of Assisi,* held on the first Saturday in October, when New Yorkers bring their pets (everything from lizards to llamas) down the aisles of the cathedral to be blessed, and the *Paul Winter Consort,* a choral group that offers a magical, musical celebration of the winter solstice in mid-December. One of the most moving times to visit is for *Christmas Eve* mass. Information: *Cathedral of St. John the Divine,* Amsterdam Ave. and W. 112th St. (phone: 212-316-7540).

CENTRAL SYNAGOGUE Founded in 1842 by *Congregation Ahavoth Chesed* (Lovers of Acts of Kindness), this is the oldest synagogue in continuous use in New York City. Although it was originally located near the tenements of Manhattan's Lower East Side, mass migrations of worshipers uptown resulted in its relocation in 1870 to the present site. The unusual Moorish Revival architecture is a true standout, and its dark, cavernous interior is adorned with miniature teardrop minarets and red, blue, ocher, and gilt stenciling along the walls. A copper, onion-shape dome, designed by Henry Fernbach, the first prominent Jewish architect in the country, dominates the building. Information: *Central Synagogue,* 123 E. 55th St. at Lexington Ave. (phone: 212-838-5122).

CHURCH OF THE TRANSFIGURATION This intimate little Episcopal church, with its tranquil garden, is better known as the "Little Church Around the Corner" and has been a favorite of actors for over a century. Its origins as a haven for the theatrical community began in 1870, when a priggish pastor of a nearby church refused to bury destitute actor George Holland there and suggested that "the little church around the corner" might be more appropriate. In response, Holland's friend and fellow actor Joseph Jefferson replied, "God bless the little church around the corner," a scene reenacted in the stained glass window of the south nave. Many memorials to theistic thespians are contained in the main building, which dates to 1849; one tribute is a bronze marker dedicated to Gertrude Lawrence. Among the marvelous stained glass windows that reproduce Raphael's *Madonna del Gran Duca* and Botticelli's *Virgin and Child* is the portrait of Edwin Booth in his role as Hamlet, located in the south transept. This is also the seat of the *Heidelburg Chamber Music Society,* which performs Baroque concerts here in December. Information: *Church of the Transfiguration,* 1 E. 29th St. (phone: 212-684-6770).

FRIENDS MEETING HOUSE This tiny church, founded in 1694, is the oldest house of worship in New York. True to the Quaker principles on which it was founded, this simple wooden structure, with its steep-hipped roof and tiny windows, has no flamboyant apses or fulsome architectural details to distract or confuse the eye. However, its austere design has an effective charm—it quickly clears the mind and encourages piety in even the most jaded churchgoer. The church has been in almost continuous use since its inception, with the exception of the British occupation from 1776–83, when it was used as a prison, barn, and hospital. Information: *Friends Meeting House,* 137-16 Northern Blvd., Flushing, Queens (phone: 718-358-9636).

RIVERSIDE CHURCH An interdenominational, interracial, and international church, this bastion of social activism has housed intellectual fire-eaters such as the Reverend William Sloane Coffin, its former spokesman and spiritual leader. Renowned for its free cultural programs, the church has always welcomed critical thinkers and nonconformists and functions as a center of religious democracy. Its ornate beauty is crowned by a 22-story, French Gothic Revival bell tower, and an agora houses administrative offices and classrooms. Here, too, is the largest carillon in the world, whose 74 bells issue lyrical peals that resound throughout the neighborhood. The entrance to this imposing church is modeled after the elaborate portals of *Chartres Cathedral,* but its interior, which seats 2,500, is quite austere. And if you ascend to the observation deck on the 20th floor (there is an elevator), the breathtaking vista overlooking the Hudson River, New Jersey, and New York's unmistakable skyline lifts the spirits even higher. The white building next to the church is known as "the God Box" because many religious organizations (among them, the *National Council of Churches* and the *Interfaith Council on Corporate Responsibility*) are based here. Information: *Riverside Church,* 490 Riverside Dr. at W. 122nd St. (phone: 212-222-5900).

ST. BARTHOLOMEW'S This Byzantine jewel, an Episcopal church with an intricately tiled dome and rounded arches, is one of the oldest and most gracious buildings on Park Avenue. The ornate, carved portico was transported from the previous *St. Bartholomew's* on Madison Avenue, which was designed by Stanford White. Inside, mosaics on the ceiling of the narthex tell the story of the Creation, and a mosaic of glass and gold leaf on the ceiling of the apse represents the Transfiguration. Information: *St. Bartholomew's,* 109 E. 50th St. at Park Ave. (phone: 212-751-1616).

ST. MARK'S IN THE BOWERY Built entirely of fieldstone, this 1799 country church was constructed on the site of Peter Stuyvesant's personal chapel. In 1828 a Greek Revival steeple was added, with an addition in 1854 of a neoclassical portico, which gives it a more formal air. Two Italian marble lions flank the broad main doorway, which opens into a straightforward Georgian interior. The church is a longtime venue for poetry readings and performances; the main sanctuary's pews have been removed to accommodate dancers and other performers. A triangular cobblestone courtyard, with patches of grass and benches, looks out on the charming vistas of townhouses along East Ninth and East 10th Streets, and provides a calming respite from the bustle of the city. Visitors can view Peter Stuyvesant's and Commodore Perry's graves in the ancient cemetery adjacent to the church. Information: *St. Mark's in the Bowery,* 131 E. 10th St. (phone: 212-674-6377).

ST. PATRICK'S CATHEDRAL Many people commonly link *Notre Dame* in Paris, *St. Peter's* in Rome, and *St. Patrick's* together as among the most beautiful churches in the world, and with good reason: All are superbly crafted architectural marvels. The largest Roman Catholic cathedral in the US, *St. Patrick's* was begun in 1858, consecrated in 1879, completed in 1906, and is now the seat of the Roman Catholic Archdiocese of New York. Among the venerable clergy who have graced the church are Popes Paul VI and John Paul II, who once said mass here. Designed by James Renwick, this Gothic hybrid of white marble and stone is reminiscent of many 19th-century European cathedrals. The façade's two square towers are topped by spires that loom 330 feet above Fifth Avenue. Inside are a gigantic organ with 9,000 pipes and an exquisite bronze canopy rising 57 feet above the high altar. Midnight mass at *Christmas* is astounding: A candlelit procession travels up the nave to the altar as thousands of voices join in celebration. Information: *St. Patrick's Cathedral,* Fifth Ave. from E. 50th to E. 51st St. (phone: 212-753-2261).

SPANISH AND PORTUGUESE SYNAGOGUE Erected in 1897, this is the fifth and newest home of *Congregation Shearith Israel* (Remnant of Israel), the nation's oldest Jewish community. Descendants of Jews who fled the Spanish Inquisition founded this group in 1654, and despite Peter Stuyvesant's overt reluctance to permit them to settle in Manhattan, this sect persevered as the city's sole Jewish congregation until 1825. Its first synagogue was erected on the Lower East Side in 1730, and many artifacts have been preserved, including the floor boards from the old reader's desk. In the late afternoon the daylight fiercely illuminates the richly colored Tiffany stained glass windows. Information: *Spanish and Portuguese Synagogue,* 2 W. 70th St. (phone: 212-873-0300).

TEMPLE EMANU-EL The world's largest Reform synagogue, this mighty edifice is located on the former site of one of Mrs. William Astor's mansions. In 1929 a solemn limestone synagogue took root at the behest of New York's German-Jewish elite. Moorish and Romanesque architectures intermingled to create a harmonious blend of Eastern and Western styles. The ceilings, columns, and great arches are covered with mosaics reminiscent of Middle Eastern basilicas. Religious symbols, such as the six-pointed Star of David and the Lion of Judah, appear frequently in the decorative patterns of the stained glass windows and mosaics in the sanctuary. The synagogue can hold up to 2,500 worshipers, which surpasses the capacity of *St. Patrick's*. Information: *Temple Emanu-El,* 1 E. 65th St. at Fifth Ave. (phone: 212-744-1400).

TRINITY CHURCH For weary Wall Street wage earners, this unpretentious little church, with its graceful spire, is a stalwart spiritual oasis in the midst of mammon. All but engulfed by the towers of commerce, this historic house of worship (the third incarnation, built in 1846) sits on more than two acres of some of the most valuable real estate in Manhattan. The marvelously wrought front doors were modeled after those designed by Ghiberti for the *Baptistery* of the *Duomo* in Florence, and architect Richard Upjohn's stained glass window in the chancel is considered one of the finest ever crafted. Some of the earliest Manhattanites are interred here, including Robert Fulton of steamboat fame, statesman Alexander Hamilton, and William Bradford, publisher of the *New York Gazette,* who first brought the printing press to New York. In good weather during the spring and summer, visitors can muse over the unusual tombstones while listening to noontime classical concerts. Information: *Trinity Church,* 74 Trinity Pl. (phone: 212-602-0800).

A Day at the Races

Only the coolest of customers remain unflappable at the sight of a horse race; the clatter of hooves and the shouts and curses of the spectators, most of them anxious bettors, are integral parts of the experience. Although numerous—and seedy—*Off-Track Betting (OTB)* offices are scattered about the city, a visit to one of these cannot compare to the actual thrill of a day at the races.

AQUEDUCT Located in Ozone Park, Queens, at 108th Street and Rockaway Boulevard, near *John F. Kennedy International Airport,* this racetrack (phone: 718-641-4700) caters to thoroughbreds. Built in 1894, it was named for the Ridgewood Aqueduct, which was the first large water system for Brooklyn and Queens. Operated by the nonprofit *New York Racing Association* (phone: 718-641-4700), it is easily accessible by subway. The horses run at the *Big A* from about mid-October to the beginning of May, when the action switches to *Belmont Park* (see below). During the cold winter months racing is conducted on an inner dirt track that resists freezing. Although there are some major stakes races at *Aqueduct,* the horses—especially in the heart of winter—don't really measure up to those at *Belmont.*

BELMONT PARK This is one of the country's most beautiful tracks. Most of New York's premier spring and autumn races are run here, topped each June by the *Belmont Stakes,* the third and final jewel in racing's *Triple Crown.* Behind the grandstand is a large park crowded with families picnicking on weekends and holidays. The stands have wide, comfortable seats that afford excellent views of the mile-and-a-half dirt track, the largest in North America. *Belmont* straddles the New York City/Nassau County line; the official address is Hempstead Avenue, Elmont, Queens (phone: 718-641-4700). It is accessible easily by car or by special *Long Island Rail Road* trains from *Penn Station* in Manhattan. Horses race here from early May through the end of July, then return for several weeks in September and October after a four- or five-week meeting in upstate Saratoga Springs.

YONKERS RACEWAY Just outside the New York City limits in northern Westchester County (phone: 914-968-4200), this well-known racetrack is the home of year-round harness racing and such classic heats as the *Cane Pace* and *Yonkers Futurity.* Though it is a little worn around the edges, *Yonkers* offers ten races every evening and an occasional day program when the city's thoroughbred tracks are closed.

MEADOWLANDS Across the Hudson River in East Rutherford, New Jersey (phone: 201-935-8500), this track hosts both standardbred and thoroughbred races, with harness races featured from January to August and flat racing from *Labor Day* to the end of December. Races are usually held in the evenings and on Sunday afternoons throughout the year—except during the football season. In addition, there are several fine restaurants with good views of the track, so you can follow your favorite horse as you dine.

Boating

Boating is a truly sybaritic pleasure. There is nothing quite like skimming over the water on a balmy summer afternoon to cool down and restore peace of mind. Most lakes in the five boroughs have on-site boat rentals. Those who wish to canoe or kayak in New York's outlying waters must obtain a permit from the *Department of Parks and Recreation* (for a nominal fee) at one of the following locations: the *Arsenal* in *Central Park,* Manhattan (Fifth Ave. and 64th St.; phone: 212-360-8133); the *Litchfield Villa* in *Prospect Park,* Brooklyn (Prospect Park W. and Fifth St.; phone: 718-965-8993); *Lost Battalion Hall* in Rego Park, Queens (93-29 Queens Blvd.; phone: 718-263-4121); *Bronx Borough Office* in *Bronx Park,* Bronx (phone: 718-430-1838); or *Staten Island Headquarters* (1150 Clove Rd.; phone: 718-390-8023).

CENTRAL PARK As soon as the snow melts, dozens flock to the *Loeb Boathouse* (park entrance at Fifth Ave. and E. 72nd St.; phone: 212-517-4723) in search of a sound vessel and a pair of wooden oars. This boathouse rents rowboats for *Central Park*'s small lake, a haven for incurable romantics and frisky children who love to trail their hands in the water. For those inclined to let someone else do the heavy work, there are strong gentlemen who propel gondolas that hold up to five people. Among the sights to see as you maneuver smoothly through the calm waters are the majestic *Bethesda Fountain* toward the south end and the quaint Bow Bridge near the woodsy western edge. If you look up beyond the treetops, the stately apartment houses of Central Park West and the hotels that line the southern edge of the park provide a splendid skyline view.

BROOKLYN There is one rental opportunity in *Prospect Park,* at the *Wollman Ice Skating Rink* (on the south side of the park near Parkside Ave.; phone: 718-287-9824), where pedal and rowboats are available. Canoe and kayak enthusiasts should visit the launch in *Canarsie Beach Park* (Seaview and Paerdegat Aves.), which is part of the *Gateway National Recreation Area* in Jamaica Bay. You can rent a canoe at Paerdegat Basin and paddle to Pumpkin Patch Channel, the populated Beach Channel area, and *Jacob Riis Park* on the Rockaway peninsula.

BRONX There is a launch site for kayakers and canoers in *Pelham Bay Park,* near the lagoon side to the west, rather than the beach side. From here you can paddle up to Pelham and New Rochelle in Westchester County, where there are plenty of docks and marinas, or around Hunters Island, past Orchard Beach, and over to busy City Island.

QUEENS You can launch a canoe or kayak from the *Bayside Marina* on Little Neck Bay (28th Ave. and Cross Island Pkwy.). Most of the western shoreline of the bay is scenic parkland, with the *Fort Totten* army base, designed by Robert E. Lee in 1857, anchoring the north end. Along the southern shoreline of Little Neck Bay are the residential communities of Douglaston and Little Neck, while the exclusive Great Neck Estates area of Nassau County is to the east. Take a breather from all that paddling and explore some of the rocky coves, where you'll probably turn up lots of mussels, clams, and perhaps some oysters, whelks, periwinkles, and crabs.

STATEN ISLAND In *Clove Lakes Park,* just north of Victory Avenue, there is a boathouse that rents rowboats and pedal boats for Clove Lake (phone: 718-442-7451). Most of the visitors to the park are local residents, so expect aggressive rowing from teens and a few boom boxes violating the "quiet zone" regulations.

One of the most breathtaking views of Manhattan's southern tip is from Staten Island; the view becomes twice as spectacular when approached from the water. There is a boat launch at *Alice Austen State Park* (Hylan Blvd. and Edgewater St.), where you can put in; you'll pass the Verrazano-Narrows Bridge to the south, with the *Staten Island Ferry Terminal* to the north as you push on to lower Manhattan. There is a lot of traffic in these waters and the currents can be tricky, so only very experienced canoers and kayakers should embark on this adventure.

Sailing

New York City, with its dense population and concrete canyons, might seem like an unlikely sailing center; however, it does boast one of the finest natural harbors on the East Coast. Old salts no longer carouse along the Lower East Side's waterfront, but there is still a lot of activity in New York Harbor. And don't forget that Manhattan is home to the *New York Yacht Club* (37 W. 44th St.; phone: 212-382-1000), the old and prestigious organization that for many years was guardian of the *America's Cup,* the world's top competitive yachting trophy.

Rentals for day sails can be made by qualified sailors at two sailing schools on City Island in the Bronx. The *Offshore Sailing School,* with affiliates in Cape Cod, Captiva Island, Florida, and St. Lucia and Tortola in the West Indies, teaches the basics with a combination of classroom instruction and hands-on training aboard its boats (phone: 718-885-3200 or 800-221-4326). The *New York Sailing School,* with a 20-boat fleet, offers instruction for both novices and experienced hands looking for refresher courses in convenient weekend sessions (phone: 718-885-3103 or 800-428-SAIL).

MANHATTAN The city's *Department of Parks* maintains the *79th Street Boat Basin* in the Hudson River on Manhattan's West Side, but the boats here seem to spend more time tied up at the docks than at sea. There are also docks at the *South Street Seaport* in the East River, the *North Cove Marina* at *Battery Park City* on the Hudson, and just west of there across the river, at *Newport Marina* in Jersey City. The last has a pump-out facility, the closest for pleasure boats in the New York Bay area. If your destination is up the Hudson, most of the waterfront amenities are on the Jersey side of the river, at least until you get above Manhattan. The tidal effect in the Hudson extends all the way north of Albany, but the lower Hudson is relatively easy to navigate since the middle grounds and steep-to shoaling don't begin until well past the Tappan Zee Bridge at Tarrytown.

Heading toward Long Island Sound via the East River requires maneuvering past the aptly named Hell Gate at the entrance; the currents here are the strongest in the harbor. Small craft can have a difficult time unless crews pay very careful attention. The sail up the river—under a half-dozen bridges and past such sights as Wall Street, the *South Street Seaport,* the *Fulton Fish Market,* the *United Nations,* Roosevelt Island, and *Carl Schurz Park*—is awesome.

BROOKLYN Though Sheepshead Bay is best known for its fishing fleet, the 1½-mile-long bay is also filled with pleasure boats. Boaters can exit the Sheepshead Bay Channel—guided by *Ambrose Light* in the lower bay—and steer east into the quiet, scenic waters of Jamaica Bay and the *Gateway National Recreation Area,* or head west and north past Norton's Point at the tip of Coney Island toward New York Harbor. The waters of the harbor are deep and well marked, but rife with tankers, freighters, passenger liners, naval vessels, and hard-working tugs and towboats—not to mention various ferries and private craft. The larger vessels are given the right-of-way because they are in tight quarters and have limited room in which to maneuver. In addition to all the craft in the harbor, major hazards are the "deadhead" objects floating just below the surface, such as railroad ties, construction debris, and utility poles. The currents in the harbor can be tricky due to the shifting tides and occasional eddies. Winds—affected by the monstrous buildings on shore—can be even trickier, and auxiliary power is recommended for sailboats.

BRONX Some of the most serious boating in the area is done on Long Island Sound out of City Island, which has a worldwide reputation as a boat-building center. (One *America's Cup* defender, the *Courageous,* skippered by Ted Turner, was built on City Island.) A truly nautical haven in New York City, tiny City Island has a number of boatyards and marinas providing moorings, dock slips, repairs, equipment, and supplies for pleasure and commercial boats. There are also a number of excellent seafood restaurants here.

The waterfronts of the East Bronx, Queens, Brooklyn, and Staten Island are sprinkled with private marinas and yacht clubs mooring primarily powerboats, but there are a surprising number of sailboats as well.

A Shutterbug's New York

An exceptionally photogenic city, New York is visually arresting at every turn. The architectural variety is astounding: From the slick, gilded exterior of *Trump Tower* to the understated elegance of the *Frick Collection* to the Athenian courtyards of *Columbia University,* there is scarcely a block that does not intrigue the eye. Natural beauty also abounds: Ivy climbs up the banisters of a brownstone, pale pink roses and lilies of the valley cluster about the walkways of a community garden, and the sun makes the rivers sparkle with thousands of diamonds of light. And there is the human element: Socialites in haute couture drinking white wine spritzers over lunch, a souvlaki seller in a long apron grilling sticks of barbecued meat, models posing for a camera in the middle of traffic islands, and a three-card monte dealer working his scam with the agility of an athlete. This is the ultimate stomping ground for enthusiastic shutterbugs. Even a beginner can achieve remarkable results with a surprisingly basic set of lenses and filters. Equipment is, in fact, only as valuable as the imagination that puts it into use.

LANDSCAPES, SEASCAPES, AND CITYSCAPES New York's bustling byways and historic buildings are most often photographers' favorite subjects. But the city's green spaces and waterways provide numerous photo possibilities as well. In addition to *City Hall,* the *Grace Building,* and *Trinity Church,* be sure to look for natural beauty: The majestic trees lining Riverside Park, the well-manicured plots of flowers in front of the *Plaza* hotel, and the rowboats that skim along the lakes in *Central Park* are just a few examples.

Although a standard 50mm to 55mm lens may work well in some landscape situations, most will benefit from a 20mm to 28mm wide-angle. The promenade next to the *United Nations*, with city skyscrapers looming in the distance, for example, is the type of panorama that fits beautifully into a wide-angle format, allowing not only the overview, but the opportunity to include people or other points of interest in the foreground. A flower, for instance, may be used to set off a view of a beautiful old brownstone; or people can provide a sense of perspective in a shot of Times Square.

To isolate specific elements of any scene, use your telephoto lens. Perhaps there's a particular carving in a historic church that would make a lovely shot, or it might be the interplay of light and shadow on a Greenwich Village street. The successful use of a telephoto means developing your eye for detail.

PEOPLE As with taking pictures of people anywhere, there are going to be times in New York when a camera is an intrusion. Consider your own reaction under similar circumstances, and you'll have an idea of what would make others comfortable enough to be willing subjects. People are often sensitive to having a camera suddenly pointed at them, and a polite request, while getting you a share of refusals, will also provide a chance to shoot some wonderful portraits that capture the spirit of the city as surely as the scenery does. For candids an excellent lens is a zoom telephoto in the 70mm to 210mm range; it allows you to remain unobtrusive while the lens draws the subject closer. For portraits a telephoto can be used effectively as close as two or three feet.

For authenticity and variety select a place likely to produce interesting subjects. The *Empire State Building* is an obvious spot for visitors, but if it's local color you're after, visit Chinatown or one of the city's many ethnic street festivals, sit at a Greenwich Village café and watch the fashion parade, or walk around *Central Park*, where elderly couples, college students, tourists, and the homeless go to enjoy a sunny day. Aim for shots that tell what's different about New York. In portraiture there are several factors to keep in mind. Morning or afternoon light will add richness to skin tones, emphasizing your subject's coloring. To avoid the harsh facial shadows cast by direct sunlight, shoot in the shade or in an area where the light is diffused.

SUNSETS When shooting sunsets, keep in mind that the brightness will distort meter readings. When composing a shot directly into the sun, frame the picture in the viewfinder so that only half of the sun is included. Read the meter, set, and shoot. Whenever there is this kind of unusual lighting, shoot a few frames in half-step increments, both over and under the meter reading. Bracketing, as this is called, can provide a range of images, the best of which may well be other than the one shot at the meter's recommended setting.

Use any lens for sunsets. A wide-angle is good when the sky is filled with color-streaked clouds, when the sun is partially hidden, or when you're close to an object that silhouettes dramatically against the sky.

Telephoto lenses also produce wonderful silhouettes, either with the sun as a backdrop or against the palette of a brilliant sunset sky. Bracket again here. For the best silhouettes wait 10 to 15 minutes after sunset. A tripod is recommended unless you are using a very fast film.

Red and orange filters are often used to accentuate a sunset's picture potential. Orange will help turn even a gray sky into something approaching a photogenic finale to the day, and can provide particularly beautiful shots linking the sky with the sun reflected on the river. If the sunset is already bold in hue, however, orange will overwhelm the natural colors. A red filter will produce dramatic, highly unrealistic results.

NIGHT If you think that picture possibilities end at sunset, you're presuming that night photography is the exclusive domain of the professional. If you've got a tripod, all you'll need is a cable release to attach to your camera to assure a steady exposure (which is often timed in minutes rather than fractions of a second).

For situations such as evening concerts in *Central Park* or nighttime harbor cruises, a strobe does the trick, but beware: Flash units are often used improperly. You can't take a picture of the skyline with a flash. It may reach out as far as 30 feet, but that's it. On the other hand, a flash used too close to a subject may result in overexposure, resulting in a "blown out" effect. With most cameras strobes will work with a maximum shutter speed of 1/125 or 1/250 of a second. If you set the exposure properly and shoot within range, you should come up with pretty sharp results.

CLOSE-UPS Whether of people or of objects such as antique door knockers, close-ups can add another dimension to your photography. There are a number of shooting options, one of which is to use a 70mm or a 210mm lens at its closest focusable distance. Unless you're working in bright sunlight, a tripod will be worthwhile. If you are very near your subject and there is a good deal of reflective light, it may pay to underexpose a bit in relation to the meter reading.

If you do not have a telephoto lens, you can still shoot close-ups using a set of magnification filters. Filter packs of one-, two-, and three-time magnification are available, converting your lens into a close-up lens. Even better is a special macro lens designed for close-up photography.

A SHORT PHOTOGRAPHIC TOUR

Here are some of New York's truly great pictorial opportunities.

STATUE OF LIBERTY Unless you plan to jump in a whirlybird and tour Manhattan at cloud height, the towering majesty of the *Statue of Liberty* is best photographed from the water. Whether you take a 90-minute cruise, sail around Manhattan on the *Circle Line,* ride the ferry to Staten Island, or hop the boat to Liberty Island itself, you'll have ample opportunity to photograph this glorious statue. Check beforehand to see if the boat sails southwest of Liberty Island; if so you'll be able to photograph against the angular panorama of Manhattan's skyscrapers. Since the statue faces east, a morning excursion will enable you to capture the serene face if you shoot with the sun behind you. As you approach, aim for a sidelong shot of the head and the upraised arm that bears the torch. Another great snap is toward the crown in late afternoon; awash in the light at sunset, the features have a beautiful purity and poignancy.

LINCOLN CENTER The central plaza of this performing arts complex is one of the busiest public spaces in Manhattan; thousands of music, dance, and drama buffs converge daily upon its theaters, pausing at the circular fountain as if it were a magnet. From the entrance on Columbus Avenue on an autumn evening, that fountain, aglow from the soft light of the *Metropolitan Opera*'s delicate chandeliers, seems to capture the quiet elegance and majesty of this city. Find the right angle, and you'll have a quintessential New York photo for your album.

ROCKEFELLER CENTER Stand at the Fifth Avenue entrance of the promenade (known as the *Channel Gardens*) for a long shot of the shops and lush, landscaped gardens that stretch down the center aisle. If you're visiting New York at *Christmastime,* focus on the angel sculptures that line the promenade. Agleam with tiny lights, they blow trumpets skyward in a silent tribute to the season. Head for the ice skating rink, forever guarded by the golden statue of Prometheus. Above the famous demigod is the magnificent *Christmas* tree, a yearly tradition that dates back to the 1930s. It is an awesome sight, bedecked in thousands of colored lights. Many dozens of international flags flank the plaza, and if you center *Prometheus* in your viewfinder, you will be able to compose a picture that has a little bit of everything in it.

BROOKLYN BRIDGE The graceful geometry of this undeniably exquisite structure is framed by double arches that rise heavenward and a curving network of cables that stretch from their towers to form gigantic celestial harps. You can photograph the bridge from virtually any angle, but a diagonal shot with the bright blue sky in contrast to the austere arches will be particularly rewarding. Try shooting from *City Hall Park* or during a stroll across the span when the sun is glinting on the filigree of cables.

CHINATOWN This enclave's narrow, crowded streets, with sprawling sidewalk markets and doorways emblazoned with Chinese ideograms, offer endless photo opportunities. You may want to snap the pagoda-topped telephone booths along Mott Street. Another eye-catcher is the colorful Hong Kong and Shanghai Bank in Chatham Square, with its sweeping tile roof and galleries. If you're fortunate enough to visit during the *Chinese New Year* celebration (the first full moon after January 21), and you can handle the din and fumes of constantly exploding firecrackers, you should get some great shots of the parading dragon dancers and local children resplendent in their holiday best.

CENTRAL PARK Marvelous photo opportunities await the photographer in every corner of the park. Warm-weather weekends will bring endless subjects, from kites streaming across the midday sky to roller-bladers demonstrating new dance steps to picnickers at all-day parties. You might want to take a picture of the sea of sun worshipers or model sailboats gliding smoothly on the Conservatory Pond. A shot of children riding on the carousel is sure to be a winner, and no one should leave the park without a close-up of a simian grin on one of the denizens at the zoo.

Directions

Introduction

"One belongs to New York instantly. . . . One belongs to it as much in five minutes as in five years." Though Thomas Wolfe wrote these words in the first half of the 20th century, when he lived in Greenwich Village, his observation is still accurate. This dynamic, fast-paced city generates a kind of excitement that is at once absorbing and exhilarating. Most adjectives run to the superlative where New York is concerned: biggest, fastest, tallest, dirtiest, most fashionable, richest, poorest, and most diverse. The world's foremost figures in business, finance, and the arts converge here—as do all the less appealing elements of urban culture. So, warts and all, New York is like nowhere else on earth—and proud of it.

To a first-timer, most of the old clichés will probably be borne out. New York's manners can be abrupt, its size overwhelming, and the cost of living a shock, but for the visitor, it's simply a matter of planning strategies for making the city manageable.

Begin with an overview. A boat trip on the *Circle Line,* which circumnavigates Manhattan, provides an excellent orientation, with premium skyline views during the whole trip. A visit to the *Empire State Building* takes you inside a grand Art Deco building and then shows you all five boroughs from the top, a stupendous viewpoint. A helicopter ride affords another type of dramatic perspective. Finally, there are numerous bus tours, whose leisurely, ground-level pace and reasonable cost attract a large portion of the city's visitors. (See *Seeing the City* in THE CITY for particulars on all of the above.)

Once you've taken a grand tour of New York, explore the city one neighborhood at a time. Chinatown, SoHo, Greenwich Village, Wall Street, and *Rockefeller Center* all have their own unique personalities.

If the roar of traffic and the rush of pedestrians who travel at a semi-sprint are too much for you, find a quiet place and take a breather. In the midst of all the concrete is an abundance of pocket parks and other quiet oases. Relax on a bench near the splendid *Temple of Dendur* in the *Metropolitan Museum of Art,* or pause to admire the charming cluster of Elizabethan-style buildings in village-like *Tudor City Park,* tucked incongruously above East 42nd Street. Other placid places include the hushed interior of Fifth Avenue's *St. Thomas Church* and the reading rooms of the *New York Public Library.*

If you are trying to find your own way, remember that most New Yorkers will help you—some may even escort you to your destination while imparting a bit of knowledge about the area. They probably also will tell you to stay out of the parks after dark, which definitely is advice to heed. During the daytime, though, as you navigate through the throngs of joggers, bikers, roller-bladers, dog walkers, and Frisbee throwers in beautifully landscaped *Central Park,* you'll realize that New Yorkers aren't so different from other people—there are just more of them.

As for seasonal diversity, New York experiences spring, summer, fall, and winter with equal zeal. Autumn in New York is inviting. The brisk air, the clear blue sky, and the relief from summer's muggy dog days add a spring to the step. Rio may have *Carnaval,* but New York has *Christmas.* During this magical and frantic December-long celebration, the city decks itself out in high style. Everything is illuminated, from the red and green lights on the *Empire State Building* to the towering tree in *Rockefeller Center.* Spring arrives in fits and starts. One day temperatures soar to promising heights, and the next morning a blast of winter confuses the cherry blossoms that have just begun to bloom. Eventually, spring settles in, and changes the treetops to a delicate shade of green; parks and plazas suddenly seem to fill with picnickers at the first hint of warmth. And though Paris may sizzle in the summer, New York ungraciously wilts. There are compensations, however; despite the deadly humidity and uncomfortable temperatures, the *Fourth of July* fireworks lift overheated spirits as they illuminate the skyline. Other perennial hot-weather treats are *Shakespeare in the Park,* and the *Mostly Mozart Festival* at *Lincoln Center.*

New York City is made up of five boroughs—Brooklyn, Queens, the Bronx, Staten Island, and Manhattan—but New Yorkers know that "The City" really refers to Manhattan alone. This narrow island, about 12½ miles long and 2½ miles at its widest, stretches along an axis tilted from southwest to northeast. Most of Manhattan is an easily navigated grid; the avenues run north and south, the numbered streets east and west. Below 14th Street disorder prevails. This is the oldest part of the city, and its streets follow long-gone property lines, streams, canals, even obsolete Indian trails. The only way to explore downtown successfully is to arm yourself with a good map and a sense of humor. Don't be concerned if you get lost once or twice—you may discover a small café or a charming antiques shop that doesn't appear on any tourist map.

Each of the following walking tours covers a special part of the city, an area that contains quintessential elements of New York. Enjoy it; after all, you belong to it already.

Walk 1: Wall Street

The Wall Street area is a history-rich part of New York where the city's constant state of flux hasn't completely eradicated signs of its past. Manhattan's first European settlement was here, at the southern tip of the island, and in the 1650s Governor Peter Stuyvesant built a wooden wall to protect the original settlers against attacks by native tribes to the north: hence the name, "Wall Street." Today the city's skyscrapers, their roofs punctuated by satellite dishes, coexist with 19th-century brick buildings, and the whup-whup-whup of helicopters mingles with the piercing cries of sea gulls.

Blessed with one of the best natural deep-water harbors in the world, New York has always thrived as a port city. This tour begins at the entrance to the *South Street Seaport* at Fulton and Water Streets. The small white lighthouse on the left is a memorial to the hundreds of victims of the *Titanic*, which sank in 1912 on its way here from England.

During the 18th and 19th centuries this was New York City's busiest port district. The area teemed with sailors and brawny dockworkers, and goods from all over the world were unloaded on the piers jutting out into the East River. When steamships replaced sailing ships, the steamers couldn't navigate the East River, and port activity switched over to the Hudson River; the ever-thriving *Fulton Fish Market* and some pleasantly seedy seafood restaurants were the only survivors here. Over the past couple of decades, however, the area has undergone extensive renovation, including the addition of a large pedestrian mall. The financial boom of the 1980s brought pricey condominiums, and the seaport gained cachet as a playground for a then burgeoning population of Wall Street yuppies.

The seaport now represents a rather sanitized version of its rollicking past. Instead of dark, dingy taverns, there are now museums, galleries, expensive restaurants and casual eateries, and popular stores—among them, *Brookstone,* the *Nature Company, J. Crew, Country Road Australia, Banana Republic,* and a miniature version of the *Strand,* the huge bookstore at Broadway and East 12th Street. During the summer Pier 17 plays host to a series of outdoor jazz and rock concerts (for more information, call 212-669-9400, or check the listings in the newspapers). On spring and summer weekends you'll have to negotiate the clusters of people watching the numerous mimes, jugglers, and musicians who perform along its main drag. On Friday nights *South Street Seaport* is a popular happy hour destination for throngs of young traders from the financial district. And on any night (weather permitting) there's a spectacular sunset harbor cruise that departs from Pier 16 aboard the schooner *Pioneer* (phone: 212-669-9400).

The piers, a quick duck across South Street under the elevated Franklin Delano Roosevelt Drive (better known as the "FDR"), are a giant stage.

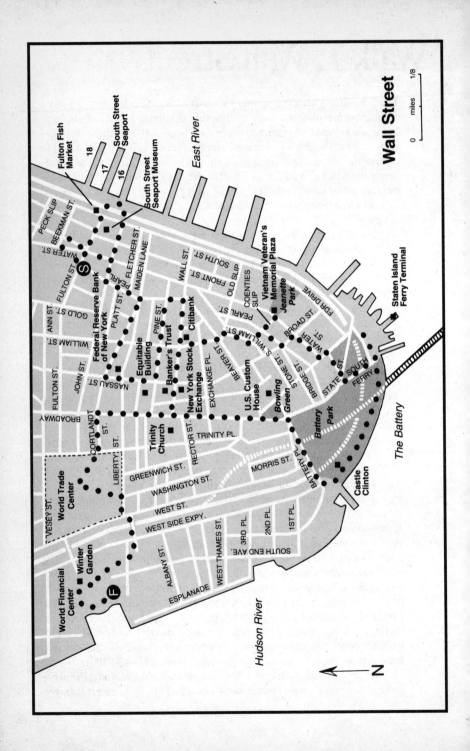

To the north is the giant *Pier 17 Pavilion,* with so-so beaneries and T-shirt emporiums. Anchored to the south are some beautiful old tall ships, including the four-masted *Peking* and the 1885 three-masted *Wavertree.*

Despite all the hoopla, the heart of the seaport remains the *Fulton Fish Market,* now located in a hygienic brick barn that also houses upscale shops and eateries. Come here after a night on the town—the joint is jumping by 4 AM, Mondays through Saturdays. From spring through fall, tours are given at 6 AM, just after the city's restaurateurs have chosen from among the catch of the day (call 212-669-9400 for reservations).

This marks the start of Schermerhorn Row, which runs from Nos. 2 to 18 Fulton Street. The row, which dates from 1811, is a group of warehouses built by merchant Peter Schermerhorn on landfill some 600 feet from the original shoreline. John Street, the back side of the block, contains the *South Street Seaport Museum,* housed in the A. A. Low Building (171 John St.; phone: 212-669-9400), a cream-trimmed brownstone built in 1850 as a countinghouse for the China trade. Next door is the *Boat Building Shop,* where skilled craftspeople are currently restoring the *Shadow,* a traditional coastal "sandbagger."

Water Street, on the opposite side of Schermerhorn Row, is the museum block, with an operating 19th-century printing shop (No. 211), the *Seaport Gallery* (No. 215), which features nautical exhibits, and the *Melville Library of Maritime History* next door (by appointment only). Bookworms who dream of sailing over the bounding main can stop in at *Books & Charts* (No. 209) and fulfill all sorts of nautical fantasies. Follow Water Street north to Beekman Street, turn right, then left on Front Street. At the northern boundary of the seaport area is quiet, cobblestoned Peck Slip, whose benches make a perfect spot for a picnic. Or sit and compare the trompe l'oeil mural of the Brooklyn Bridge to the real thing just beyond it. Now do an about-face and head south on Water Street.

At One Seaport Plaza, at the corner of Water and Fulton Streets, the mood dramatically shifts into the 20th century. Water Street, with its buildings and plazas interspersed with more buildings and more plazas, looks like it was designed by architects who overdosed on Lego as children. One block south, at the corner of John Street, a commercial building (No. 127) is a delightful conglomeration of brightly colored metal tubes and canvas canopies. The calendrical device outside—it's too big and complex to call it a mere clock—further accents the mood.

Turn right on John Street and then left on Pearl Street. The best time to visit this section of town is on weekdays, when everything from churches to office buildings is open. Try not to get caught in the narrow streets at lunchtime, however; shoving your way through a sea of pinstriped suits is enough to induce a severe case of *Brooks Brothers* agoraphobia.

Using Pearl Street as your main thoroughfare, feel free to make detours. Two blocks to the right on Maiden Lane (named for the young girls who did the family washing in a brook that once flowed here) is an appropriately impregnable stone fortress that houses the *Federal Reserve Bank of New York* (33 Liberty St.). Modeled after a Florentine Renaissance palazzo, this stronghold stores one-quarter of the gold of 80 countries—even more than *Fort Knox*. There are free one-hour tours of the building (call 720-6130 at least one week in advance to make reservations). Opposite the bank stands a sandstone skyscraper (33 Maiden La.), whose turrets mimic those of the *Fed*.

Follow Maiden Lane to Nassau Street and turn left. Walk down these dark, narrow, canyon-like streets framed by towering skyscrapers; it will help you understand why executive suites are on the top floors: No sunlight can penetrate down to street level. Turn left on Pine Street and follow it two blocks down to Pearl Street, then turn right and walk one block to Wall Street.

Wall Street was named for the wall built by Peter Stuyvesant in 1653; it was torn down by 1699, when there was no longer a threat of attack from the north. As you walk up Wall Street, the Greek Revival *Citibank Building* (55 Wall), with its magnificent Ionic and Corinthian colonnade, is on the left. The building was designed to resemble a Greek and Roman forum and marketplace; it served as the *New York Stock Exchange* until 1854, when it was acquired by the National City Bank, and until 1899 housed the *US Custom House*.

Stocks have been traded up and down Wall Street since government bonds were first issued in 1790. The forerunner of the Big Board dates from May 1792, when a group of brokers who used to meet under a sycamore (or buttonwood) tree in front of what is now part of *J.P. Morgan* (see below) signed the Buttonwood Agreement, which established commissions and pledged the signers to give preference to each other in trading. The peripatetic traders had a number of other headquarters before taking up permanent residence in the present neo-Renaissance structure, a block up on the left at Wall and Broad Streets, in 1903. Free tours leave weekdays from the *New York Stock Exchange Visitors' Center* at 20 Broad Street (phone: 212-656-5168); tickets are distributed at 9 AM.

Catercorner to the *New York Stock Exchange* is the *Federal Hall National Memorial* (phone: 212-264-8711). This Doric structure stands on the site of the first *English City Hall,* which was extensively remodeled in 1788–89 to become the first *US Capitol* (in 1790 the capital of the country was moved to Philadelphia). George Washington took the presidential oath of office from a balcony here on April 30, 1789, and a bronze statue on the steps by John Quincy Adams Ward commemorates the event; inside there are exhibits on American history.

Patriotism once again is subsumed to commerce among *Federal Hall*'s neighbors. At the corner of Wall and Nassau Streets is the 39-story *Banker's Trust Building,* erected between 1910 and 1914. The site originally cost $825 per square foot, the highest price ever paid for land anywhere in the world at the time. Even in these recessionary times, the same space would go for thousands of dollars per square foot.

At No. 23 Wall stands the anonymous bulk of the old *J.P. Morgan* building. Now headquartered at 60 Wall, the company was founded in 1913 by financier J. Pierpont Morgan. Although Morgan deliberately chose an understated design in which to house his millions, a horse-drawn cart carrying explosives pulled up in front of the building in 1920, and moments later the cart blew up. The blast, which killed 33 people and injured hundreds of others, left numerous pockmark scars on the building's façade, which are still visible.

For a respite from the hurly-burly, continue up Wall Street and seek sanctuary in the neo-Gothic *Trinity Church,* a spiritual and architectural oasis. Built in 1846, it was once the tallest structure in Manhattan; now gleaming from a recent exterior cleaning, it is truly a sight to behold. In its secluded graveyard are the tombstones of Alexander Hamilton and Robert Fulton. This is also a fair-weather venue for free concerts in the yard outside the church.

Walk back down Wall Street and turn right onto William Street. Check out the bronze doors on No. 22 William (a.k.a. 20 Exchange Place) at the southeast corner, with their beautiful carvings depicting different modes of transportation; across the top are cartouches of European countries. At the junction of William, South William, and Beaver Streets is the triangular building (56 Beaver St.) that housed *Delmonico's* restaurant (closed in 1993). Once the haunt of such legendary big spenders as Diamond Jim Brady, and the city's premier dining spot in the "Gay" 1890s, *Delmonico's* was the place where lobster Newburg and sole Véronique were introduced.

Continue along South William Street, and make a detour on Coenties Slip to Water Street to the *Vietnam Veterans Memorial Plaza* (55 Water St.), a translucent block of glass engraved with letters from soldiers who fought in Vietnam. It is especially moving—and legible—at dusk, when interior lights make the letters glow.

Retrace your steps to Pearl Street and turn left along the block of 18th- and 19th-century buildings that lead to *Fraunces Tavern* (54 Pearl St. at Broad St.; phone: 212-425-1776). The three-story, Georgian brick building holds an honored place in American history: Purchased by innkeeper Samuel Fraunces, the tavern was a meeting place for the Sons of Liberty, a group of merchants who established the chamber of commerce here in 1768. It was also here that a triumphant George Washington bid farewell to his troops on December 4, 1783, at the end of the Revolutionary War. The museum contains war memorabilia, and the colonial dining room is a real charmer. The food holds a less-than-honored place in American gastronomy, so enjoy this old watering hole for what it is without any undue culinary expectations.

Turn left on Broad Street, then right on Water Street, and continue along it to South Ferry. Along the way you'll pass the plaza behind No. 17 State Street, which contains an exhibit of urban archaeology called "New York Unearthed," on loan from the *South Street Seaport Museum.* Around the corner at No. 7 is the former James Watson House, a fine example of Federal architecture, whose white Ionic columns are believed to have been crafted from ships' masts. Housed here is the *Shrine of St. Mother Elizabeth Ann Seton* (1774–1821), the first American-born saint, who founded the first order of nuns and established Catholic parochial schools in the United States.

You are now standing on what was once the shoreline of Manhattan. In later years it became a fashionable residential center inhabited by wealthy merchants who could keep a watchful eye on their cargoes being loaded and unloaded from ships in the harbor. Many of these houses were truly elegant; the mansion of one Carey Ludlow was lauded as a "center of fashion, intellect, and refinement" in 1792. In a civic gesture, Ludlow had 300 trees planted on the stretch of landfill that is now *Battery Park*.

Before stopping to enjoy this delightful park (plan to stop here on the way back), continue along the path to the southernmost tip of the island and head up the ramp that leads to the *Staten Island Ferry Terminal;* from this vantage point you have an inspiring view of the harbor. Ferry service began in the 1680s—it consisted of a rowboat that sailed from the present Peck Slip to what is now Fulton Street in Brooklyn. Regular service on the East River was inaugurated about a decade later between Fly Market Slip (Maiden Lane) and Brooklyn, and by the 1750s, commuter ferries shuttled back and forth between South Ferry and Staten Island. One of New York's great inexpensive thrills, today's ferry affords glorious views of Manhattan and upper New York Bay, passing by Governors Island and Liberty Island—and the fare for the ride is still a bargain at 50¢ round-trip.

Battery Park was named for the battery of cannons that protected Manhattan Island at Battery Place. Cooled by sea breezes, with the noise of city traffic drowned out by the cries of sea gulls and the cheerful blasts of ships' horns, the park hosts a daily invasion of lunchtime hordes of white-collar workers from the financial district and weekend tourists. Try to visit early in the morning, when the water glows with lambent light and the members of the Jamaican steel-drum band that normally serenades people waiting in line for the *Statue of Liberty Ferry* are still asleep. The circular sandstone fort in the park was originally built as the *Southwest Battery* to blast the British in the War of 1812, and was once located on a small island, connected to the mainland by a causeway.

In 1824 the city renamed the fort *Castle Garden* and used it as a place for public entertainment. The facilities were subsequently used as the immigrant landing depot: Between 1892 and 1924 more than 12 million immigrants passed through here on their way to a new life (a statue outside depicts their hope and apprehension upon their arrival). In 1941 extensive remodeling of *Castle Garden* resulted in its reincarnation as the *New York Aquarium.* The fish later were transferred to Brooklyn, and the fort was restored to its original state in 1945. Now called *Castle Clinton,* tickets for Liberty and Ellis Islands are sold here (call 212-269-5755 for information).

From outside *Castle Clinton,* the *Statue of Liberty* seems to speak the words engraved on its base—the poem "The New Colossus," written by native New Yorker Emma Lazarus: "Give me your tired, your poor, your huddled masses yearning to breathe free. The wretched refuse of your teeming shore. Send these, the homeless, tempest-tost to me, I lift my lamp beside the golden door." The colossal statue rises 151 feet atop a pedestal that adds another 89 feet. Its creator, the French sculptor Frédéric Auguste Bartholdi, originally planned that the noble figure would reside in Alexandria, Egypt, but it was later decided that she would better serve as a goodwill ambassador between France and the United States. Polished and restored for the 1986 centennial, the Lady of the Harbor is an uplifting and timeless expression of the American dream.

Lines for the ferry can be quite long, and the wait for the elevator to the observation deck in the base of the statue can be even longer, especially in the summer and on weekends. A climb up the additional 171 steps that lead to the crown (there are no elevators here, and the unventilated heat in summer can test even the most enthusiastic) is rewarded by a spectacular view of the harbor.

The same ferry that calls at the *Statue of Liberty* stops at Ellis Island. Restored to its original 1918–24 appearance, the main building houses the *Ellis Island Immigration Museum* (phone: 212-363-3200), with fascinating exhibitions that include thousands of personal items, such as toys, articles of clothing, and musical instruments brought by immigrants from around the world. Everything from a Russian balalaika to a Chinese abacus are on display, and there is also an extensive collection of documents, photographs, films, and other paraphernalia that describe the arduous series of physical and mental examinations the immigrants had to endure.

Head north as you disembark the ferry and turn right at Battery Place to reach Broadway. To the right, in front of you is the massive former *US Custom House,* built in 1907 by architect Cass Gilbert (who also designed the *Woolworth Building* on Broadway and the *US Courthouse* on Foley Square). It is one of the city's finest examples of the ornate American interpretation of Beaux Arts style. The entrance sculptures, *The Four Continents,* by Daniel Chester French (who was also responsible for the statue of Lincoln in the *Lincoln Memorial* in Washington, DC), include a sleeping Africa and an energetic America, while above them on the cornice 12 statues representing commercial powers gaze down beneficently.

Across from the *Custom House* is *Bowling Green;* originally called the *Playne* and then the *Marketfield,* it was the city's first park. In 1645 the Dutch signed a treaty with the Indians here; in 1732 three enterprising New Yorkers leased the land for one peppercorn per year, manicured the sward, and used it as a bowling alley. The park was once presided over by a statue of King George III. When crowds first heard the reading of the Declaration of Independence in 1776, they became so incensed that they toppled the statue and melted it, along with the crowns that once topped the iron fence along the perimeter. At the north end of the park stands the bronze sculpture *Charging Bull,* by Arturo DiModica, its horn tips and muzzle buffed to a high sheen by visitors, who rub it for good luck (no one knows just when—or how—this superstition originated).

Head north on Broadway, once called "Steamship Row." The immense, Renaissance-style building at No. 25 was designed by Benjamin Wistar Morris for the *Cunard Line.* It now has a rather boring fate as a post office, but its lavish interior, with an intricate ceiling and ornate frescoes, is worth noting. Another fine lobby is across the street (No. 26) in the former headquarters of the Standard Oil Company.

Continue up Broadway past *Trinity Church* on the left and turn left on Cortlandt Street. You might want to take a deep breath (or two) before you contend with that immense bastion just ahead: the *World Trade Center.* When Minoru Yamasaki's 110-story "Twin Towers" first opened in the early 1970s, their stripped-down, unadorned height seemed to mock the attendant romantic skyscrapers with their ornate details. The scale of the brown glass buildings—boasting works of art by Joan Miró, Louise Nevelson, Fritz Koenig, and Alexander Calder—dwarfs all who stand before it. Besides the thousands who work here and the additional throngs who just come to visit, the soaring structures have proved irresistible to many daredevils: A tightrope artist once walked across a wire suspended from the two roofs, a mountain climber once scaled one of the structures, and even King Kong straddled the towers in the remake of the movie. Unfortunately, in February of 1993, the Twin Towers also proved an irresistible terrorist target: A massive car bomb exploded in the complex's underground garage, killing six. Although (amazingly) the structure itself was not damaged, the buildings were closed for about a month for repairs, and security has been permanently upgraded.

Most of the people who work in the area barely notice the outside of the complex, availing themselves of its many services through a series of underground concourses that house more than 60 shops and restaurants. Those interested in theater should take note of one of New York's best-kept secrets: The *TKTS* booth on the mezzanine level of *2 World Trade Center,* the south tower, sells half-price tickets for Broadway and off-Broadway shows on the day of the performance (for matinees, the day before), and the line here is practically nonexistent compared with the gigantic one that forms around its counterpart in Times Square (phone: 212-768-1818).

The crowds here are in the line for the observation decks on the 107th and 110th floors of the south tower (be prepared for a long wait—sometimes as long as two hours in peak tourist season). Another way to see the view is to take the high-speed elevators to the *City Lights* bar at *Windows on the World* (*1 World Trade Center;* phone: 212-938-1100) for a drink, or grab a bite at the appropriately nicknamed *WOW* restaurant; it's pricey, but the new American fare almost equals the view. Call ahead to be sure the restaurant is open, as it had a long shutdown after the bombing in 1993.

Although it's difficult to top the sleek elegance of the *World Trade Center,* the *World Financial Center* just across the street certainly is a worthy contender. Turn right on Liberty Street and take the pedestrian footbridge over West Street to this exciting vision of a city within a city. The four 34- to 51-story towers sheathed in granite and reflective glass, topped by geometric copper roofs, house such financial district patricians as Dow Jones, American Express, and Merrill Lynch. A glance at the news kiosk on the corner of Liberty and West Streets gives you an idea of who lives and works in this pristine playground: the *Financial Times,* the *Wall Street Journal, Investors Daily,* the *International Herald Tribune,* and the *Globe & Mail.* These publications are required reading for the many successful young stockbrokers, lawyers, and bankers and their families who live in the adjacent condominiums, patronize the tony shops such as *Barneys New York, Platypus, Tahari, Rizzoli,* and *Il Papiro* in the *WFC* concourses, dine at the restaurants, and enjoy the park-like landscape and riverside promenade.

Try to visit here on a sunny day, when the light streams into the *Winter Garden* (phone: 212-945-0505), a 120-foot-high vaulted glass-and-steel conservatory graced by palm trees; many excellent free concerts are held here during lunchtime and after work, often including big-name performers. Stop for a lobster club sandwich at the *Pipeline* (*2 World Financial Center;* phone: 212-945-2755), a wonderful eatery with outdoor seating that overlooks the marina. (The *Pipeline* also offers take-out food, if you want to create your own picnic.) Just around the corner *Edward Moran* (*4 World Financial Center;* phone: 212-945-2255) serves basic burgers and sandwiches with the stunning southern view as an appetizer. For an altogether drop-dead dining experience—waterfront view, plush surroundings, very haute American fare, and a fleet of Rolls-Royces at the door—you can't do better than the *Hudson River Club* (*4 World Financial Center;* phone: 212-786-1500). End the day with a post-prandial moonlit stroll (the area is generally safe) along the promenade. (For more information on many of the sights mentioned above, see *Special Places* in THE CITY.)

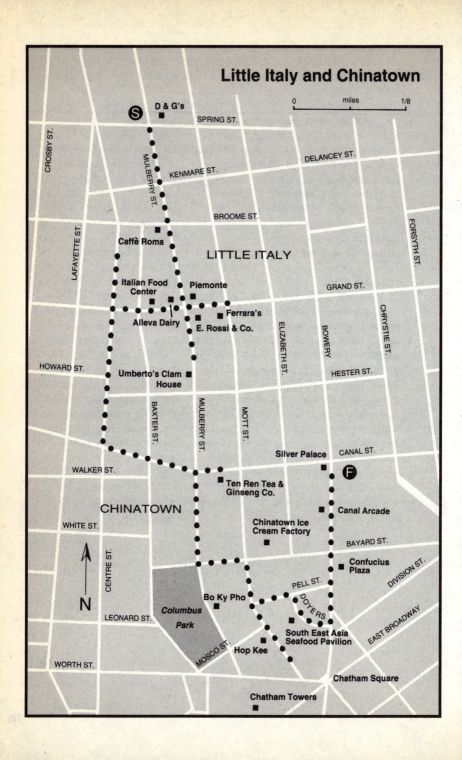

Walk 2: Little Italy and Chinatown

Any walking tour of Little Italy and Chinatown also must be considered an eating tour. Little Italy, continually shrinking in size due to the emigration of its sons and daughters and the encroachment of ever-growing Chinatown, nonetheless still likes to put a good spread on its restaurant tables and serve up strong coffee in its cafés. As for Chinatown, every now and then some enterprising statistician tries to add up the number of restaurants here, but the task has proven as futile as trying to count grains of sand.

Visitors should bear in mind that they will satisfy their stomachs best south of Canal Street, the traditional dividing line between Little Italy and Chinatown, because the culinary code in Little Italy these days seems to be quantity rather than quality. Most of the restaurants specialize in passable southern Italian food characterized by the color of the sauce—red or white. And their numbers are dwindling. Even along Mulberry Street, Little Italy's geographical and spiritual main artery, the visitor can spot signs of the northward-moving Chinese: a tiny storefront noodle shop; a sign advertising *Hop Shing Hong Imports,* half hidden by its neighbor's Italian flag; the aroma of soy sauce and scallions insinuating itself between whiffs of garlic sautéed in olive oil.

Yet there's still a lot of exuberance that courses through Mulberry Street and its tributaries. Restaurants flaunt their signed portraits of Frank Sinatra, souvenir shops proudly display posters of the 1982 *World Cup*–winning Italian soccer team, sinister-looking black stretch limousines glide through the streets, and young men in sharp suits stand watch in front of the blind bricks of "social clubs." Shades of *Godfather*-style shootouts haunt *Umberto's Clam House* (129 Mulberry St.; phone: 212-431-7545), where, in 1972, an alleged member of the Colombo crime family gunned down rival Joey Gallo. *Umberto's* has preserved the bullet holes in the swinging kitchen door, but, thankfully, today's street scene is far quieter.

Two of the most enthusiastic displays of Italian-American pride occur during the *Feast of St. Anthony* (in June) and the *Feast of San Gennaro* (a 10-day food fest in September). Depending on your point of view, the *San Gennaro* festival is either the best or the worst time to visit Little Italy (the *Feast of St. Anthony* is only slightly less frenetic). Named after the patron saint of Naples, the *San Gennaro* fair reflects the southern Italian origins of Little Italy's original residents. Thousands of people—Italian-Americans and others—come to share the experience and to sample the food—everything from hot sausages to *scungilli*—served in local restaurants and at sidewalk stands. A statue of the saint, decorated with dollar bills, is carried to a special grandstand, where it presides over the festivities.

Start a tour of Little Italy at *D&G's* (45 Spring St.; phone: 212-226-6688), one of the finest bakeries in the city. Although it's technically located on the periphery of Little Italy, its delicious spicy pepperoni loaf—perfect for munching along the way—is strictly Italian. Head south on Mulberry Street. The first of the grand cafés you'll encounter is *Caffè Roma* (385 Broome St.; phone: 212-226-8413), at the southeast corner of Mulberry and Broome Streets. There's lots of marble: on the walls, on the tiny, tippy tabletops, on the counters next to the display cases. There's also lots of food: cannolis, almond *biscotti,* puff pastry stuffed with sweetened ricotta, and a host of traditional, cloyingly sweet Italian confections. Wash it all down with an excellent espresso, a cup of cappuccino, or a wine spritzer flavored with *sciroppo di amarena* (bitter cherry), *granatina* (grenadine and raspberry extract), or *arancia* (bitter orange). Try to plan a return visit for lunch or dinner at *Grotta Azzurra,* directly across the street (see *Eating Out* in THE CITY).

One block south, at the intersection of Mulberry and Grand Streets, is the heart—and the stomach—of Little Italy. Flanking Mulberry Street on the north side of Grand are *Piemonte* (190 Grand St.; phone: 212-226-0475), the *Alleva Dairy* (188 Grand St.; phone: 212-226-7990), and the *Italian Food Center* (186 Grand St.; phone: 212-925-2954), a trio of first-rate food shops. Pasta is the specialty at *Piemonte,* established early in this century, which makes dozens of different kinds, like fresh pumpkin tortellini; it also sells a variety of homemade sauces. *Alleva* has been making fresh ricotta and mozzarella since 1892; it also sells its own sausage and will gladly slice off a hunk of prosciutto for you from the piece that hangs over the counter. The *Italian Food Center* is a mini-mart–cum-delicatessen. For those who want to make a cauldron of chowder, here's where to find that three-pound can of clams. There are prepared foods to go (you can sit on the bench outside and munch); those unconcerned about cholesterol should try one of the huge deep-fried, cheese-filled rice balls.

Souvenir hunters will appreciate *E. Rossi & Co.* (191 Grand St. at Mulberry; phone: 212-226-9254), which sells everything from Italian magazines, tricolor hats, and espresso sets to T-shirts that proclaim, "I survived an Italian mother." With its small plaster crèches and attendant angels and martyrs prominently displayed in the window, *Rossi* is where old people still gather to gossip in Italian and discuss soccer scores. If you prefer less crowded surroundings for your souvenir shopping, *Forzano Italian Imports* (128 Mulberry St.; phone: 212-925-2525) is just down the street.

Before continuing down Mulberry, detour east (left) for one block on Grand Street toward Mott Street. A quarryful of marble must have gone into the making of *Ferrara's* (195 Grand St.; phone: 212-226-6150). With its scores of glass-fronted display cases, it's a wonderfully kitschy barn, popular with the tour-bus crowd and pastry-cream addicts—a good place to go for dessert after dinner in Little Italy or Chinatown. At Mott Street, turn left and look north for a classic New York view: The towering spire of the *Empire State Building* is neatly framed by the street's tenements. And if hunger strikes just at this moment, stop in at *DiPalo's Fine Foods* on the corner (206 Grand St.; phone: 212-226-1033) for homemade and imported Italian cheese. Back on Mulberry, go south about half a block. On a wall on the east side is a signed trompe l'oeil mural of old storefronts by Richard Haas, which adds a nice touch amid the garish tiles and chianti flasks.

Going farther west on Grand Street, you'll pass the *Pearl River* department store (200 Grand St.; phone: 212-966-1010); an example of Chinatown's inexorable expansion, it carries a wide selection of Chinese merchandise. Note its beautiful copper dome which looms above the clustered tenements to the west. Turn north on Centre Street to the former New York City police headquarters (240 Centre St.). A Renaissance-style palazzo built in 1909, this massive building, with its cavernous lobby and steep staircases, is impressive—and intimidating. Although the police moved out in 1973 and the building has since been converted into condominiums, echoes of lineups and interrogations remain. (The upper floors are off limits to the public, but you can look around the lobby.)

Turn around on Centre Street and continue south for two blocks to Canal Street. Named for the 40-foot-wide canal dug on the site in 1805 to drain the water from the Collect Pond (then New York City's reservoir) into the Hudson River, Canal Street is a colorful, crowded, noisy thoroughfare anchored by the Holland Tunnel to New Jersey on the western end and the Manhattan Bridge to Brooklyn on the eastern end. Canal Street is the northern border of Chinatown, an ever-expanding enclave of American-born Chinese, many immigrants from mainland China, an increasing number of Hong Kong Chinese who have chosen to leave before the communist takeover, and a large population of Southeast Asians. The historic and spiritual heart of the area is the triangle formed by Canal Street, Mulberry Street to the west, and the Bowery to the east. The adventurous walker who wanders farther east on the streets between the Manhattan Bridge overpass (an area dubbed "DUMBO," for *D*irectly *U*nder the *M*anhattan *B*ridge *O*verpass) and the Brooklyn Bridge approach will find a less glitzy and more spacious Chinatown undiscovered by most visitors.

Chinatown is New York's most ethnically distinctive neighborhood. The signs in the streets and the subway station are in Chinese as well as English, and many structures—notably public phone booths—are topped with bright red pagodas, as is the building on the northwest corner of Canal and Centre Streets. There are seven local Chinese newspapers; more than 150 restaurants, stand-up lunch counters, tea parlors, and noodle shops; as well as garment sweatshops, exotic import/export stores, and places that sell medicinal herbs and the precious goods of the east: jade, pearls, and silk. The opium dens that brought Chinatown notoriety at the turn of the century have been replaced by gambling dens for mah jongg, poker, and fan-tan, which are controlled by the same tong (gang) factions. Chinatown even has its own distinctive smell, an aromatic cloud of frying garlic, minced ginger, fresh fish, and vegetables you may never have seen before (some showing signs of their long journey to market).

This is no place for those with sensitive stomachs (food is displayed everywhere) or for agoraphobics; be prepared to be jostled, nudged, shoved, and swept along in the constant crowds, which are especially noticeable on weekends. Chinatown gets even more packed with animated celebrants during the *Chinese New Year* festival held on the night of the first full moon after January 21, when giant man-managed dragons undulate through the streets, merrymakers jam the restaurants, and firecrackers explode nonstop.

Cross to the south side of Canal Street, and head east. Every other storefront seems to be a greengrocer, fishmonger, or market (savvy Occidental cooks shop here for some of the freshest and least expensive fare in the city). Jewelry shops sell gilt baubles, and the streets reverberate with the sounds of piped music from the numerous music stores and the high singsong of Chinese shoppers haggling with the merchants. If you're buying, remember that prices are negotiable on everything from fish to knock-off Rolex wristwatches.

Between Mulberry and Mott Streets is *Kam Man* (200 Canal St.; no phone), a two-story supermarket offering the area's widest selection of ingredients, cooking utensils, soaps (this is the place to buy boxes of Bee & Flower–brand sandalwood soap at half the price they're sold uptown), unusual pharmaceuticals, and chopsticks. Modernized a few years ago, *Kam Man* is a pasteurized version of its former days, although its wares haven't changed. To see the real thing, backtrack and turn south on Mulberry Street. Half a block down on the west side, a couple of steps lead down to the *Chinese American Trading Co.* (91 Mulberry St.; phone: 212-267-5224), where the aisles are narrow and crowded, no one speaks English, and a pervasive odor of preserved fish fills the air; the shop also stocks a wide selection of ingredients for Japanese and Vietnamese cooking.

Continuing south on Mulberry Street, *Saigon II* (89-91 Bayard St. at Mulberry; phone: 212-732-8988) serves delicious Vietnamese food, which is generally lighter than Chinese and distinctively seasoned with *nuoc mam,* a pungent fermented fish sauce. Bayard Street forms the northern border of *Columbus Park.* As Chinatown's only open space, it is often frequented by people practicing the slow, mesmerizing movements of t'ai chi, softball teams, martial artists young and old, and those who just come to sit and socialize. In the summer the annual *Festival of Performing Arts,* a free program of Oriental dance, music, and theater, further enlivens the park. On the eastern border is *Bo Ky Pho* (80 Bayard St.; phone: 212-406-2292), a Vietnamese restaurant that specializes in *pho,* a delicious and satisfying soupy stew.

Turn east on Bayard Street and continue north on Mott Street, Chinatown's main drag. Any one of the eateries that line the block promises an excellent, inexpensive meal, or you can stop for a bite at a tea house (they look like Occidental coffee shops), which offer pork buns and custardy snacks. Nearby is the *Ten Ren Tea and Ginseng Co.* (75 Mott St. between Bayard and Canal Sts.; phone: 212-349-2286), where hundreds of kinds of teas are prepared for uses that range from the medicinal to merely thirst quenching. You can buy tea in myriad Chinatown shops, but the proprietor here, Li Ming Xing, is one of the area's undisputed mavens.

For bibliophiles the *Hong Kong Bookstore* (72 Mott St.; no phone) and *Chinatown Books* (70A Mott St.; phone: 212-966-1599), also between Bayard and Canal Streets, carry good selections in both Chinese and English; they also sell beautiful calligraphy brushes and ink pads. Burn a joss stick for good luck and pick a fortune at the *Eastern States Buddhist Temple* (64 Mott St.; phone: 212-966-4753). *Tai Heng Lee* (60 Mott St.; no phone) and *Quong Yuen Shin* (32 Mott St.; no phone) are both good places to buy rice-pattern tea sets, porcelain tableware, embroidered silk garments, sandalwood fans, and little plastic pagodas that are perfect for an aquarium. Take a break at the *New Lung Fong Bakery* (41 Mott St.; phone: 212-233-7447), where you'll find a great assortment of homemade pastries.

Still hungry? The *Chinatown Ice Cream Factory* (65 Bayard St., between Mott and Elizabeth Sts.; phone: 212-608-4170) offers 36 homemade flavors, including chow mein, almond cookie, lichee, ginger, papaya, and green tea. (Less adventurous palates can cool off with vanilla and rocky road.) The *Mee Sun Mee Tea House* (48 Mott St.; no phone) serves lotus-seed and loquat ice cream and sesame-seed balls in a setting reminiscent of an old-fashioned soda shop. South of Pell Street, on the southwest corner of Mott and Mosco Streets, is a two-tiered dining treat: Downstairs is *Hop Kee* (21 Mott St.; phone: 212-964-8365), a deservedly popular Cantonese restaurant; upstairs (at street level) is the *Sun Hop Shing* tea house (21 Mott St.; phone: 212-267-2729), which serves delicious dim sum—an ever-changing selection of sweet and savory snacks—in a diner-like atmosphere. Just across the street is *20 Mott St.* (phone: 212-964-0380), a dining spot whose dim sum and other dishes are so good that it needs no fancy name to advertise itself.

Dim sum has its own delightful etiquette; it's usually served from about 9 AM to 2 PM daily, and is especially popular for Sunday brunch among both Chinese and westerners. Try to arrive before Chinese church services have ended (at 10:30 AM), or you'll have to wait for a table. Usually you'll share one with people you've never met; though you don't have to socialize, it helps to compare notes on the food. Waitresses push carts up and down the crowded aisles, singing out their wares, and each customer indicates his or her choice by pointing. The bill is computed by counting the number of dishes on the table.

If you want to explore more of the twisting, turning maze, backtrack and turn right on Pell Street. *Mueng Thai* (23 Pell St.; phone: 212-406-4259) serves authentic and inexpensive Thai food. Turn right on Doyers Street and descend a flight of stairs to the *Viet Nam* restaurant (11 Doyers St.; phone: 212-693-0725), which has minimal decor but delicious food; the coffee is a true standout.

Doyers Street leads into the Bowery at the northern tip of Chatham Square (Mott Street intersects it at the southern tip), a traffic snarl where seven streets converge. It's distinguished by the modern apartment buildings of Chatham Towers (170 Park Row) and Chatham Green (85 Park Row), as well as by the curved, red brick tower of Confucius Plaza, with its bronze statue of the sage by Tiu Shih. Those who choose to explore the warren of tenements and crooked streets to the east will discover such architectural nuggets as the *Mariners' Temple* and *Baptist Meeting House* (12 Oliver St.); the 1837 *St. James Roman Catholic Church* (32 St. James Pl.); No. 6 Bowery (the site of the former *Olliffe's Apothecary,* the oldest drugstore in America, which dates back to 1803); a Federal-style house built in 1785 (18 Bowery); and the Chatham Square branch of the *New York Public Library* (33 E. Broadway). Also nearby is the *Golden Unicorn,* another delicious dim sum detour (see *Eating Out* in THE CITY).

On the west side of the Bowery, named for the road that originally led to Peter Stuyvesant's farm, or *bouwerie,*, walk north and keep a sharp eye out for the *Canal Arcade,* an unobtrusive, block-long passage on the left. Just a few steps north of this is the *Silver Palace* (52 Bowery; phone: 212-964-1204), where patrons are whisked upstairs via two escalators to a dining room the size of a football field. It's so large that the maître d' has to direct his staff via a cordless phone. Although conversation is almost impossible amid the cacophony of English and Chinese, the food is delicious and the prices very reasonable. Stop here at the end of your walk to refresh yourself with some jasmine tea. It's said to soothe the spirit and restore the equilibrium.

Walk 3: SoHo and TriBeCa

SOHO

Since it was first settled in the early 1800s, SoHo, the area *So*uth of *Ho*uston (pronounced *How*-ston in New York) Street, has risen as an urban phoenix; it is a neighborhood that renews itself with gritty determination each time its latest source of vitality burns out. In its current incarnation, SoHo epitomizes everything chic: Art, food, and fashion thrive here. In an area where (almost) everything is relentlessly new, the imposing structures that dominate the SoHo Cast-Iron Historic District form the largest concentration of such architecture in the country.

The importation of cast iron from England was responsible for a construction boom that lasted in this neighborhood from 1860 until 1890, and even today it defines SoHo's intriguing architectural texture. Before the introduction of cast iron, masonry and stone walls had to be made thicker as buildings grew taller in order to support the increased weight. Cast-iron buildings, however, consist only of a frame of rolled-iron beams; exterior brick walls were attached to the skeleton, and cast-iron ornamentation was added to the outer walls to help ground the buildings. (Cast iron acts as a lightning rod by carrying electricity safely into the ground.)

Since decorations such as columns, lintels, friezes, and cornices could be made easily by casting them in molds, architects used them lavishly. Even the web of fire escapes draped across each façade looks like a deliberate and clever part of the plan. Despite the fact that the storefronts have been often and radically altered, these cast-iron beauties retain a quiet dignity.

Around 1965 an influx of artists, many driven out of neighboring Greenwich Village to the north by escalating rents, began moving into SoHo and transformed the industrial lofts into large, well-lighted, and inexpensive studio spaces, despite the fact that many buildings lacked such basics as modern plumbing. Galleries, restaurants, and boutiques soon joined the studios, and the area gained a cachet as the city's artistic hub. Today SoHo has become so pricey that most of the artists originally drawn here have moved once again, and cutting-edge art has begun to emerge in the western reaches of TriBeCa, the East Village, Queens, Brooklyn, the Bronx, and Hoboken, New Jersey, just across the Hudson River. Tales of SoHo's imminent demise are now as popular as its trendy bars, but a stroll down any one of its streets instantly refutes the rumors.

Happily, SoHo has not been completely homogenized by fashion; many rough edges still abound. Quite a number of buildings are still fronted by

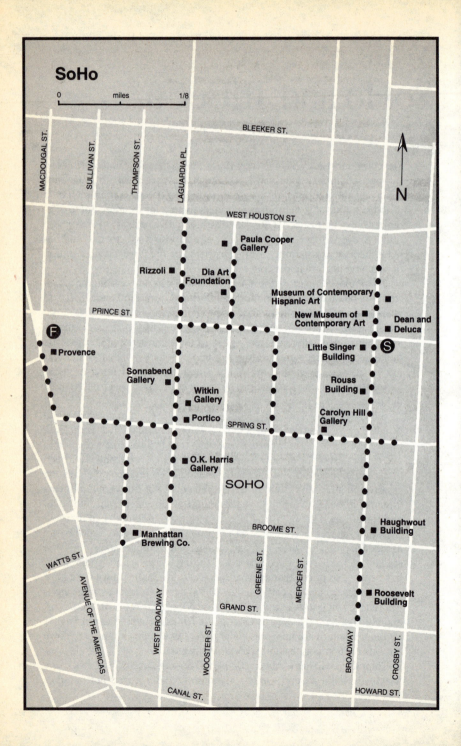

steep, broad steps that once were loading docks, and in some cases still serve the same purpose. Expensive, upscale lofts stand side by side with dilapidated, offbeat structures.

The heart of SoHo is contained within the rectangle of West Houston Street to the north, Canal Street to the south, and from West Broadway four blocks east to Broadway. There also is plenty of spillover to Lafayette Street on the east and Sullivan Street on the west side. Despite its relatively compact size, it can be overwhelming on a busy Saturday afternoon.

Many people choose a theme walk—an art tour, a shopping spree, or a search for historic landmarks—before they set out for a day in SoHo. A must for art aficionados is the *Gallery Guide;* available free at any of the numerous galleries, it contains current listings of shows. The following trek combines a gallery tour, a shopping trip, and a dash of cast-iron lore. The best times to explore the area are Wednesdays through Sundays, despite the fact that the galleries are closed on Sundays, as are many stores. When the galleries shut down, the cultural remains are an engaging and motley combination of restaurants, cafés, and shops.

A good place to begin a SoHo tour is at Prince Street and Broadway. On the southwest corner is the slender *"Little Singer Building,"* the smaller sibling of the sewing machine company's larger headquarters on lower Broadway (now demolished, it was once the world's tallest skyscraper). SoHo's *Singer* combines cast-iron and terra cotta panels, and is considered one of the architectural gems of the area.

Dean & Deluca (560 Broadway; phone: 212-431-1691), among the city's many astonishingly well-stocked food emporiums, is located on the opposite corner in an elaborate brick-and-stone building. Food is the art form here, and it's temptingly arranged to break down even the staunchest dieter's resolve. (The high prices may help the willpower, however.) Upstairs are art galleries, including the *Max Protech Gallery* (phone: 212-966-5454), where blueprints by such renowned architects as Frank Lloyd Wright, Robert Venturi, and Aldo Rossi are displayed as works of art in themselves. The *Guggenheim Museum Soho* (575 Broadway at Prince St.; phone: 212-423-3500) houses the larger works from the main museum's vast collection uptown, and much of the art on display here has never been exhibited before.

As you complete a loop up and down Broadway, stop in at the *New Museum of Contemporary Art* (583 Broadway; phone: 212-219-1355), which showcases the works of emerging artists; the building was erected on the site of John Jacob Astor's house. Stroll north up Broadway and cross the street to No. 594, the *Alternative Museum* (phone: 212-966-4444), which hosts exhibits with a social or political message. Also at No. 594 are the *Heineman Galleries* (phone: 212-334-0821), which in 1994 opened a special exhibition space devoted to cartoon and graphic art. South of this at No. 578 is a Renaissance Revival structure built by art dealer George B. Post, a preeminent architect of the late 19th century who also designed the

New York Stock Exchange. One of art dealer Leo Castelli's galleries is located here. At No. 568 you'll find *A/X* (phone: 212-431-6000), Giorgio Armani's pricey and stylish version of *The Gap,* where white T-shirts cost around $40.

Cross Prince Street again and take a look at 555 Broadway, the *Rouss Building.* An impressive gray granite edifice with cast-iron decorations, it was designed by Alfred Zucker for Charles Rouss as a celebration of the latter's rags-to-riches success story. Rouss arrived in New York from Virginia just after the Civil War with practically nothing, and eventually made a fortune as a wholesale merchant. He was so grateful that he legally adopted "Broadway" as his middle name.

Go left on Spring Street to the *New York Open Center and Bookstore* (83 Spring St.; phone: 212-219-2527), a source for books with spiritual and holistic themes. The center also offers lectures and demonstrations on physical and emotional healing. The *D&G Bakery* (45 Spring St.; phone: 212-226-6688) is tiny, but its delicious Neapolitan bread, baked in a coal-fired brick oven, should not be missed. Right next door is *Rocky's* Italian restaurant (45 Spring St.; phone: 212-334-8178), a cozy place for classic Italian fare.

Now go back to Broadway; on the left is the *Broadway Panhandler* (No. 520; phone: 212-966-3434), a cook's delight that specializes in basic and hard-to-find kitchenware. SoHo's largest store, the *Canal Jean Co.* (502-504 Broadway; phone: 212-226-1130), carries a wide variety of jeans, T-shirts, and other casual clothing. The building in which it's housed dates from 1860 and has two-story carved stone arches and an unusual façade decorated in a "sperm candle" motif (named after the shape of whale-oil candles). Inside, elaborately topped columns, exposed brick walls, industrial staircases, and wide-planked, creaking floors form the backdrop for the affordable vintage and new clothing.

At Broome Street cross to the southwest corner for a glimpse of the *Haughwout Building* (488-490 Broadway), which is sometimes called "The Parthenon of Cast-Iron Architecture in America." Connoisseurs admire its beautifully balanced façade of Corinthian columns and arch-topped windows, but even the uninitiated can appreciate its somber beauty. History buffs should note that the first commercial steam-powered elevator built by the Otis Company operated here. The *Haughwout,* which resembles an Italian Renaissance palazzo, was one of the first New York City buildings to be declared a landmark. It has remained intact and now houses the *SoHo Mill Outlet* (phone: 212-226-8040), offering a wide selection of fine sheets, towels, and bathroom accoutrements at low prices.

As you continue down Broadway, note the *Roosevelt Building* (Nos. 478-482). Designed by Richard Morris Hunt, the architect of the *Metropolitan Museum of Art* and the base of the *Statue of Liberty,* this is his only extant commercial building. The superb façade is composed of tall cast-iron columns separated by broad, high windows and topped by delicately carved, cast-iron arches. Among the many stores that occupy its street level, *Pure Madderlake* (phone: 212-941-7770) is an upscale, innovative florist.

The year-round Sunday flea market at Grand Street and Broadway is a great place to pick up an Art Deco toaster or a slightly worn wool sport coat, or just to browse through the mélange of toys, old military insignia pins, and antique jewelry. (If the flea market doesn't tempt you, turn right on Broome Street. Individually artistic buildings that also complement one another—the harmonious result of the effort of various architects—line this street.)

From the flea market backtrack up Broadway two blocks to Spring Street. At this point it can be difficult to decide which way to turn, but it really doesn't matter—there are worthwhile sights in every direction. To maintain some sense of purpose, however, make a left on Spring and continue for two blocks to Greene Street. Turn right on Greene Street for a long block, then left again on Prince Street (you can make an optional detour on Wooster Street), and continue two blocks west to West Broadway.

This zigzag path leads through the heart of SoHo. Gallery banners flap briskly in the breeze, lacy cast-iron fire escapes throw shadows on the intricate façades, and cafés beckon with the promise of a steaming cup of cappuccino. Along the way are a number of places of interest. The *Dyansen Gallery* (122 Spring St.; phone: 212-226-3384) displays Erté bronze sculptures and LeRoy Neiman paintings. *Shabby Chic* (93 Greene St.; phone: 212-274-9842) sells the ultimate in casual furnishings. The rumpled sofas and burlap chairs look like they've shared a previous life with a band of rambunctious adolescents, but all this informality carries a very high price tag. An equally pricey shop is *Zona* (97 Greene St.; phone: 212-925-6750), which carries much tonier furnishings and accessories for the home. Everything here is either beautifully packaged, useful, or appealing, including fruit that appears perishable but is, in fact, marble.

Those with weary feet and parched throats will appreciate a stop at the *SoHo Kitchen and Bar* (103 Greene St.; phone: 212-925-1866), a longtime neighborhood favorite. Designed by Henry Fernbach, the building dates back to 1879. Brick walls, a tin ceiling, and a large open kitchen at the rear create a very au courant yet comfortable atmosphere. It's a good place to relax over a glass of wine. *Jerry's* (101 Prince St.; phone: 212-966-9464), a bistro-cum-diner of deliberately nondescript decor, is popular among established and struggling artists alike. Note the east wall of Nos. 112-114 Prince Street, which has an excellent trompe l'oeil mural of a cast-iron building. You also might want to stop at the *Prince Street* restaurant (125 Prince St.; phone: 212-228-8130) for a quick cheeseburger, or at *Harriet Love* (126 Prince St.; phone: 212-966-2280) for new clothes with a vintage feeling, and a large collection of authentic vintage jewelry.

Two galleries on Wooster are definitely worth a detour. One of the *Dia Center for the Arts*' two SoHo locations (141 Wooster St.; phone: 212-431-9232) is here; it offers an unusual tribute to the environment. Walter DeMaria's *New York Earth Room,* a permanent exhibit, is staggering: an entire gallery space filled three feet high with soil. Farther along is the *Paula*

Cooper Gallery (155 Wooster St.; phone: 212-674-0766), the first one to open in SoHo. Artists Elizabeth Murray and Jonathan Borofsky are among those who have shown their work here.

A block west of and parallel to Wooster Street is West Broadway, SoHo's original "Main Street" and home of many of the first galleries that ventured into the area during the late 1960s and early 1970s. If you have time to visit only one street in the SoHo/TriBeCa area, make it this one. At the intersection of West Broadway and Prince Street, turn north (or right) up West Broadway toward West Houston Street. The *Sally Hawkins Gallery* (448 West Broadway; phone: 212-477-5699) sparkles with artistic jewelry. Next door, the small *Rizzoli* bookstore (454 West Broadway; phone: 212-674-1616) pleases the eye with hefty art tomes and the ear with gentle music.

Across the street are *I Tre Merli* (463 West Broadway; phone: 212-254-8699) and *Amici Miei* (475 West Broadway; phone: 212-533-1933), two first-rate Italian eateries. *Amici Miei*'s outdoor café, which spills onto the corner of West Houston and West Broadway, is the kind of place where New Yorkers are content to put up with the street noise and grime just to be seen lounging over the Italian *nuova cucina*.

Backtrack south to the West Broadway block between Prince and Spring Streets, which is lined with upscale shops and renowned galleries. *Joovay* (436 West Broadway; phone: 212-431-6386) carries high-style silk and satin lingerie. The original SoHo home of the *Leo Castelli Gallery* (420 West Broadway; phone: 212-431-5160) is located here, and the *Sonnabend Gallery* (phone: 212-966-6160), on another floor of this cavernous space, is now a landmark on the contemporary art scene. Across the street the *Witkin Gallery* (415 West Broadway; phone: 212-925-5510) is one of the oldest in the city to exhibit photography. *Mary Boone* (417 West Broadway; phone: 212-431-1818) is considered a kind of SoHo barometer, an epicenter for up-and-coming art trends and artists.

Continuing south, next is a string of "lifestyle" emporiums, names that pop up repeatedly as shopping sources in magazines such as *HG* and *Elle Decor*. *Ad Hoc Softwares* (410 West Broadway; phone: 212-925-2652) carries trendy household items; *America West* (386 West Broadway; phone: 212-966-9378) is stocked with trendy Santa Fe–style furniture; and *Portico* (379 West Broadway; phone: 212-941-7800) sells hand-crafted copies of Shaker furniture. The shop extends through to Wooster Street; midway through is a cappuccino bar where an assortment of pretty little tables and chairs are all for sale. Look into the *O. K. Harris Gallery* (383 West Broadway; phone: 212-431-3600), one of the mainstays of the SoHo art establishment. Nearby are two popular watering holes where you can also get meals: the *Broome Street Bar* (363 West Broadway; phone: 212-925-2086) and the *Cupping Room Café* (495 Broome St.; phone: 212-925-2898).

Return north to Spring Street and go left. *Spring Street Books* (169 Spring St.; phone: 212-219-3033) also stocks foreign magazines and stays open very late for insomniac bookworms. The next cross street is Thompson, which has fewer galleries but lots of interesting shops. Turn left on Thompson Street to *Il Bisonte* (72 Thompson St.; phone: 212-966-8773) for fine leather goods straight from Florence. Not far away, *Ceramica* (59 Thompson St.; phone: 212-941-1307) is the kind of pottery store that makes you feel as if you're shopping in an Italian hill town. *Classic Toys* (69 Thompson St.; phone: 212-941-9129) carries both old and new nonelectronic playthings.

If you can't bear to leave the neighborhood, head back to Spring Street to linger at *Nick and Eddie* (203 Spring St.; phone: 212-219-9090), the kind of dining establishment that instantly makes you feel at home. *Café* (210 Spring St.; phone: 212-274-0505), owned by the grandson of Pablo Picasso, offers fabulous French fare. Or push on a bit, walking north on MacDougal Street after it intersects West Houston Street to *Provence* (38 MacDougal St.; phone: 212-475-7500) for southern French fare and some of the best *crème brûlée* in the city.

TRIBECA

The latest in Manhattan's alphabet soup of neighborhood names, TriBeCa (pronounced Try-*beh*-cuh) is an acronym for *Tri*angle *Be*low *Ca*nal. It is on the Lower West Side, below Greenwich Village and SoHo, and is defined roughly by Canal Street to the north, Broadway to the east, and the Hudson River to the west. The two main arteries are West Broadway, as it continues south from SoHo, and Hudson Street; these streets converge and form the tip of the triangle at Chambers Street.

Locating TriBeCa proves far easier than describing it. It is a neighborhood in transition, although chic restaurants and equally snazzy residents have populated the area for years. Just as in SoHo, trucks rumble through the streets by day, and the smell of exhaust fumes can be slightly overpowering on a steamy summer afternoon. By early evening, however, the side streets are deserted, the warehouses and businesses are closed, and as many of the restaurants open their doors to customers, savory scents fill the air.

TriBeCa began as a spillover from SoHo, a new home for artists who needed more affordable loft space and for whom SoHo represented "the establishment." A few experimental galleries followed, and once the artists paved the way, others came in search of the New York dream: more space for less money in an as yet ungentrified neighborhood. Since TriBeCa is also convenient to the financial district, many bankers, stockbrokers, and businesspeople have put down tangible roots here, and businesses have followed suit: Shearson Lehman Hutton's gleaming headquarters on Greenwich Street stands out amid the crumbling warehouses, renovated lofts, and intimate restaurants. Yet TriBeCa lacks the cohesion of SoHo; there are few fancy boutiques, and the general pace is rather disjointed. The area is like a movie soundstage, waiting for actors to arrive on the set and begin the scene.

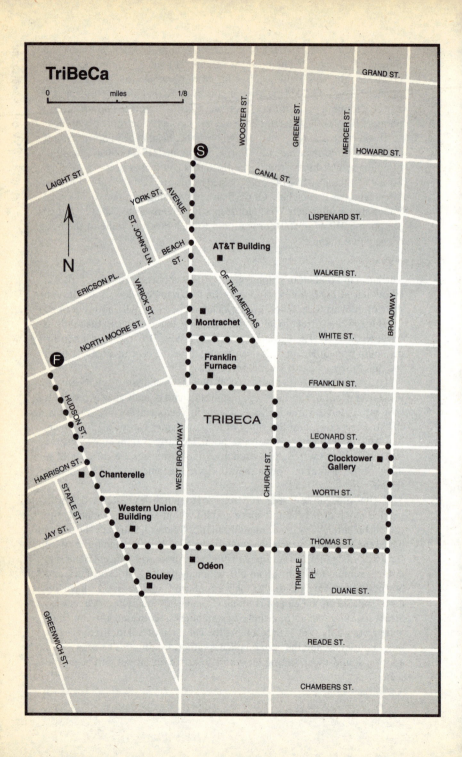

The best time to come here is in the late afternoon or early evening, when the galleries are nearly empty and the area changes gears. After dark the streets are quiet, and although there is not yet anything especially sleazy about the neighborhood, you should still avoid wandering alone in any deserted part of the city at night. The tour begins at West Broadway and Canal Street, an intersection near which a confusion of tiny streets shoot off at odd angles. Use the tall, brick *AT&T Building* as a beacon to guide you south to the intersection of Beach Street, West Broadway, and the Avenue of the Americas. Here, in the little park with cobbled pavement and a few benches under the trees, is a good place from which to view the *American Thread Building* (260 West Broadway), which curves along the corner. This sturdy brick building has been converted to luxurious lofts and is one of the toniest addresses in TriBeCa. Walk down the left side of West Broadway; *Montrachet* (No. 239) looks very unassuming amid a block of crumbling buildings just a few doors down from the park, but it is one of the finer French eating spots in town (see *Eating Out* in THE CITY). Just south of *Montrachet* is a cluster of alternative art spaces, featuring the work of artists who have not yet become part of the mainstream. The *Artists' Space* used to be here, at 223 West Broadway, an avant-avant-garde, not-for-profit gallery that showcased undiscovered artists; Laurie Anderson, Robert Longo, Cindy Sherman, and Jonathan Borofsky all displayed their offbeat work here. (The *Artists' Space* is now at 38 Greene St., Third Floor, SoHo; phone: 212-226-3970.)

Turn left (or east) off West Broadway onto White Street. At the corner notice odd little No. 2, a brick-fronted frame house with a curved gambrel roof and dormers. Built in 1809, it is now a landmark, albeit a rather dilapidated one. No. 10 is a handsome cast-iron building converted to lofts. The *SoHo Photo Gallery* (15 White St.; phone: 212-226-8571) is an artist-run photography gallery that occupies several floors. At the corner of White Street across the Avenue of the Americas, the *Farm & Garden Nursery* (2 Ave. of the Americas; phone: 212-431-3577) cuts a refreshing, green swath of horticulture through this intensely urban landscape.

Just around the corner *Franklin Furnace* (112 Franklin St.; phone: 212-925-4671) is difficult to locate amid the industrial buildings on the block (look for the green columns). This experimental center launched such multimedia performance artists as Karen Finley and Eric Bogosian, whose work has caused consternation among some conservative members of Congress. Limited editions of artists' books are on sale here.

Turn right on Church Street and walk down to Leonard Street, a typical TriBeCa mixture of trucks, textile wholesalers, and lofts. Walk east along Leonard Street to the *Clocktower Gallery of the Institute for Art and Urban Resources* (108 Leonard St.; phone: 212-233-1096) on the corner of Broadway. This ornate white building stands out against the sky and is hard to miss; the gallery is on the top floor and extends right into the tower itself. Talented artists are regularly awarded working space here and give shows several times a year. The view up Broadway from the terrace (lined with discount stores and delicatessens) is spectacular.

Now look down Broadway from the *Clocktower Gallery.* The massive pink granite edifice at Broadway and Worth Street is the *AT&T Building,* a windowless tower filled with telephone-switching equipment. Happily, its sculptural shape and soft-colored stone keep it from intruding on the horizon.

Walk down Broadway and turn right on Thomas Street toward West Broadway. Stop to look at No. 8, a cast-iron building decorated in atypical Gothic style. At the corner of West Broadway and Thomas Street is the stylish *Odéon* (see *Eating Out* in THE CITY). Continue along Thomas to Hudson Street and turn left for one block to Duane Street. Surrounding this little green space are wonderful buildings that make the area so architecturally alive. Some are warehouses for egg wholesalers whose loading docks are in constant use; one, No. 165 Duane, has been elegantly restored and houses a fine French and American eatery, *Bouley* (see *Eating Out* in THE CITY).

Turn back up Hudson Street and on the right (at No. 60) is an Art Deco building built in 1930 by the Western Union Company and decorated with bricks of various colors; from the corner of Jay and Hudson Streets, note the gold-leaf decorations over the door. Now look south down Hudson Street for a glimpse of the lower Manhattan skyline. The standouts are the Gothic roof of the *Woolworth Building* and the tower of the *Municipal Building.*

A block north on Hudson to the left, Harrison Street has charm and authenticity, which are thrown into stark relief by harsh, modern Independence Plaza at the end of the street. *Commodities* (117 Hudson St.; phone: 212-334-8330), a natural foods supermarket set in a cavernous space, is further evidence that the area is more domesticated than it appears. The *Mercantile Exchange,* built in 1886, dominates the corner of Harrison and Hudson Streets; composed of red brick and granite, its arches, columns, and gables give it a businesslike air. *Chanterelle* (2 Harrison St.; see *Eating Out* in THE CITY) serves very fine French cuisine.

Only the most urban personalities tend to live in TriBeCa—Harvey Keitel, Robert De Niro, and Martin Scorsese are among those who have occupied converted lofts at 151 Hudson Street. On the building's street level the *Thai House Café* (phone: 212-334-1085) serves wonderful food. Other nearby culinary landmarks include the *Tribeca Grill* (375 Greenwich St.; see *Eating Out* in THE CITY) and the much-lauded *Capsouto Frères* (451 Washington St.; phone: 212-966-4900), which serves French fare in an 1891 landmark building.

Walk 4: Greenwich Village

Prior to the 18th century, Greenwich Village (pronounced *Gren*-itch) was a rural refuge, far from the densely populated area of Manhattan to the south. It is still filled with tree-lined streets and pretty 18th- and 19th-century row houses on a manageable, human scale. The atmosphere is easygoing and somewhat bohemian, due to the dozens of offbeat boutiques and lively jazz venues, and the sidewalks often clog with sightseers, shoppers, and barhoppers. There is also a thriving gay community here, one of the city's most concentrated.

Overall, it is safe to walk here (but stick to the general New York rule of avoiding parks, including *Washington Square,* at night). Sometimes, though, it's confusing. Since streets here follow old property lines, cow paths, and vestiges of the early farms and estates that once blanketed the area, the grid system that makes Manhattan an easy city to navigate simply dissolves (especially at points west and south). There's Greenwich Street and Greenwich Avenue; West Fourth Street bends to cross West 10th, 11th, and 12th Streets; and Seventh Avenue South runs through like a fault line, setting the streets on either side at peculiar angles.

The settlement of the Village, as it is usually referred to today, began in earnest in the early 1800s, when waves of people and businesses sought to flee the yellow fever epidemics rampant in lower Manhattan. By 1822 Bank Street—aptly named for all the Wall Street banks that resettled here—was home to many houses of finance. When the nearby river shore developed into a busy, industrial waterfront some years later, fashionable folk moved farther north, and artists, writers, and various groups of immigrants moved into the area. Edgar Allan Poe, Henry James, Winslow Homer, Mark Twain, and O. Henry were just a few of the literary and artistic types who once called Greenwich Village home. By the early years of this century the Village had become America's bohemia. Until the 1980s at least, free love and social change were debated in its coffeehouses, and quaint brownstones were easily rented at low prices—another very attractive lure for struggling artists.

Today rents are too high for all but the most well-heeled artists, writers, and actors. Consequently many of the city's artists live in the East Village. With roughly the same north and south borders as Greenwich Village, it begins east of Broadway and trails into "Alphabetland," Avenues A and B. For information on the East Village, see "Lower Manhattan" in *Special Places,* THE CITY.

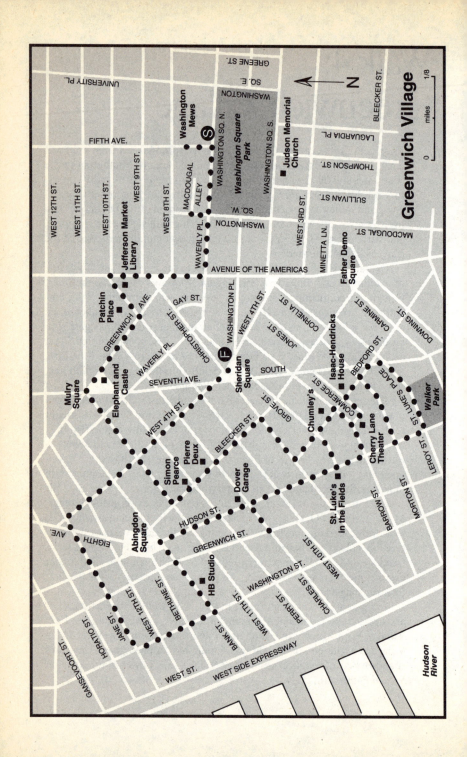

The eccentric personality of Greenwich Village (which includes the West Village, the area west of Seventh Avenue South) is still evident, however, especially at night, when the streets around *Washington Square* and along the broad avenues are teeming with tourists and New Yorkers alike in search of a great jazz, salsa, or comedy club. This walk winds through some of the loveliest and liveliest areas of the Village, and also through streets west of the usual tourist haunts. It begins at the majestic arch in *Washington Square Park,* a massive, marble structure that opens onto Fifth Avenue to the north. Designed by Stanford White in 1891 to commemorate the centennial of George Washington's inauguration, it looks like the very embodiment of civic nobility. *Washington Square* started out as a marshland and then became a potter's field; later it was a spot where public executions were carried out. Today it is a smallish but vibrant open area that draws hundreds of *New York University* students (who attend classes in the surrounding buildings), avid chess players, performance artists, families with children in strollers, vendors pushing food carts, and a few (usually) unaggressive marijuana salespeople at the fringes. It is a relaxed place, though, and fairly well policed at night.

Along Washington Square North, Nos. 21 to 26 are among the finest Greek revival houses in the country. Henry James's novel *Washington Square* was set at his grandmother's home (No. 18). Unfortunately, the house and the neighboring buildings were demolished in 1952 to make way for a large apartment house at 2 Fifth Avenue. The houses from Nos. 7 to 13 are really the front of an apartment building constructed behind the old façades, the result of a clever renovation job. Walk up Fifth Avenue a few steps to look behind them into Washington Mews, a cozy, flowery passage at the end of a colonnade; a life-size statue of Cervantes bows at the very back. Its houses originally were the stables for the horses and carriages of high society.

Now walk back toward the arch and turn right along Washington Square North; the Italianate campanile visible across the park is the bell tower of the *Judson Memorial Church,* a Village landmark. Turn right on MacDougal Street for a look at another secluded mews. Like its Fifth Avenue neighbor, MacDougal Alley once was home to the stables for the fine houses that face the park.

Back at the square, turn right along Waverly Place, lined with an eclectic group of brick, stone, and painted stucco townhouses, some trimmed with curlicued, wrought-iron banisters; this tree-lined street is a particularly welcome respite from the noisy Avenue of the Americas ahead. Turn right on the Avenue of the Americas (though it was thus named in 1945 by Mayor Fiorello La Guardia, it will be known forever as Sixth Avenue to New Yorkers). As soon as you round the corner, the *Jefferson Market Library,* a fanciful, turreted building of red brick banded with white stone, dominates the avenue. One of the most beloved Village oddities, it was built as a courthouse in 1874–78, and was listed as one of the 10 most beautiful buildings in America at the time. Renovated by architect Giorgio Cavaglieri, it's now a branch of the *New York Public Library*.

For a good view of the library, stand at the east corner of West 10th Street and the Avenue of the Americas. We should warn you that, one block south, *Balducci's* (424 Ave. of the Americas; phone: 212-673-2600) will prove a mighty distraction. One of the city's premier food shops, it sells delicacies such as imported figs and lobster ravioli, and arranges displays worthy of a still life. Happily, it has a mail-order department, so you can send goodies home.

Cross the Avenue of the Americas at West 10th Street, and take a look at the row of brick houses set at an angle facing the avenue. A few steps farther west on West 10th Street, stop for a peek into Patchin Place, whose small brick buildings were constructed in the mid-19th century to house the workers from the posh *Brevoort* hotel, once situated on Fifth Avenue. This quiet cul-de-sac was later popular among the literary set: e. e. cummings lived at No. 4; and John Masefield and Theodore Dreiser were also former residents of the area.

Stroll down West 10th Street and stop at the *Jefferson Market Gardens,* a lushly planted spot adjacent to the library; filled with blooms of all colors and varieties, it is open on weekend afternoons, when volunteers tend the flowers, shrubs, and paths.

Turn right up Greenwich Avenue, past Charles and Perry Streets to West 11th Street. At the southeast corner *Elephant and Castle* (68 Greenwich Ave.; phone: 212-243-1400) is a popular spot for a hamburger or a sandwich. At this point Seventh and Greenwich Avenues and West 11th Street come together in one of the Village's confounding, star-shape intersections. Watch the street signs carefully, cross the avenues with *Elephant and Castle* at your back, and walk down West 11th Street.

For the rest of this walk, you will be startled at how much this part of Manhattan feels like a village. Occasionally, a traffic-filled thoroughfare intrudes upon the scene, but all you have to do is turn another corner to avoid the congestion.

Tree-lined West 11th Street is neighborly and quiet; Nos. 238 and 240 are charming, as are Nos. 241 and 243 just across the street. Although there is little historical significance to these homes, this area is pretty and welcoming, typical of this part of the Village. At the corner of Bleecker Street, turn left. Two interesting shops face each other across Bleecker Street at West 11th Street: *Bird Jungle* (401 Bleecker St.; phone: 212-242-1757) resounds with chirps and screeches of brilliantly colored birds, many sitting uncaged on perches, preening and watching the customers watch them; in contrast, the tiny *Biography Bookshop* (400 Bleecker St.; phone: 212-807-8655) is very quiet, with books on some of the Village's illustrious residents.

Walk down Bleecker Street several pleasant blocks toward Christopher Street. This is the quieter end of Bleecker, with interesting stores and restaurants. *Simon Pearce* (385 Bleecker St.; phone: 212-924-1142) left Ireland to make his hand-blown glass in Vermont; his city shop stocks his pleasing, simple designs, as well as pottery by his brother and other designers. Seconds in glassware are almost half price here, and are usually all the more endearing for their flaws. Take a peek in at *Godfrey M. Simpson* (375 Bleecker St.; phone: 212-242-7815) for what he calls "the English cluttered look." Authentic, elegant antiques are a few doors down at *Pierre Deux* (369 Bleecker St.; phone: 212-243-7740). Across the street *Cucina della Fontana* (368 Bleecker St.; phone: 212-242-0636) combines southern Italian cooking with a charming bar, a pretty garden dining room, and a cabaret.

Turn right on Christopher Street, a lively street rife with fascinating shops and even more fascinating Village characters. Here and there are boutiques that cater to the most flamboyant tastes. The fragrant *McNulty's Tea & Coffee Company* (109 Christopher St.; phone: 212-242-5351) is a little shop lined with over 100 varieties of tea on one side and 50 blends of coffee on the other. Those with a sweet tooth should drop in at *Li-Lac Chocolates* (120 Christopher St.; phone: 212-242-7374); the buttercrunch, a local favorite, has just the right balance of chocolate and crunch. Be sure to sample a homemade chocolate bar, too.

Stop for a minute to look at the marquee of the *Lucille Lortel Theater* (121 Christopher St.; phone: 212-924-8782) before turning left onto Bedford Street. Originally called the *Theatre de Lys,* this historic stage (a former meat-packing warehouse) has hosted scores of off-Broadway hits, including Kurt Weill's *Threepenny Opera,* which had its New York premiere here.

The next few blocks along Bedford and the adjoining streets are the epicenter of Greenwich Village history. The quaint old houses and narrow streets seem to have been left over from another time. The row of houses that begins at Christopher Street and runs most of the length of Bedford to Grove Street is particularly noteworthy. Nos. 107 and 109 are original Federal-style houses; note the crescent moons cut out of the shutters. No. 102 Bedford is an odd, half-timbered house with a twin-peaked roof. Built in 1835 in the Federal style, it was remodeled into this whimsical structure in 1926 as a home for creative artists.

At the corner of Grove Street two charming wooden buildings are joined by a tall fence. Sash maker William Hyde lived in the house at 17 Grove Street; the structure at 100 Bedford Street was his workshop. While Grove Street is lovely on both sides of Bedford Street, turn right for a peek at Grove Court, which used to be called Mixed Ale Alley and was built as laborers' quarters. Its present incarnation is much more elegant: Red brick houses with white shutters now look out over a lushly planted courtyard. The sense of privacy here is punctuated by the locked gate. The nearby houses at Nos. 4 to 10 Grove Street are lovely authentic Federal-style buildings. Cross the street and stand in the school building entrance to get a good look at the charming and unique dormers—typical of this type of architecture—at the top of each house.

Return to Bedford Street, and walk south to *Chumley's* (86 Bedford St.; phone: 212-675-4449), a former speakeasy and still popular bar. Its unmarked exterior harks back to Prohibition days, when a knock at the door prompted the opening of a small, barred window through which one announced one's identity before the door would be opened. A "secret" doorway still opens onto an alley around the corner on Barrow Street; this was the escape route for patrons when the police raiding the place came in the front entrance.

The next block, Barrow Street, is named for artist Thomas Barrow, who lived here in the early 19th century; detour in either direction if you would like a closer look at this lovely street. Continue on Bedford Street and cross Commerce Street. The oldest house in the Village is the Isaacs-Hendricks House (77 Bedford St.), a lovely brick building on the corner of Commerce. Its sadly neglected next-door neighbor is the famous No. 75½ Bedford, the narrowest house in the city. Only nine and a half feet wide, this once was the home of John Barrymore, and later of Edna St. Vincent Millay.

Cross Morton Street, and stay on the right side of Seventh Avenue South, only briefly stepping out of the shelter of the small, cozy lanes. Just after the bend in Seventh Avenue South, turn right into St. Luke's Place, one of the most photographed blocks in Manhattan. A row of 15 elegant townhouses that form a harmonious streetscape, this short block has had its share of famous residents: Novelist Theodore Dreiser lived at No. 16; poet Marianne Moore lived at No. 14; and No. 12 was home to playwright Sherwood Anderson. Roaring Twenties Mayor Jimmy Walker lived at No. 6, the house with two pretty lanterns on the stoop. Television fans might recognize No. 10 as the home of the Huxtable family of "The Cosby Show." For a broader perspective walk along the large park across the street. Even the park's swimming pool has been on camera: In the movie *Raging Bull* this was where Robert De Niro first met Cathy Moriarity.

Follow St. Luke's Place to Hudson Street and turn right. Along this side of Hudson three charming cafés beckon footsore travelers. *Anglers & Writers* (420 Hudson St.; phone: 212-675-0810) occupies a bright, comfortable room decorated with old fishing baskets, rods and reels, and a rolltop desk. Each of the tiny tables is unique, and the room feels cozy but not crowded. Afternoon tea here is very good, too. *Café Maurizio* (434 Hudson St.; phone: 212-929-9170) is just what you imagine a Village coffeehouse to be: dimly lit with brick walls, tiny tables, a fireplace, and wonderful-looking cakes that go well with a good cup of java. In summer the tiny garden is a perfect venue for outdoor dining—much more relaxing and private than a sidewalk café. The *Village Atelier* (436 Hudson St.; phone: 212-989-1363) is another lovely little spot, full of character.

Turn right into Morton Street for a loop that swings back to Bedford Street and into Commerce and Barrow Streets before returning to Hudson Street. As soon as you turn the corner from Hudson, Morton is quiet and tree-lined, with a blend of architecturally intriguing townhouses. Turn left on Bedford Street and left again onto Commerce Street. This short street bends sharply, the most dramatic example of the Village's crooked ways. In 1822 it was called Cherry Lane because it was lined with blossoming cherry trees, but when the Village began to develop as a commercial hub, so many businesses settled here that its name was changed to Commerce Street. Notice the *Cherry Lane Theater* on the left at No. 38; founded by Edna St. Vincent Millay, it is the perfect setting for an off-Broadway house. Across the street are a pair of matching faded brick houses—dubbed "the twins" by locals—built in 1831 and connected by a small courtyard.

Where Commerce Street runs into Barrow Street, turn left and walk the short block back to Hudson Street. You can then proceed immediately across Hudson Street to charming *St. Luke's Gardens,* enclosed by a brick wall. Look down Barrow Street toward Greenwich Street, past the delightful brick houses that overlook the gardens, to the arches of the *Federal Archives Building* (641 Washington St.). Built in 1899, this is considered New York's best example of an all-brick industrial building.

The *Church of St. Luke in the Fields* dominates the west side of Hudson from Barrow to Christopher Street. Although the traffic whizzes up Hudson, the streetscape here has a small-town feeling. The simple brick church, the lovely gardens, and the brick houses on either side maintain the intimate scale.

Although it is a busy, noisy artery, Hudson Street is very much a part of the Village, unlike the avenues to the east which slice garishly through the tiny streets. Many of the buildings along Hudson are brick, and most are only a few stories high. Shopping is amazingly varied here; salespeople are almost always friendly, and the restaurants seem to be vying to see which can have more "character." The length of Hudson Street up to Bank Street holds many delights. *Lucy Anna Folk Art & Quilts* (502 Hudson St. at Christopher St.; phone: 212-645-9463) is a tiny shop decked in pretty quilts and inhabited by a herd of patchwork stuffed animals. The scene stealers are the chenille bears and dogs, which are irresistible to children of all ages.

This is a good time and place to sit for a while. If coffee and a sweet seem in order, *Caffè ShaSha* (510 Hudson St.; phone: 212-242-3021) offers both with operatic music in the background; if it's a nice day, sip a cappuccino in the little garden in the back—from here you can still hear strains of *La Bohème.* For more substantial sustenance cross over to the *Cowgirl Hall of Fame* (519 Hudson St.; phone: 212-633-1133) for a barbecue in a noisy Western setting. The lamps over the bar are made from antlers, and expect to be asked to check your six-shooter at the door. For strolling snackers a stop into *Taylor's* (523 Hudson St.; phone: 212-645-8200) is a must. This tiny shop is crammed with homemade muffins, cookies, pies, and cakes. (There's a bench just outside if you don't want to eat on the go.)

The vintage clothing at *Panache* (525 Hudson St.; phone: 212-242-5115) looks neat and clean, and the shop is just what one would hope a good thrift shop would be—no pretense but lots of character. More vintage atmosphere fills *Fish's Eddy* (551 Hudson St.; phone: 212-627-3956), a small place selling industrial china from the 1930s to the present. The stock is ever changing, but there are always some very inexpensive and quirky pieces of Americana. Turn left on Charles Street for a view of one of the Village's many wonderful little surprises: At the corner of Greenwich Street, a picket fence surrounds a tiny wooden house, complete with a lawn.

Back on Hudson Street, keep your eye out for the *Dover Garage* (534 Hudson St.), at the opposite corner of Charles Street. If it looks familiar, it is because it was the setting for the TV show "Taxi."

At Bank Street turn left off Hudson Street and head west. These next blocks of the walk are strictly non-tourist country, a neighborhood that is quiet by day and not much noiser when the nightlife begins. Bank Street, like many of the others here, is cobbled along this block. Artistic types, eccentrically dressed and almost uniformly good-looking, lounge outside No. 120, the site of the famous *HB Studio*. The list of well-known actors who have studied here with the founder, the late Herbert Berghoff, and his wife, Uta Hagen, includes Jill Clayburgh, Robert De Niro, Jack Lemmon, Al Pacino, and Bette Midler.

The looming bulk of *Westbeth* (463 West St. at Bank St.) provides low-cost housing for artists. Formerly the headquarters of Bell Telephone's Western Electric Laboratories, this was where the pioneering work that brought sound to moving pictures was done. Bell eventually left for the suburbs, and in 1970 *Westbeth* became the city's first conversion of an industrial building to loft housing, touching off a lifestyle tidal wave that has swept the downtown area.

Take a look into *Automatic Slim's* (733 Washington St.; phone: 212-645-8660), a tiny, authentic musician's bar at Washington and Bank Streets that calls itself "One Bar under a Groove." The streetfront is painted black, with one white column marking the corner doorway; locals praise the food. Now walk up Washington Street to Jane Street and make a right. Some of these quiet, leafy streets are cobbled, and a tiny wedge of a garden has been planted at the intersection of Jane and Eighth Avenue, an expression of the intense neighborhood pride here. Cross Eighth Avenue at Jane Street, and then turn right immediately onto West Fourth Street. This is the last leg of the tour, continuing along a quiet, pretty stretch of West Fourth across Seventh Avenue South to Sheridan Square. At each corner look in both directions down the cross streets—West 12th, Bank, West 11th (which should look familiar from the early part of the walk), Perry, Charles, and West 10th; each offers another Greenwich Village tableau.

La Focaccia (51 Bank St. at W. Fourth St.; phone: 212-675-3754) is an Italian restaurant with painted tiles on the walls and tabletops. Not surprisingly, *focaccia* (a flat, round bread with various toppings) is one of the house specials; a wood-burning fireplace turns out tasty grilled chicken and chops. For a real treat stop at the well-known *Pâtisserie J. Lanciani* (271 W. Fourth St.; phone: 212-929-0739) and take home the Grand Marnier cake (the lemon tart is a close second).

In the space of the next block you can choose from French, Italian, or Spanish fare. *Carmella's Village Garden* (49 Charles St.; phone: 212-242-2155) offers excellent Italian food. Across Charles Street the *Sevilla* restaurant (62 Charles St.; phone: 212-929-3189) serves paella, garlic shrimp, and other Spanish delicacies. Walk a block farther along West Fourth to West 10th Street. Here is the tiny and ultra-charming restaurant *La Metairie* (189 W. 10th St.; phone: 212-989-0343). If they can't accommodate you, try *Chez Ma Tante* next door (189 W. 10th St.; phone: 212-620-0223). Both establishments are very pretty and serve delicious French dishes.

Continue along West Fourth Street, which meets Seventh Avenue South and Christopher and Grove Streets at Sheridan Square. *Christopher Park* is the official name of the patch of greenery at one end of the square, although most Villagers would not recognize it by that name. A statue of General Philip Henry Sheridan in his Civil War uniform stands at the apex of the park, a reminder that New York's infamous 1863 Draft Riots took place on this spot. Across Christopher Street is the *Lion's Head* (59 Christopher St.; phone: 212-929-0670), where actress Jessica Lange was working as a waitress when Dino DeLaurentis "discovered" her and cast her in his remake of *King Kong*. This basement pub also has a long history as a writer's hangout, and Norman Mailer used it as his campaign headquarters when he ran for Mayor of New York City back in the 1970s. A few doors down is the *Stonewall* (53 Christopher St.; phone: 463-0950), famous for a 1969 clash between gay patrons and raiding police, generally considered the beginning of the American gay rights movement.

Rockefeller Center and Fifth Avenue

0 miles 1/4

N

- Central Park
- Grand Army Plaza
- CENTRAL PARK SOUTH
- Plaza Hotel
- WEST 58TH ST. / EAST 57TH ST.
- WEST 57TH ST. / EAST 56TH ST.
- WEST 56TH ST. — Fifth Ave. Presbyterian Church — Trump Tower
- WEST 55TH ST. — Penninsula Hotel — EAST 55TH ST.
- WEST 54TH ST. — St. Regis — EAST 54TH ST.
- WEST 53RD ST. — St. Thomas Church — Samuel Paley Plaza — EAST 53RD ST.
- WEST 52ND ST. / EAST 52ND ST.
- WEST 51ST ST. / EAST 51ST ST.
- Radio City Music Hall — ROCKEFELLER — St. Patrick's Cathedral
- WEST 50TH ST. / EAST 50TH ST.
- GE Building — Saks Fifth Avenue
- WEST 49TH ST. / EAST 49TH ST.
- CENTER
- Barnes & Noble — Brentano's
- WEST 48TH ST. / EAST 48TH ST.
- WEST 47TH ST. / EAST 47TH ST.
- Atrium
- WEST 46TH ST. / EAST 46TH ST.
- Fred F. French Building
- WEST 45TH ST. / EAST 45TH ST.
- Algonquin Hotel
- WEST 44TH ST. / EAST 44TH ST.
- WEST 43RD ST. / EAST 43RD ST.
- WEST 42ND ST. / EAST 42ND ST.
- WEST 41ST ST. — Bryant Park — EAST 41ST ST.
- WEST 40TH ST. — New York Public Library — EAST 40TH ST.
- WEST 39TH ST. / EAST 39TH ST.
- WEST 38TH ST. / EAST 38TH ST.
- WEST 37TH ST. / MURRAY / EAST 37TH ST.
- WEST 36TH ST. / HILL / EAST 36TH ST.
- WEST 35TH ST. / EAST 35TH ST.
- WEST 34TH ST. / EAST 34TH ST.
- Empire State Bldg.
- WEST 33RD ST. / EAST 33RD ST.
- WEST 32ND ST. / EAST 32ND ST.

BROADWAY, SEVENTH AVE., FIFTH AVE., MADISON AVE., VANDERBILT AVE., PARK AVE., PARK AVENUE SOUTH, LEXINGTON AVE., THIRD AVE.

Walk 5: Rockefeller Center and Fifth Avenue

This walk of roughly 15 blocks begins at the *Empire State Building,* moves up Fifth Avenue, pauses for a look at *Rockefeller Center,* and then finishes at Grand Army Plaza, where the leafy expanse of *Central Park* spreads out at the feet of some of the city's most impressive buildings. Bisecting the east and west sides of town, Fifth Avenue is Manhattan's spine; lined with high-priced boutiques, airline offices, and electronics stores, and populated by society matrons and street people, it is also New York's heart.

One of the city's best-known sites, the *Empire State Building* (350 Fifth Ave.; phone 212-736-3100) fronts an entire block of Fifth Avenue from West 33rd to West 34th Street. Soaring 102 stories, it was for many years the tallest building in the world (only the *Sears Tower* in Chicago and the twin towers of the *World Trade Center*—all built much later—now surpass it). Many who have looked down from these heights agree that nothing can match the thrill of seeing New York City from the outdoor observation deck on the 86th floor of the *Empire State.* The building's top 30 floors are always illuminated at night, often in colors to mark important holidays: all-American red, white, and blue for the *Fourth of July;* red and green for *Christmas,* and so on. If you are able, visit the observation deck once during the day and then again in the evening, when the city is illuminated by hundreds of thousands of shimmering lights. Daily hours are from 9:30 AM to midnight; last tickets are sold at 11:30 PM, which is often a good time to avoid lines, not to mention being a magical hour at which to view the city.

Walk uptown (north) on Fifth Avenue to *Lord & Taylor* (424 Fifth Ave., from W. 38th to W. 39th St.; phone: 212-391-3344), the last of the elegant (if conservative) specialty and department stores that once dominated this part of the avenue. At *Christmastime* people stand in line just to view the charming storefront windows, decorated with mechanized dolls in elaborate period settings. For a quick but delicious lunch, try the store's terrific *Soup Bar* on the 10th floor. One block north on the same side of the street is the *Republic National Bank Building,* an ornate confection of a mansion originally designed to house the Knox Hat Company. It is a lovely reminder of Fifth Avenue's history as a posh residential neighborhood.

On the west side of Fifth Avenue from 40th to 42nd Street stands one of New York's architectural gems, the central research (main) branch of the *New York Public Library* (phone: 212-930-0800; 212-661-7220 for recorded information). Although its design includes some ornate flourishes, everything about this building is dignified yet welcoming, beginning with the two massive stone lions that flank the front entrance. The stately white Vermont marble façade, with its enormous columns, triple-arched portico, and pediment, opens onto a wide terrace where office workers and shoppers stop to rest, and where musicians and street performers entertain the crowds. When the library opened in 1911, it represented the merger of three fine private libraries, the Astor, Tilden, and Lenox. Among those who contributed to its construction was Andrew Carnegie, who presented the builders with a $52 million grant; President William Howard Taft was on hand for the dedication. Even if you venture no farther than the vaulted entrance hall with its twin magnificent staircases, you will have a wonderful sense of the scope of the building.

It's worth a longer look, however, to visit the *Gottesman Exhibition Hall,* the *De Witt Wallace Periodical Room,* with its mix of marble and walnut paneling, and the *Edna Barnes Salomon Room,* where the library's Gutenberg Bible is kept. Don't miss the monumental and famous *Main Reading Room* upstairs; a graceful and impressive expanse, 297 feet long and 78 feet wide, it sits atop several floors of stacks which accommodate over 88 miles of bookshelves. Free tours of the library last an hour and are given Tuesdays through Saturdays at 11 AM and 2 PM; tours of the current exhibits (in 1993 and 1994 these have included the hugely popular Dead Sea Scrolls and a "Compleat Charles Addams") leave at 12:30 PM and 2:30 PM (phone: 212-930-0501 for tour information). Just behind the library is beautifully restored *Bryant Park,* with cultivated gardens and velvety grass, where movies are occasionally screened in summer. Inside the park is the *Bryant Park Ticket Booth* (phone: 212-382-2323), where you can buy half-price tickets for same-day music, dance, and some opera performances.

As you continue north on Fifth Avenue across 42nd Street, look down West 43rd Street to see the banners of many exclusive clubs. The *Century Association* (7 W. 43rd St.) was designed in 1891 by architects McKim, Mead & White to resemble a solemn Italian palazzo. Time has only enhanced its classical façade; the staid *Princeton Club* (15 W. 43rd St.) almost looks modern by contrast. Keep an eye out for the cast-iron Seth Thomas clock that stands on the sidewalk between West 43rd and West 44th Streets; it's an anachronistic remnant of pre-wristwatch days (though we don't recommend setting your watch by it).

Take a detour on West 44th Street to get a closer look at the architectural details that adorn the fronts of more private clubs. The *Harvard Club* (27 W. 44th St.) was built in 1894 of red Harvard brick, presumably to warm the hearts of alumni with a reminder of the good old days. The *New York Yacht Club* (37 W. 44th St.), which administers the *America's Cup* race in the US, catches even a landlubber's eye with its ornately carved windows in the shape of a ship's stern and its decorative stone waves and dolphins. The nautical theme continues in the sleek *Royalton* hotel across the street, whose lobby resembles the grand salon of an ocean liner.

Farther along, the *Algonquin* hotel (59 W. 44th St.; phone: 212-840-6800) is another architectural treat and a famous literary landmark. In the

1920s renowned literati such as Dorothy Parker, Ring Lardner, Robert Benchley, and George S. Kaufman formed a mock social club and dubbed it the "Round Table"; they met in the *Algonquin*'s *Oak Room* to sharpen their rapier wits. Legends of the entertainment industry, such as Douglas Fairbanks and Mary Pickford, were also drawn to this lively atmosphere. The cozy lobby and upscale surroundings still draw literary, theater, and Hollywood types; good for people watching, this is an excellent place to pause for a cup of tea before continuing on the walk.

Head back to Fifth Avenue. On the northeast corner of Fifth and 45th Street is the *Fred F. French Building,* with its rosy brick and exotic decorations that combine Aztec and Egyptian motifs. Stand at the corner of Fifth Avenue and West 44th Street for the best view of the top ornament, which depicts a sun moving through the heavens. The building adds a graceful note to this part of Fifth Avenue, which is otherwise largely populated by garish "going out of business" electronics shops.

The *Atrium* (575 Fifth Ave. at E. 47th St.), an upscale shopping complex and oasis for the footsore, is the latest in the architectural vernacular for public places. Among its beauties is a stained glass trompe l'oeil ceiling, the largest of its kind built in the city in the last 50 years. Baseball fans should stop at the *New York Mets Clubhouse Shop* (phone: 212-986-4887) in the lower concourse; this is the place to stock up on everything from tickets for this season's games to baseball caps to items that look like either tattered old jackets or precious relics, depending on your point of view. *Rusty Staub's on Fifth* (phone: 212-682-1000), just across the concourse, is a good place to satisfy hunger pangs (and you might even see this former *Expo* and *Met*).

Those in search of jewelry should visit the diamond district, which occupies the block of West 47th Street between Fifth and Sixth Avenues. Most of the wholesale diamond trade in the city—if not the country—is conducted here, mainly by Orthodox Jews; though some retail trade goes on in the rather dingy storefronts, the real action is behind the scenes. There is one literary landmark among all these gems: the *Gotham Book Mart* (41 W. 47th St.; phone: 212-719-4448), where as-yet-unknown writers such as Henry Miller, John Dos Passos, and Edmund Wilson used to gather in the 1920s to read from their works-in-progress. Founder and former owner Frances Steloff held the philosophy that all fine literary talent should be nurtured; consequently, the bookshop is still crammed with tomes by up-and-coming authors, as well as the classics.

Two large bookstores face each other across Fifth Avenue between 48th and 49th Streets. On the west side the large and recently refurbished *Barnes & Noble* (600 Fifth Ave.; phone: 212-765-0590) is part of a chain that carries many best sellers at discounted prices, as well as a good selection of college and instructional textbooks. Across the avenue is the historic black and gilded iron and glass front of *Brentano's* (formerly *Scribner's;* 587 Fifth Ave.; phone: 212-826-2450).

Saks Fifth Avenue (611 Fifth Ave., from E. 49th to E. 50th St.; phone: 212-753-4000) is a haven for well-heeled, fashion-conscious shoppers. The eighth-floor restaurant, *Café SFA,* is a nice spot for a light lunch, complemented by a view of *St. Patrick's Cathedral.* Even if you must spend all afternoon looking for the perfect outfit for next season, be sure to allow time to savor one of the most wonderful of urban panoramas: *Rockefeller Center.* Located just across the street from *Saks,* this splendid sight is a favorite among tourists and New Yorkers alike. Stand in front of the store and look across the street down the *Channel Gardens* (so called because they separate the *British Building* to the right and the *Maison Française* to the left) all the way to the soaring tower of the *GE Building* (formerly the *RCA Building*). Built in the early days of the Depression, the mixture of tall buildings and open spaces was designed to lift spirits and encourage business. Public interest and enthusiasm were so great when *Rockefeller Center* was under construction that John D. Rockefeller Jr. had holes cut in the construction barriers to facilitate viewing. Today over 240,000 people work and visit here daily.

After savoring the view from *Saks,* cross Fifth Avenue and walk down the *Channel Gardens* (creative floral displays that change with the seasons) toward the sunken ice rink and the golden statue of *Prometheus* by Paul Manship. At *Christmastime* a towering tree illuminated by tens of thousands of tiny, colored lights stands on the plaza just above the statue (see *Quintessential New York* in DIVERSIONS). Ringing the ice rink are the flags of all the countries that are members of the United Nations. (In warm weather wall-to-wall umbrellas shield diners in the sunken plaza.)

Take a few moments to visit the interiors around *Rockefeller Center.* Walking into the sleek lobby of *30 Rockefeller Plaza* is like walking into a black-and-white 1930s movie. Above the entrance is the José María Sert mural *American Progress,* an allegory of the country's development. (The original mural by Diego Rivera was removed when John D. Rockefeller Jr. objected to its inclusion of Lenin.) On the ceiling is *Time,* another Sert work; the huge figures, with their feet braced on marble columns, seem to lean in different directions as you walk under them.

Tickets for *NBC Television Studio* tours are available at the West 50th Street side of this lobby. Tours leave every 15 minutes Monday through Saturday and last about an hour. Fans of "Saturday Night Live," the "Today Show," and "Phil Donahue" can view the premises where it all happens (phone: 212-664-3055 for recorded information); at press time tickets cost $8.

An extensive underground concourse filled with shops, a post office, and several restaurants connects all the *Rockefeller Center* buildings. One of the most interesting corners in this maze is an alcove at the foot of the escalator in *30 Rockefeller Plaza;* it contains a permanent exhibit of the history of the complex, including photographs of construction in progress and newspaper clippings that capture the excitement and enthusiasm of the time. The *Sea Grill* (phone: 212-246-9201), specializing in fresh seafood, is an elegant spot for lunch or dinner, especially in winter, when skaters whiz by the windows. Just next door is the *American Festival Café* (see *Eating Out* in THE CITY), with alfresco dining on the ice rink in summer.

Also part of *Rockefeller Center*, *Radio City Music Hall* (Ave. of the Americas and W. 50th St.; phone: 212-247-4777; 212-632-4041 for tour information) was the largest theater in the world when it opened in 1932, and is still one of the most impressive. When its family entertainment programs became passé in the 1970s, the building was threatened with demolition, but in 1978 a citizens' group campaigned to have the glorious Art Deco interior declared a landmark and saved it. Now the great stage hosts a variety of entertainers from Frank Sinatra, k. d. lang, Tina Turner, and Bette Midler to the *Moscow Circus*. The *Rockettes* still show off their perfectly synchronized kicks, and the traditional *Christmas* and *Easter* extravaganzas draw enormous crowds of loyal fans each year. Even if you don't see one of the shows, the view of the lobby, with its sweeping staircase and two-ton chandeliers, is breathtaking.

Walk back along West 50th Street to 630 Fifth Avenue, between West 50th and West 51st Streets, for one more memorable sight. The famous statue of Atlas, struggling with his worldly burden, stands just in front of the doorway. If you enter the building, ride up the escalator and look back through the window. The façade of *St. Patrick's Cathedral* that looms just beyond is a memorable sight. Cross the street to the steps of the cathedral, and look up Fifth Avenue at the flags flapping and the bustling traffic. The green trim of the luxurious *Peninsula* hotel stands out at West 55th Street, and farther up a haze of trees marks the start of *Central Park*. The stroll from 50th Street up to 59th Street is lovely—there are beautiful churches, elegant shops, world-famous jewelers, and grand hotels.

Named for the patron saint of Ireland, *St. Patrick's Cathedral* nearly overwhelms the avenue, a reminder of the influence wielded by the church in the late 1800s, when it was built. Awesome though it is, *St. Patrick's* is not always a quiet place; the constant flow of worshipers and tourists lends an air of rush-hour devotion.

Farther up Fifth Avenue at the southeast corner of 52nd Street is the Italian Renaissance mansion built in 1905 that now houses *Cartier* (phone: 212-753-0111). Fortunes are spent on its beautifully set gems. As at many other stores along this glamorous strip, window shopping may be as close as you want to get.

St. Thomas Church, across the avenue at West 53rd Street, is a place for quiet contemplation even if you are not Episcopalian. Built in 1914, it boasts a beautiful Gothic façade, but it is the interior that is a must-see. An elaborate reredos, a wall of beautifully carved stone, is behind the main altar; representations of angels, saints, and a few honored clergy "float" in a heavenly vision. Music is also an important feature of this church, and it is delightful to wander in when an organist or the famous all-male choir is practicing. (For evensong and high mass schedule, call 212-757-7013.) Around the corner, on West 53rd Street between Fifth and Sixth Avenues, is the *Museum of Modern Art* (phone: 212-708-9400; 212-708-9480 for recorded information) with one of the world's finest and most comprehensive collections.

Samuel Paley Plaza (created by CBS founder William S. Paley and named for his father) is a tiny, restful park with a wall of water just around the corner from Fifth Avenue on the north side of East 53rd Street. It tends to be crowded at lunchtime, but is a lovely place to relax with a cup of coffee; sandwiches and hot and cold drinks are sold in one corner.

Back on Fifth Avenue at the northwest corner of 54th Street sits the *University Club,* looking as dignified and unflappable as its members, who occasionally can be seen through the windows, reading their newspapers. Although from the outside this structure looks like a three-story Renaissance palazzo, it actually rises seven stories.

The *St. Regis,* an elegant hotel just off Fifth Avenue on East 55th Street, is worth a look, if not a lingering stay (see *Checking In* in THE CITY). Built by John Jacob Astor in 1904, it was so luxurious it even had marble boiler rooms. Recently renovated, it is said to have the costliest accommodations in New York today.

The austere *Fifth Avenue Presbyterian Church* shares the block between West 55th and West 56th Streets with four brownstones that are home to *Henri Bendel,* one of the city's trendiest yet upscale stores for women (phone: 212-247-1100). Just before these buildings were scheduled for demolition, an architectural historian uncovered a cache of buried treasure that saved them from the wrecker's ball. Windows designed in 1912 for cosmetics czar François Coty by René Lalique, a master jewelry and glass designer, were discovered hidden under decades of accumulated urban grime. The restored windows, a delicately colored, molded trellis of vines and poppies, now form the focal point of a beautiful atrium just inside the store. The Lalique windows, the lovely brownstone façades, and their more somber Presbyterian neighbor are best viewed from across the street, in front of *Steuben Glass* (717 Fifth Ave.; phone: 212-752-1441), whose famous hand-blown glass animals and commemorative pieces are displayed in a hushed atmosphere more reminiscent of a museum than a shop (a small number of items are priced for everyday budgets). One of the city's most aristocratic jewelers, *Harry Winston* (718 Fifth Ave.; phone: 212-245-2000), has its own gem-like site on the southwest corner of 56th Street.

Our walk continues on to *Trump Tower* (Fifth Ave. and E. 56th St.), Donald Trump's glittering monument to capitalism. There are always visitors ambling through the Florentine marble atrium to look if not to shop. At less crowded times it is pleasant to ride the escalators up along the waterfall wall or to sit and sip an expensive cappuccino at the *DDL Bistro.* The *Terrace* restaurant on the top floor of the atrium is a quiet oasis for lunch (phone: 212-319-5341). If you really must, there is a newsstand that sells souvenir Trump T-shirts for about $30. Filled with shops whose merchandise carries out-of-this-world price tags, *Trump Tower* is truly an exercise in conspicuous consumption (see "Malls" in *Shopping,* THE CITY).

Continue your dose of decadence next door at *Tiffany & Co.* (727 Fifth Ave. at E. 57th St.; phone: 212-755-8000). Truman Capote's character Holly Golightly was absolutely on target when she sighed, "Nothing bad can ever happen to you in a place like this," in the short story (and the film) *Breakfast at Tiffany's.* From the impeccably polite salespeople to the exquisite merchandise, browsing and buying here are true pleasures. Also at Fifth and 57th, on the northeast corner, is one of the most animated retailers in this luxurious shopping district. The *Warner Bros. Studio Store* (1 E. 57th St.; phone: 212-754-0300) sells cartoon character theme items—from potholders to pricey sportswear. Superman hoists the glass elevator from floor to floor, and the exterior's stone façade is carved with other well-known characters like Sylvester.

Across Fifth Avenue it's all seriousness again at *Van Cleef & Arpels* (744 Fifth Ave. at W. 57th St.; phone: 212-644-9500), one of the city's most exclusive purveyors of jewelry. Next door, *Bergdorf Goodman* (754 Fifth Ave.; phone: 212-753-7300) has long carried the very ultimate in fashionable female apparel and accessories; its equally upscale men's store is just across the avenue.

Alongside *Bergdorf's,* Fifth Avenue opens onto Grand Army Plaza, the space in front of the château-like *Plaza* hotel, whose romantic entrance and interiors have been captured in many movies. The vista here combines the ornateness of the *Plaza,* the forthrightness of the *General Motors Building* across Fifth, and the refreshing openness of *Central Park* to the north. Tucked in a corner of the *General Motors Building, FAO Schwarz* (767 Fifth Ave., but with a larger entrance on Madison Ave.; phone: 212-644-9400), the quintessential toy store, keeps youngsters and adults alike amused year-round, although it's a special treat at *Christmastime.*

There's no better way to finish a Fifth Avenue walk than with tea at the *Plaza's Palm Court* (phone: 212-546-5493). If you desire something stronger, have a cocktail in the timeless *Oak Bar.* Look for the portrait in the hotel lobby of the fictional Eloise, that mischievous and lucky little girl who once called the *Plaza* home.

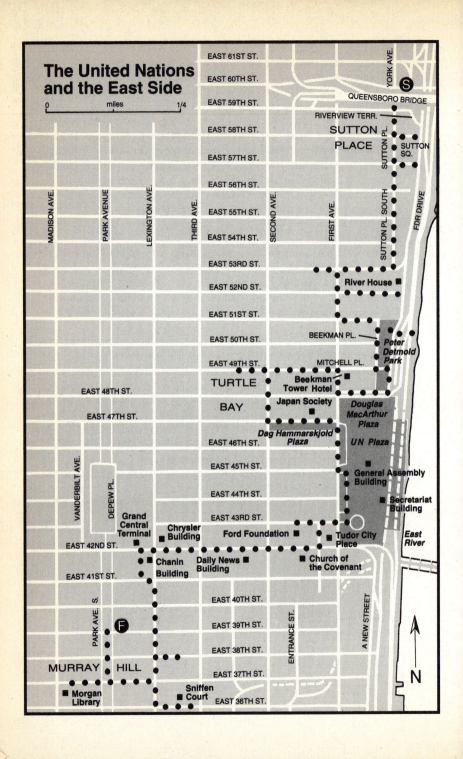

Walk 6: The United Nations and the East Side

This is a tour of contrasts. The most effete and the most democratic institutions in the world coexist here, such as the old-world, private residential enclave of Sutton Square and the contemporary *United Nations* complex. The walk zigzags from street to street, and begins under the Manhattan side of the Queensboro Bridge. Better known by locals as the 59th Street Bridge because of its entrance on that street, this giant erector set of cantilevered steel construction was made famous in an early *Simon and Garfunkel* song named after it. Built in 1909, it originally carried the old Second Avenue elevated trolley line between Manhattan and Queens as well as vehicular traffic, but it is now limited to the latter.

Heading south under the Queensboro Bridge along York Avenue, you will see that the street simultaneously changes its name and its identity. Suddenly you're on Sutton Place, one of the city's most elegant residential streets. Here you'll find traces of bygone days, as chauffeured limousines wait at the curb and life goes on at a pace untouched by the rhythms of commerce just blocks away. Each of the streets from East 56th to East 59th ends at the East River; this waterfront "community" enjoys a sense of quiet and isolation despite the traffic rumbling on the bridge above and the FDR Drive below. East 58th Street's cul-de-sac is called Sutton Square, a lovely group of townhouses that share a common garden. Similar to many appealing New York neighborhoods, much of its charm is a result of its diverse architecture: One house has a French provincial air, others are serenely Georgian, and one distinctly resembles a Beverly Hills mansion. At the very end of East 58th Street is Riverview Terrace, an even more exclusive little street, not open to the public; the five houses on its west side have an enviable view of the river.

Return to Sutton Place and turn left; walk down one block to East 57th Street and turn left (toward the river) again. Lillian Gish lived for over 50 years at 430 East 57th Street, and in the late 1950s Marilyn Monroe, then Mrs. Arthur Miller, lived at No. 444. At the end of East 57th Street is *East River Park*, a little green space suspended like a balcony over the East River. Sutton Place is blessed with unobstructed river views along its entire length, due to the fact that the busy FDR Drive runs through a tunnel beneath it. The views from nearly every other East Side location (including lovely Beekman Place, which is farther along on this walk) unfortunately have to contend with the noise and visual distraction of this main north-south artery.

Turn left back onto Sutton Place and head south, descending slightly downhill. Individual townhouses give way to large, elegant, but fairly unimaginative apartment houses. An exception is 1 Sutton Place South; designed by Rosario Candela in 1927, its elegant façade opens onto a lobby which in turn opens onto a private garden overlooking the river. Although the gardens are not open to the public, a polite request to the doorman *might* be rewarded with a peek.

Sutton Place South ends (or begins, depending on which way you're walking) at East 53rd Street. Just before you turn right on East 53rd Street, there is another little park at the bend of the street. Walk along East 53rd Street, cross First Avenue, and look for 312 East 53rd Street, a landmark wooden house built in 1866. Go back across First Avenue, turn right, and walk down to East 52nd Street, then turn left toward the river. On the left, near the end of the street at No. 435, is the gated entrance to the courtyard of *River House*. The generous open space is somewhat marred by the balconies of newer neighboring buildings, but no matter: There is a spacious drive-in entrance that leads to this luxury apartment building. The end of the street looks out onto a wide space of sky and the broad East River. If you peek through the wrought-iron fence and down to the right, you can catch a glimpse of a private sculpture garden; this pretty patio extends for a length of about four townhouses and is draped with a blanket of ivy.

As you walk back to First Avenue on the east side of the street, you'll spot an unmarked storefront with two large amphorae planted with wisteria vines which curl up the front of the building. Nothing so crass as a sign announces that this is *ZeZe* (398 E. 52nd St.; phone: 212-753-7767), a sophisticated florist. Walk down First another block to East 51st Street. Before turning left at the corner, drop into *Ideal Tile of Manhattan* (405 E. 51st St.; phone: 212-759-2339). In addition to a wide selection of hand-painted and imported wall and floor tiles, there are pottery jugs, plates, and figurines for sale. Walk toward the river on East 51st Street to the Beekman Place district, which is as exclusive as Sutton Place yet smaller and quieter. Beekman Place itself extends from East 51st Street to Mitchell Place, its southern boundary. The area was named for James Beekman, owner of the Beekman estate and son of William Beekman, who sailed to America with Peter Stuyvesant. His manor house, *Mount Pleasant,* originally stood on the high ground between East 51st and East 52nd Streets, east of First Avenue. This storied little corner is rich in history: During the American Revolution, General Howe made his headquarters on the estate; patriot Nathan Hale was captured and hanged nearby; and it was here that Major John André made arrangements to meet the infamous Benedict Arnold to secure plans for the fort at *West Point.* After the war George Washington, the new President of the United States, was a frequent visitor. The Beekman family resided here until 1854, when a cholera epidemic broke out; *Mount Pleasant* was demolished about 20 years later. Among the well-known residents of the neighborhood over the years were John D. Rockefeller II, Irving Berlin, Ethel Barrymore, and the fictional Auntie Mame.

Walk to the end of East 51st Street and down the steps to *Peter Detmold Park* (we'll return to Beekman Place later). Walk over the footbridge that spans the park and the FDR Drive for some memorable views. The first thing you notice as you stand on the bridge is that you are looking down on a seemingly endless line of cars. The traffic never stops—except when it ceases altogether from sheer volume and results in an ever-unpopular New York traffic jam. To the north lies Cannon Point, where the FDR disappears into the tunnel beneath Sutton Place.

Walk back over the bridge for a backstage view of Beekman Place, with its wonderful assortment of little houses. Go down the steps into the park, where local residents exercise their dogs and sit in the sun. Rest here a while and look up at the 59th Street Bridge as it spans Roosevelt Island and stretches to Queens. The park feels like the back lot of a Woody Allen movie; in fact, it often appears in his and other directors' films.

At the top of the park steps, walk the short distance to Beekman Place and turn left. From here the glass towers of 860 and 870 United Nations Plaza block the view south to the *UN,* yet, oddly enough, they don't diminish the charm of these small houses. Instead, the towers make Beekman Place cozier, and their expressionless façades emphasize the unique personality of each of the homes.

Walk west on Mitchell Place toward First Avenue and, reluctantly, back to the real world. The *Beekman Tower* hotel (3 Mitchell Pl.; phone: 212-355-7300), with its distinctive Art Deco details, is your final glance at this neighborhood's elegant atmosphere. The nighttime view from the *Beekman's Top of the Tower* piano bar is delightful.

Turtle Bay is the next neighborhood on the tour, an area of the East 40s above 42nd Street from Third Avenue to the East River. The avenues have become more impersonal as one office tower after another has been built; happily, the cross streets are still lined with brownstones and a few medium-size apartment buildings. The intensity of the traffic on these streets makes them slightly less appealing than the uptown enclaves, but they still provide a glimpse of how Manhattan used to look. Cross First and Second Avenues along the left side of East 49th Street to a group of houses called *Turtle Bay Gardens.* One of the most exclusive areas on the walk, this group of vintage back-to-back brownstones was transformed in the early 1920s; among other improvements, their backyards form a large and lush common garden for the use of residents (Katharine Hepburn lives on the East 48th Street side).

Across East 49th Street is *Amster Yard* (211-215 E. 49th St.), another private place worth a peek through the gate. These late 1860s buildings have been converted into a charming courtyard of offices. Named for James Amster, an interior decorator who bought the property in 1945, it is now a designated historical district. Considering the canyon of office buildings that characterize Third Avenue, the survival of this enclave is something of a miracle.

Now walk down Second Avenue to East 47th Street and turn left, back toward the East River. In the mid-1600s, when Manhattan was still a sparsely populated island and Turtle Bay indented the coast (now the site of the *United Nations*), this area was part of Turtle Bay Farm. Dag Hammarskjold Plaza—named for the Secretary General of the *United Nations* who was killed in a plane crash in 1961 while on a peace mission to the Congo—occupies the block between First and Second Avenues. Its broad sidewalk along the south side is frequently the site of demonstrations by those eager to bring their issues to the attention of *UN* delegates and the world. Across the plaza, note the elegant simplicity of the *Japan Society Building* (333 E. 47th St.; phone: 212-832-1155); lectures, classes, and exhibits on Japanese art and culture are frequently offered here.

Walk east to First Avenue, where the *United Nations* complex (called *United Nations Plaza*) dominates the skyline. This part of the East Side formerly had been an area of run-down tenements, coal docks, breweries, and slaughterhouses; architecture critics give the *UN* complex mixed reviews. While it's true that it has a hodgepodge quality, it remains an impressive sight—a thrilling experience for the millions of visitors who come here every year. Its highlight is the gleaming *Secretariat Building;* its ever-expanding number of flagpoles fly the banners of all member nations. Behind the flags is a circular marble reflecting pool donated by American schoolchildren. The *Hammarskjold Library* anchors the complex at its southernmost end at East 42nd Street.

Nestled between the crescent of flags and the *Secretariat,* the curve of the *General Assembly Building* creates a graceful panorama. The formal park to the north and the wide plaza around it are a hive of activity when the *General Assembly* is in session (from September to December), but at any time of year the plaza teems with people of all nationalities.

Walk down First Avenue to the visitors' entrance, between East 45th and East 46th Streets. Guided tours leave frequently from here and include parts of the *Secretariat, General Assembly,* and *Conference Buildings* (for more information, see *Special Places* in THE CITY). If you would rather stay outdoors, walk along the esplanade near the visitors' entrance and stroll through the gardens, which are especially lovely in the spring.

Some visually arresting buildings face the *UN* across this wide avenue. The most spectacular is *1 United Nations Plaza,* which acts as a vertical reflecting pool for the complex; its blue-green glass is broken into a grid of tiny squares. The *UN Plaza Park Hyatt* hotel occupies part of the building, and its *Ambassador Grill* (phone: 212-702-5014), always filled with visiting diplomats, is one of the best places to dine and people watch in the neighborhood. The hotel lobby faces East 44th Street, and is worth a short detour for a peek at its sleek decor.

Walk 7: Upper Midtown and Madison Avenue

This walk meanders on and off Madison Avenue from East 58th Street to East 82nd Street. Within a few short blocks, the roar of midtown traffic gives way to a gentler, more sophisticated neighborhood; with many buildings along this stretch only two or three stories high, the atmosphere is reminiscent of a main street—albeit a very posh one—in a small town. Shops that sell the finest chocolates, antiques, jewelry, and clothing, as well as art galleries rich with everything from ancient artifacts to modern masters, line Madison Avenue.

At the beginning of this century many well-heeled New Yorkers migrated from midtown to the Upper East Side and built magnificent mansions. As property values rose on Fifth Avenue, the homes eventually were torn down to make room for large apartment buildings. Happily, the side streets were less suited for this kind of development, and many of the lovely houses were spared. In the late 1980s the Upper East Side and the area around the *Metropolitan Museum of Art* were declared historic districts by the *New York City Landmarks Preservation Commission*.

Our slightly uphill climb begins at the "back" of the sleek, white *General Motors Building* at Madison Avenue and East 58th Street. Across the avenue is a parade of elegant shops. *Cardel* (621 Madison Ave.; phone: 212-753-8690) is a treasure trove of fine china and tableware; *Baccarat* (625 Madison Ave.; phone: 212-826-4100) is synonymous with exquisite crystal; and *Movado* (625 Madison Ave.; phone: 212-688-4002) marks the time in style with understated watches. *Bottega Veneta* (635 Madison Ave.; phone: 212-371-5511) is one of the most luxurious places in town for leather goods; *Boyd's of Madison* (655 Madison Ave.; phone: 212-838-6558) is the place to go for personalized makeup and imported cosmetics and brushes; and the *Macklowe Gallery* (667 Madison Ave.; phone: 212-644-6400) offers a wealth of Art Nouveau and Art Deco pieces—everything from antique vases and Tiffany lamps to estate jewelry. For a look at the latest in polished but casual apparel, stop in at *InWear/Matinique* (650 Madison Ave.; phone: 212-750-2165). The *Niessing Collection* (675 Madison Ave.; phone: 212-752-5920) features modern jewelry by the designer who has long provided rings for virtually every bride and groom in Germany (don't miss the striking interior by Japanese architect Toshiko Mori).

Undoubtedly the most publicly heralded newcomer to the elitist world of Madison Avenue shopping in recent times is the uptown branch of *Barneys New York* (660 Madison Ave.; phone: 212-826-8900). This is its third and largest Manhattan location (the flagship store is on Seventh Ave. from W.

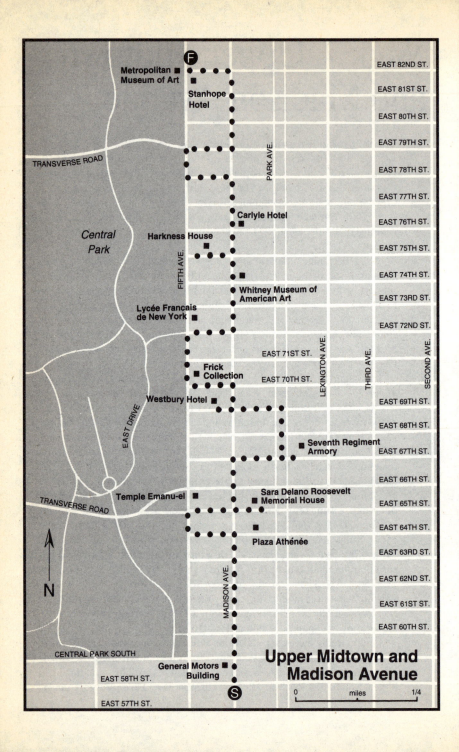

16th to W. 17th St.; a second outlet is in the *World Financial Center*). For years a leader in cutting-edge fashions for men and women, Barneys has prices that can be intimidating, but there is a spirit of fun, too, at this haunt of the well-heeled. Even if you are not buying clothes, you might try the handsome espresso bar and restaurant downstairs.

At the corner of Madison Avenue and East 62nd Street, look west (left) for a glimpse of 11 East 62nd Street, a French bonbon of a townhouse built in 1900. Its little balconies trimmed with grillwork make this a real charmer. Drink in the atmosphere of the *Sherry-Lehmann* liquor store (679 Madison Ave.; phone: 212-838-7500), home of one of the country's best selections of rare and fine French and American wines. Then stop into the nearby *Julie Artisans Gallery* (687 Madison Ave.; phone: 212-688-2345) for an intriguing look at clothing-as-art. For a terrific souvenir of New York's show-biz scene, the *Margo Feiden Gallery* (699 Madison Ave.; phone: 212-223-4230) specializes in Al Hirshfeld's unmistakable caricatures. *Laura Ashley Home Furnishings* (714 Madison Ave.; phone: 212-735-5000) is a flowery country refuge of accessories, upholstery fabrics, wallpapers, linens, and more. The bed linens at *E. Braun & Co.* (717 Madison Ave.; phone: 212-838-0650) are likewise the stuff of sweet dreams. Upstairs, *Erica Wilson's* needlework shop (phone: 212-832-7290) stocks supplies for a variety of projects, from petit point to crewel embroidery.

Look right at the corner of East 64th Street and note the canopy of the *Plaza Athénée* hotel, which adds a regal touch to an already handsome block. The lobby is sumptuous yet comfortable and discreet. A stroll down East 64th Street in the other direction (toward *Central Park*) affords a short art break. The street is lined with ornate townhouses, many of whose ground floors are occupied by important galleries, such as *Félix Vercel* (17 E. 64th St.; phone: 212-744-3131) and *Wildenstein & Co.* (19 E. 64th St.; phone: 212-879-0500). *Emilio Pucci* (24 E. 64th St.; phone: 212-752-8957) is a gallery of Italian fashion. Among the architectural features that grace some of these buildings are gabled roofs and dormer windows; also note the grimacing bas-relief griffins on the top floor of No. 20.

At Fifth Avenue, East 64th Street opens into *Central Park*. Nearing the corner, take a look at the oval windows and large dormers of 3 East 64th Street, which was built by the same architects who designed the fanciful *New York Yacht Club* on West 44th Street. At this entrance to the park is a brick building called the *Arsenal*. Built in 1851 to store arms and ammunition, it is better known as the first home of the *American Museum of Natural History,* which now has far more grand quarters across town. This English manorial-style fortress currently is the headquarters of the city's *Parks Department*.

Walk up Fifth Avenue for one block to the massive *Temple Emanu-El,* the country's largest synagogue, at the corner of East 65th Street. Its Romanesque bulk dominates the street, which also boasts some beautiful townhouses. History buffs can walk east toward Park Avenue to see the

Sara Delano Roosevelt Memorial House (47-49 E. 65th St.), a double townhouse that belonged to FDR's indomitable mother. It was here that the president first stayed after he was stricken with polio.

Back on Madison Avenue, shopping opportunities show no signs of flagging. *Walter Steiger* (739 Madison Ave.; phone: 212-570-1212) is renowned for fine women's shoes. *Léron* (750 Madison Ave.; phone: 212-753-6700) will custom-embroider or appliqué table linens and sensuous Egyptian cotton and silk bedding. The *L. S. Collection* (765 Madison Ave.; phone: 212-472-3355) is the place for original postmodern items for the home, such as a futuristic silver-plated tea set that stands at so pitched an angle that it seems to travel at high velocity. On the northeast corner of Madison and 66th Street is a building that blends an eclectic mix of Elizabethan and Gothic details; notice the way it curves gracefully around the corner. Downstairs in this wonderful structure is *Fred Leighton* (773 Madison Ave.; phone: 212-288-1872), a glittering shop for precious jewelry. Now look back down Madison; the steady rise of the avenue offers a dramatic perspective, with the glass-and-steel skyline of midtown seemingly light years away.

A treat for tired feet and jaded palates awaits in *Godiva Chocolatiers* (793 Madison Ave.; phone: 212-249-9444). Its small café, with large windows that look out onto the avenue, makes nibbling a sophisticated experience. Turn right onto East 67th Street to find *Didier Aaron Antiques* (32 E. 67th St.; phone: 212-988-5248), whose tasteful pieces carry astonishingly high price tags.

Take a break from shopping and continue along East 67th Street over to Park Avenue, to the *Seventh Regiment Armory* of the US National Guard. Built between 1877 and 1879, and looking more like a castle than an armory, this stalwart brick building is a memorial to members of the 107th Infantry who died in World War I. It regularly hosts antiques shows and posh charity functions.

The buildings along the west side of Park Avenue between East 68th and East 69th Streets are worthy of note. Commissioned during the early part of this century by several wealthy businessmen, they are the work of three different architectural firms that worked together to design a harmonious grouping without sacrificing individuality. In 1965 the four structures constituted the last block front of early-20th-century houses left on Park Avenue, and had been sold and scheduled for demolition. Fortunately, the Marquesa De Cuevas, one of John D. Rockefeller's granddaughters, responded to public agitation and rescued them from the wrecker's ball. No. 680 now houses the *Americas Society*. The first of the four to be built, it served as the *Soviet Mission* to the *United Nations* in the 1950s.

At East 69th Street turn left, back toward Madison Avenue. On this block is *Spazio Romeo Gigli* (21 E. 69th St.; phone: 212-744-9121), whose outré designs have included a metal trapeze jacket and a see-through blazer made from banana fibers. At the corner of Madison Avenue is the cosmopolitan *Westbury* hotel.

The roster of tenants inhabiting the stretch of Madison Avenue from East 67th to East 69th Street reads like a who's who of haute couture, most hailing from Italy: *Tahari* (802 Madison Ave.; phone: 212-535-1515); *Emanuel Ungaro* (803 Madison Ave.; phone: 212-249-4090); *Giorgio Armani* (815 Madison Ave.; phone: 212-988-9191); *Gianni Versace* (men's fashions: 816 Madison Ave.; phone: 212-744-5572; women's fashions: 817 Madison Ave.; phone: 212-744-6868); *Jaeger* (818 Madison Ave.; phone: 212-628-3350); and *Valentino* (825 Madison Ave.; phone: 212-772-6969).

Missoni (836 Madison Ave.; phone: 212-517-9339), stocked to the rafters with splendidly patterned signature knits, is just one of the fine shops along the next block. *Hitoshi Tamura* (838 Madison Ave.; phone: 212-288-4625) carries beautifully designed Japanese *chirimen* silk, while *Minna Rosenblatt* (844 Madison Ave.; phone: 212-288-0257) specializes in Tiffany and other Art Nouveau glassware. The *Madison Avenue Bookshop* (833 Madison Ave.; phone: 212-535-6130) lends a cerebral touch. If you have a feline friend back home, visit *Mabel's* (849 Madison Ave.; phone: 212-734-3263) for whimsical, one-of-a-kind gifts inspired by the shop's namesake, a black-and-white cat.

At East 70th Street turn left for a delightful walk toward *Central Park* and the *Frick Collection*. Especially along the north side, this block is graced by exceptional townhouses that combine Italian Renaissance and French styles. (If you have time, walk east on this street too; townhouses stretch as far as Lexington Avenue.) *M. Knoedler & Co.* (19 E. 70th St.; phone: 212-794-0550), a distinguished art gallery, is located in one of these buildings.

The *Frick Collection* (it fronts Fifth Ave., but the entrance is at 1 E. 70th St.; phone: 212-288-0700; also see *Museums* in THE CITY), the crowning glory of all this sumptuous architecture, was built between 1913 and 1915 by Carrère and Hastings, the firm that designed the *New York Public Library*. Originally the home of coke and steel magnate Henry Clay Frick, the mansion was built as a showplace for his extraordinary art collection. After a visit here, return to Madison Avenue. For a touch of the French countryside, walk up to East 71st Street, where *Pierre Deux* (870 Madison Ave.; phone: 212-570-9343) has a stockpile of colorful Provençal fabrics, furniture, and home accessories. Continue up Madison to East 72nd Street; on the corner stands the *Rhinelander Mansion,* another wedding cake of a house. Built in 1895–98 for an eccentric society matron who never lived here, it is now the home of *Polo/Ralph Lauren*'s classic clothing and home furnishings (867 Madison Ave.; phone: 212-606-2100). The store prides itself on its oh-so-elegant yet relaxed atmosphere, where open fires crackle in winter and merchandise is displayed in armoires instead of on ordinary racks or shelves. The Lauren empire has expanded to include *Polo Sport* just across the street in a far more modern building (888 Madison Ave.; phone: 212-434-8000). To the left, between Madison and Fifth Avenues at 9 East 72nd Street, is another Carrère and Hastings design; its next-door neighbor—carved from stone that appears almost malleable—was built two years later, in 1898–99, by Flagg and Chambers as a complement to the other building. Both structures now belong to the prestigious *Lycée Français de New York.*

A few tiny but lavish shops dot the short distance back on Madison from East 72nd Street to the *Whitney Museum of American Art,* three blocks north. *Portantina* (895 Madison Ave.; phone: 212-472-0636), for instance, carries hand-painted Venetian velvet clothing and fabrics with the sumptuousness and depth of color of aged port. The window at *Bardith Ltd.* (901 Madison Ave.; phone: 212-737-3775) resembles an unusual patchwork quilt made from a wild assortment of precious porcelain plates. *Au Chat Botté* (903 Madison Ave.; phone: 212-772-7402) is ideal for extravagant grandparents who love to spoil their grandchildren with expensive clothing.

A detour west (toward Fifth Avenue) on East 73rd Street will take you past the delicious geometric display at *La Maison du Chocolat* (25 E. 73rd St.; phone: 212-744-7117) and to the mansion where press baron Joseph Pulitzer plotted his newspaper war against William Randolph Hearst. The Italianate columned home (11 E. 73rd St.) was designed by the prominent architectural firm of McKim, Mead & White.

Back to Madison and on to the *Whitney Museum of American Art* (945 Madison Ave. at 75th St.; phone: 212-570-3600; also see *Special Places* in THE CITY), whose massive and somewhat forbidding exterior seems almost a violent reaction to the ornate architecture that surrounds it. But this belies its bright and lively interior, in which powerful, intellectually challenging exhibits are held. Don't miss the nearby bookstores: *Archiva* (944 Madison Ave.; phone: 212-439-9194) has a broad selection of art tomes; and *Books & Co.* (939 Madison Ave.; phone: 212-737-1450) keeps its customers abreast of what's current in the publishing world by sponsoring intimate readings with the latest literati.

A block west of the *Whitney* at 1 East 75th Street is the *Harkness House,* another beautiful Italian Renaissance–inspired mansion, built of Tennessee marble. Return to Madison Avenue to *Florian Papp* (962 Madison Ave.; phone: 212-288-6770), which offers fine European and English antique furniture. More upscale antiques shops are close by. The specialty at *Time Will Tell* (962 Madison Ave.; phone: 212-861-2663) is vintage watches. *Leo Kaplan Ltd.* (967 Madison Ave.; phone: 212-249-6766) is known for its 18th-century English pottery, porcelain, and paperweights.

The *Carlyle* hotel (35 E. 76th St. at Madison Ave.; see also *Checking In* in THE CITY) is one of the city's landmark establishments; it was a favorite of presidents Truman and Kennedy. Sophisticated entertainment abounds here: In *Bemelmans Bar* (decorated with murals by the illustrator of the *Madeleine* children's books), Barbara Carroll makes frequent appearances at the piano; if you are fortunate, you may also catch the incomparable Bobby Short at the *Café Carlyle.*

High-fashion shops—*Vera Wang Bridal House* (991 Madison Ave.; phone: 212-628-3400), *Issey Miyake* (992 Madison Ave.; phone: 212-439-7822), and a branch of *Charivari* (1001 Madison Ave.; phone: 212-650-0078)—contrast nicely with the stalwart former home of *Sotheby's* auctioneers (980 Madison Ave.), a controversial, strikingly sheer box of a building whose entryway is presided over by gluttonish figures created by sculptor Wheeler Williams. The building's ground floor now houses several museum-like art galleries, including the *Weintraub Gallery* (phone: 212-879-1195), which displays works by such modern master sculptors as Moore, Calder, and Marini.

Alicia Mugetti (999 Madison Ave.; phone: 212-794-6186) carries a hand-painted line of magnificent silk scarves and blazers. For a light meal or refreshing cappuccino or espresso in a Milanese setting, stop at *Sant Ambroeus* (1000 Madison Ave.; phone: 212-570-2211). Tiny *G & M Pastries* (1006 Madison Ave.; phone: 212-288-4424) specializes in delicious Old World treats; the danish and cookies are wonderful, but sample the jelly donuts and marble crumb cake—they're the best in town.

Continue up to East 78th Street and turn left. The stately mansion on the northeast corner of Fifth Avenue was once the home of James B. Duke, a poor farmboy who eventually became president of the American Tobacco Company. Built in 1910–12, the house was modeled after a Louis XV *hôtel particulier* in Bordeaux. In 1957 Duke's daughter, Doris, donated the house to *New York University;* it now serves as its *Institute of Fine Arts.*

Now turn right onto Fifth Avenue. Around the corner at No. 972 is the former *Payne Whitney Mansion,* now the cultural, press, and information offices of the *French Consulate.* This lovely granite-faced building has an impressive entrance bay and combines elements of an Italian palazzo with classical French touches. At Fifth Avenue and East 79th Street is another fantastic mansion, a turreted confection that marks the beginning of a very lavish block of townhouses and art galleries heading east. *Acquavella Galleries* (18 E. 79th St.; phone: 212-734-6300) deals in 19th- and 20th-century masters. *Salander-O'Reilly Galleries* (20 E. 79th St.; phone: 212-879-6606) displays the works of Old Masters and modern photographers behind its iron-grilled windows. And even if you don't plan on making an haute couture purchase, visit *Hanae Mori* (27 E. 79th St.; phone: 212-472-2352) simply to experience one of the city's most inscrutable examples of modern architecture.

The wide intersection of Madison Avenue and East 79th Street is flanked by art galleries of all descriptions. *Perls Galleries* (1016 Madison Ave.; phone: 212-472-3200) proffers first-rate contemporary drawings and paintings. *Magidson Fine Art* (1080 Madison Ave.; phone: 212-288-0666) specializes in American pop art. On the dusty, narrow, second-floor balcony of the *Burlington Bookshop* (1082 Madison Ave.) is *The Compulsive Collector* (phone: 212-879-7443), a treasure trove of antiquarian books. For those who are suffering hunger pangs, *E.A.T.* (1064 Madison Ave.; phone: 212-772-0022) has delicious salads and prepared foods to eat on the premises or take home—at astronomical prices.

As soon as you turn left off Madison Avenue onto East 82nd Street, the imposing entrance to the *Metropolitan Museum of Art* fills the streetscape like a painting overflowing its frame. Take a look at 998 Fifth Avenue, the first apartment house built on Fifth Avenue when it was still a street of private homes. Designed by McKim, Mead & White, it is still one of the city's swankiest addresses.

The walk ends at the *Stanhope* hotel (995 Fifth Ave.; also see *Checking In* in THE CITY). If the weather is fine, sit at its outdoor café (considered one of the best in the city) and look across Fifth Avenue at the *Metropolitan Museum,* with its classical Beaux Arts façade and immense staircase, where New Yorkers have lunch or arrange to meet friends. Venture inside the museum, and a whole other world awaits you (see *Special Places* in THE CITY).

Walk 8: Brooklyn Heights

Soon after regular steam-ferry service between Brooklyn and Manhattan began in 1814, the borough established a firm toehold as New York City's first suburb. Conceived as a bucolic oasis just minutes from the urban business center, Brooklyn Heights has managed to retain its small-town air despite threats of urban renewal, commercial development, fiscal upheaval, and even rampant trendiness. Its tree-lined streets and handsome townhouses, many more than a century old, won historic landmark status in 1965, so now more than 600 homes are protected and preserved for future generations to enjoy.

Brooklyn acquired the nickname "Borough of Churches" in the 19th century, due to the number and distinction—both architectural and clerical—of its religious institutions. While many no longer exist, enough still stand to fill the Heights with a delightful carillon on Sunday mornings. Another good time to visit is at twilight, when nearby Manhattan sparkles across the river and the lights inside Brooklyn's brownstones are turned on, giving passersby a view of the interiors.

The Heights is a distinct neighborhood, bordered by the Brooklyn Bridge to the north, Atlantic Avenue to the south, Court Street to the east, and, to the west, the Promenade (also known as the Esplanade), the pride of the Heights, which meanders along the bluff above the East River. It simultaneously protects residents from the noise and fumes of the Brooklyn-Queens Expressway beneath it and provides a delightfully airy park with a breathtaking view of lower Manhattan.

Any walk through this residential neighborhood is rewarded by views of many fine examples of American architecture, ranging from Federal to Greek Revival, Gothic Revival, Renaissance Revival, and, more obscurely, to neighborhood revival. Architecture buffs may want to pick up a copy of *Old Brooklyn Heights: New York's First Suburb* by Clay Lancaster (Dover Books; $7.95), which gives a detailed history of 619 landmark houses. The *Fund for the Borough of Brooklyn* (16 Court St.; phone: 718-855-7882) also offers a pamphlet, priced at $5, with an extensive walking tour of downtown Brooklyn including the architectural genealogy of the notable buildings.

Many subway lines stop in or near the Heights. For our walk, disembark from the *IRT* Seventh Avenue line (No. 2 or No. 3 train) at the Clark Street station, located in the lower level of the *St. George* hotel. Once the largest hotel in New York City, the present tower complex contains apartments and a health club; however, the area around the subway station is seedy.

A quick right on Henry Street after exiting the station leads to more genteel surroundings. The Gothic *First Presbyterian Church* (124 Henry St.) was built in 1846 and boasts many exquisite stained glass windows by Louis

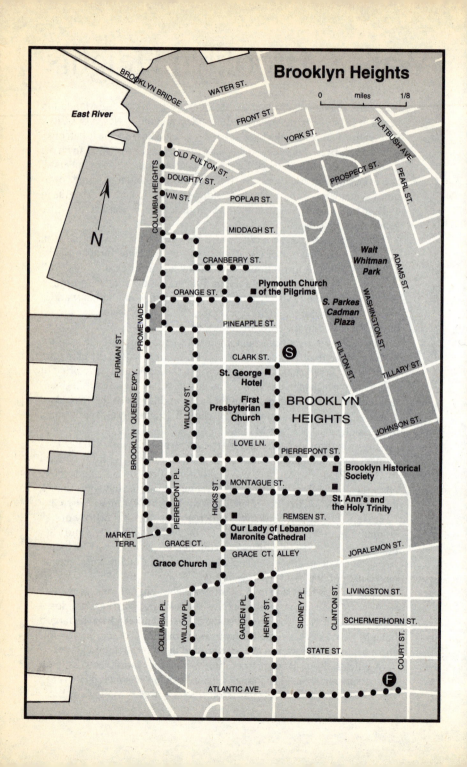

Tiffany. Just down the street at Nos. 132–138 are a series of three-story, mid-19th-century brick houses decorated with a continuous façade. Across the street four clapboard frame houses (Nos. 137–143) built in 1829 have survived in fine style.

At Pierrepont Street the ornate, turreted château on the southwest corner (No. 82) is a youngster by Heights standards; it's barely a century old but has housed many unusual people. Originally a mansion built for merchant Henry Behr, it then became a hotel, then a brothel, before achieving redemption as the dormitory for a Franciscan seminary. Now it's a conventional apartment building.

Continuing east on Pierrepont, the *Brooklyn Historical Society* is one block down to the left at the corner of Clinton Street (No. 128). Its detailed exterior includes carved inscriptions, medallions, cornices, and terra cotta sculptures of a Viking and an Indian. The second-floor library is a 19th-century sanctum, complete with carved wooden pillars and leather-top work tables with green glass–shaded lamps.

Backtrack west along Pierrepont Street, and take some time to admire the beautiful cast-iron fence at No. 36, erected in 1845; the mullioned-glass bay window at No. 10; and the balustrade on the sandstone-and-brick beauty at No. 6. The Promenade beckons at the end of the street, but try to ignore it for now and turn left onto Pierrepont Place.

If the rather gloomy brownstone at No. 3 Pierrepont Place looks familiar, you may recognize it as the mansion of Mafia chief Don Corrado in John Huston's film *Prizzi's Honor*. The house was built by architect Richard Upjohn (his work can be seen throughout the Heights) in 1857 for wealthy local Abiel Abbot Low.

Where the home of the Misses Julia and Anna Pierrepont once stood at 1 Pierrepont Place is now the *Pierrepont Playground*. In the 1940s this was the only playground in the Heights and had an exclusive reputation: Visitation was by invitation only, and mothers and their children were interviewed before permission to use it was granted.

Montague Terrace, the southern extension of Pierrepont Terrace, is a fine block of Gothic Revival houses, with long, narrow, forbidding wooden porches. Writer Thomas Wolfe lived here from 1931 to 1935 (he spent two years at No. 5) and customarily meandered along the streets during respites from writing *Of Time and the River* (which refers to the Hudson River, not the river just yards from here).

Turn right at the end of Montague Terrace onto Remsen Street, and go up the short ramp to the southern end of the Promenade. The view from this spot is unsurpassed: There's no vantage point of which we know where the skyline of lower Manhattan is more dramatic. The Promenade is a romantic lover's lane and the perfect place from which to watch the *Fourth of July* fireworks on the East River.

The Promenade also provides sneak peeks at the gardens and backs of the houses on Columbia Heights. The lacy cast-iron balconies and old brick of No. 192 evoke images of New Orleans; in fact, these fretted balconies were typical of the Renaissance Revival style in fashion from about 1850 through the end of the century. Simultaneously, industrial development had made possible the mass production of cast iron in delicate patterns that had formerly required the skills of a master craftsperson; everything from bedsteads to lampposts to fancy window guards and balconies was suddenly available for a fraction of the previous cost.

Where Clark Street intersects with the Promenade, turn around and look across the harbor and straight up Manhattan's Wall Street to *Trinity Church*. The Promenade officially ends at Orange Street and merges with Columbia Heights. Both the geography and the affluence rapidly go downhill after Middagh Street. You can now choose to remain on the high ground or explore the low road.

The modern office complex as the road drops belongs to the *Watchtower*, a publication of the Jehovah's Witnesses, who are one of the area's largest landowners. On the right at the bottom of the hill is a weathervane of a horse running into the wind, the site of former stables. This building and the massive red brick pile of the former Eagle Warehouse behind it are now pricey co-op apartments, the result of Brooklyn Heights's most recent real-estate boom.

Continue straight and cross Old Fulton Street, the original Brooklyn ferry landing. Part of the US Army embarked from here for the Revolutionary War on August 29, 1776; a tablet marks the spot. *Bargemusic* (Fulton Ferry Landing; phone: 718-624-4061), a floating concert hall, presents chamber music recitals on Thursdays and Sundays for a fee. Both the music and the view are magnificent. The pleasant little garden straight ahead belongs to the *River Café* at 1 Water Street (see *Eating Out* in THE CITY). To avoid too much wear and tear on the wallet and to make the most of the view, come for brunch instead of dinner.

The Brooklyn Bridge looms on the left as you continue along Old Fulton Street. Rather than trying to cross the off ramp of the Brooklyn-Queens Expressway, retrace your steps and climb back up Columbia Heights until you reach Middagh Street. From Middagh Street south to Pierrepont Street, the streets between Columbia Heights and Hicks Street are a treasure trove of architectural graces, leafy trees, friendly cats, and their equally neighborly owners. At the corner of Willow Street, No. 24 Middagh Street, the two-and-a-half-story, coffee-colored clapboard house, was listed in the original 1829 city directory. Its carriage house is still connected, although it's now used as a home in its own right; note that the wooden arches that define the ground-floor windows were once its doors.

Walk down Willow Street and turn left on Cranberry Street; make a right on Hicks Street, and then left again on Orange Street. Cranberry, Orange, and Pineapple Streets were named by brothers John and Jacob Middagh Hicks, two early 19th-century landowners who foresaw the economic potential of Brooklyn Heights and divided up their holdings into 25-

by-100-foot building lots. Halfway down the block is *Plymouth Church of the Pilgrims,* where Henry Ward Beecher served as pastor from 1847 to 1887. His passionate sermons on the immorality of slavery and other great issues of the day attracted thousands to this place, once the largest hall in Brooklyn.

Backtrack along Orange Street to Columbia Heights and turn left. The block between Pineapple and Clark Streets is a street of splendid doors. At Nos. 148 and 150 note the gloomy Gothic architecture; No. 181 is a delightful red brick carriage house; cast-iron scrolling is the lure at Nos. 187 and 210. Willow Street, which parallels Columbia Heights, boasts one of the best restored carriage houses in the Heights (No. 151). The most menacing door, at No. 124, is complete with medieval-looking iron hinges and gargoyle knockers; at No. 110 is a hilarious scene of Pan playing his pipes on a cornice above a second-floor bay window.

Continuing south, turn left on Pierrepont Street and then right on Hicks Street. You will soon come upon Montague Street, the main thoroughfare of the Heights, lined with ice cream shops, a few art galleries, bookstores, and several moderately priced, convivial spots for a refreshment: the *Montague Street Saloon* (122 Montague St.; 718-522-6770); *Slade's* (107 Montague St.; phone: 718-858-1200); *Leaf & Bean* (136 Montague St.; phone: 718-855-7978); and *Peter Hilary's Bar and Grill* (174 Montague St.; phone: 718-875-7900). *Henry's End* (44 Henry St.; phone: 718-834-1776) regularly features pheasant, quail, bear, and even buffalo. The extensive beer list features 25 brands from which to choose. For spiritual sustenance stop at *St. Ann's and the Holy Trinity Church* (Clinton and Montague Sts.), an 1847 Gothic Revival masterpiece designed by architect Minard Lafever; the stained glass windows by William Jay Bolton were the first to be crafted in the United States.

Back on Hicks Street walk one block farther south to Remsen Street— as charming as Willow Street, but with a bonus view of the water. The outstanding building on the corner is *Our Lady of Lebanon Maronite Cathedral,* formerly the *Church of the Pilgrims.* The stained glass windows were taken out and installed in the *Plymouth Church of the Pilgrims* when the two institutions merged; the magnificent doors were salvaged from the steamship *Normandie,* which caught fire and sank in 1942 while docked at a Hudson River pier.

Some of Remsen's architectural delights include Nos. 52, 54, and 58, three-story Greek Revival row houses with a continuous brick façade. The mansard roof edged with cast-iron fretwork at No. 58 strongly resembles the Bankses' family house in the movie *Mary Poppins.*

As you head south on Hicks Street, the next block crosses two captivating dead-end streets. On the left is Grace Court Alley, a collection of stables and carriage houses that have been converted into residences. You can still see the hooks over the door that held pulleys used to hoist bales of hay up into the lofts. (Another nearby mews is Hunter Alley, one block off Henry St.) On the right is Grace Court, which takes its name (as does Grace Court Alley) from *Grace Church,* an 1847 Gothic Revival brownstone designed by Richard Upjohn. There's a little walk along the south side of the church that leads to a secluded, sunny spot with benches. If you're lucky enough to happen by when the *Grace Choral Society* is rehearsing, this is a perfect place to sit and listen. The northern side of Grace Court skirts the backyards of the houses on Remsen Street, offering a fascinating view of individual gardens.

To understand the true definition of "height" in the Heights, turn to the right at Joralemon Street. This marks the beginning of the southern third of the neighborhood, whose houses are less grand than those farther north. Many of them are original Greek Revival row dwellings dating from the middle of the 19th century, and still retain their original pilastered doorways and iron railings. At the foot of the hill near the southwest corner of Columbia Place you can spot the *Riverside Houses,* model tenements built in 1889–90 by Alfred T. White. On the south side of the block at 58 Joralemon Street stands an 1847 Greek Revival house that has been converted to a ventilator for the *IRT* subway. Turn left on Willow Place, a block with such strong community spirit that the area is known as "Willow Town." Four Gothic Revival houses with a continuous façade, coupled porches, and clustered columns anchor the northwest corner of the block at Nos. 2–8; another four Greek Revival abodes, whose shared colonnaded portico is reminiscent of Regency crescents in London and Bath, hold down the southeast corner.

Turn left on State Street, walk two blocks, then turn left again onto Garden Place, much of whose charm derives from the dappled sycamore trees that line the block. Its early residents were a typical mixture of contemporary Brooklyn Heights citizens: A shipmaster once lived at No. 9; a grocer at No. 10; a broker at No. 32; and a distiller at No. 35. Since Garden Place wasn't built until the early 1840s, there are no Federal-style houses here. However, almost every other style of architecture popular during Brooklyn Heights' development takes a bow, including Greek Revival, Renaissance Revival, a pre–Civil War carriage house, a conglomeration of all previous styles (called the Queen Anne style), 20th-century "tapestry brick," and even a small-scale apartment building.

Turn to the right on Joralemon Street, and note the working gaslight at No. 98, still faithfully tended by the residents on the block. Turn right again on Henry Street and follow it two blocks to Atlantic Avenue.

One of Brooklyn's main thoroughfares, Atlantic Avenue picks up the traffic from the Brooklyn-Battery Tunnel via the Brooklyn-Queens Expressway and funnels it through the entire borough east to Long Island. The section between Henry and Court Streets is the center of New York's (and America's) largest Arab community. Stop in at *Rashid* (191 Atlantic Ave.; phone: 718-852-3295) for books, magazines, and Middle Eastern cassette tapes. Some of the best food shops, many of which offer takeout as well as ingredients for cooking, are *Sahadi* (187 Atlantic Ave.; phone: 718-624-4550), which stocks 16 types of olives, five-pound bags of pistachios, and roasted chick-peas by the gallon; *El-Asmar International Delights* (197 Atlantic Ave.; phone: 718-855-2455), the self-proclaimed "Manufacturers of Oriental Pastry and Turkish Delight," which also sells different kinds of rice and seven types of feta cheese; and *Malko Karkanni* (174 Atlantic Ave.; phone: 718-834-0845), a neighborhood hangout where you can find old men drinking Turkish coffee and singing in Arabic; sold here are walnut, cashew, almond, and pistachio baklava.

If you'd like to sit down and eat, try the *Moroccan Star* (205 Atlantic Ave. at Court St.; phone: 718-643-0800), a white-tablecloth eatery with reasonable prices; the stripped-down *Yemen Café* (176 Atlantic Ave.; phone: 718-834-9533), whose prices are the least expensive of the group and its clientele the most colorful; or *Tripoli* (156 Atlantic Ave. at Clinton St.; phone: 718-596-5800), which serves very good Lebanese food at moderate prices in a pleasant setting.

Index

Abyssinian Baptist Church, the Bronx, 143
Accommodations, 90–105
  bed and breakfast, 90–91
  hotels, 90–105
    grand hotels, 91–96, 130
    rental options, 90–91
Afternoon tea, 121
Airplane travel, 9–12
  charter flights, 10
  consumer protection, 12
  discounts on scheduled flights, 10–12
    bartered travel sources, 12
    consolidators and bucket shops, 11
    courier travel, 10–11
    generic air travel, 12
    last-minute travel clubs, 11–12
  insurance, 17
  scheduled flights, 9–10
    baggage, 10
    fares, 9
    reservations, 10
    seating, 10
    smoking, 10
    special meals, 10
  transportation from the airports to the city, 12–13
American Craft Museum, 65
American Museum of Natural History, 51, 75
American Museum of the Moving Image, Queens, 58–59
Amster Yard, 207
Antiques, 69–70, 133–36, 138
Aquarium for Wildlife Conservation (New York Aquarium), 55
Aqueduct Raceway, 147

Art galleries
  SoHo, 179–82
  TriBeCa, 185–86
  upper Madison Avenue, 211, 215
Asia Society, 65
Atlantic Avenue, Brooklyn, 54, 222–23
Auction houses, 136–38
Automated teller machines (ATMs), 23
Automobiles. *See* Car, traveling by
Avenue of the Americas (Sixth Avenue), 41–42, 46

Banking hours. *See* Business and shopping hours
Baseball, 57, 78
Basketball, 78
Battery Park, 35, 166
Battery Park City, 35, 36
Bay Ridge, Brooklyn, 55
Bed and breakfast establishments, 90–91
Beekman Place, 206–7
Belmont Park, 147–48
Bicycling, 78–80
Billiards, 80
Bleecker Street, 41
Boating, 148–49
  See also Ship, traveling by
Booth Theater, 142
The Bowery, 38–39
Bowling, 80
Bowling Green, 35, 167–68
Bowne House, Queens, 58
Boxing, 80
Broadway and the Theater District, 45, 84–86, 127, 141–43
Broadway musicals, 127

The Bronx
  biking, 79
  boating, 149
  golf courses, 81
  horseback riding, 83
  places of special interest, 56–57
  sailing, 151
  special events information, 65
Bronx Museum of the Arts, 56–57
Bronx Zoo (International Wildlife Conservation Park), 56
Brooklyn
  biking, 79
  boating, 149
  golf courses, 81
  places of special interest, 31–32, 53–56
  sailing, 150–51
  special events information, 65
  walking tour, 217–23
Brooklyn Academy of Music, 86, 140
Brooklyn Botanic Gardens, 54
Brooklyn Bridge, 37, 154, 220
Brooklyn Heights, 53–54
  map, 218
  walking tour, 217–23
Brooklyn Heights Promenade, 31–32, 129, 217–20
Brooklyn Historical Society, 219
Brooklyn Museum, 54–55
Bus, traveling by, 13, 32–33, 61–62
Business and shopping hours, 23

Canoeing, 149
Car, traveling by
  insurance, 13, 17
  renting a car, 13–14
  views from the road, 32
Carl Schurz Park, 50
Carnegie Hall, 86, 139
Cash machines. *See* Automated teller machines
Castle Clinton (Castle Garden), 35, 166–67
Cathedral of St. John the Divine, 51, 143–44

Central Park, 48, 155
  biking, 79
  boating, 148–49
  horseback riding, 82
  Shakespeare in the Park, 127
Central Park Wildlife Conservation Center, 48
Central Synagogue, 144
Charter flights, 10
Chelsea, 43
Children's Museum of the Arts, 66
Chinatown, 38, 126, 154–55
  Little Italy and
    map, 170
  walking tour, 170–76
Christie's, 138
Christmas in New York, 127–28, 197, 201
Chrysler Building, 45
Church of the Transfiguration, 144–45
Circle in the Square Uptown, 142
City Center, 86, 139–40
City Hall, 37
Climate, 9
Cloisters, 52
Colleges and universities, 51–52, 68–69
Columbia University, 51–52
Coney Island, Brooklyn, 55
Conference House, Staten Island, 60
Consumer protection, 12
Cooper-Hewitt Museum, 66, 76
Cort Theater, 142
Credit cards, 23
  telephone calls with, 24
Cruises. *See* Ship, traveling by

Dag Hammarskjold Plaza, 208
Disabled travelers, 17–20
Discounts
  on music and dance tickets, 87, 198
  on scheduled flights, 10–12
  on theater tickets, 85, 139, 168
Driving. *See* Car, traveling by

Easter Parade, 128
East Side
  lower, 39, 67, 126, 133
  United Nations and
    map, 204
    walking tour, 204–8
  upper, 48–50
    map, 210
    walking tour, 209–16
East Village, 40
Edgar Allan Poe Cottage, the Bronx, 57
Ellis Island Immigration Museum, 34, 129, 167
Emergencies
  medical assistance, 25
  telephone number in New York, 25
Empire State Building, 32, 44, 66, 129, 130, 197

Federal Hall National Memorial, 36, 164
Federal Reserve Bank of New York, 164
Ferries. *See* Ship, traveling by
Festivals, 38, 52–53, 171–72, 174
Fifth Avenue, 47, 48–49
  lower, 41
  parades, 128–29
  Rockefeller Center and
    map, 196
    walking tour, 196–203
Fifth Avenue Presbyterian Church, 202
First Presbyterian Church, Brooklyn, 217–18
Fitness centers, 80
Flushing Meadow-Corona Park, Queens, 59
Football, 80
Forbes Magazine Galleries, 66
Ford Foundation Building, 45
Ft. Tryon Park, 52
Four Seasons, dining at, 125
14th Street to 34th Street, places of special interest, 42–43
Fraunces Tavern Museum, 66, 75, 165

Frick Collection, 66, 213
Friends Meeting House, Queens, 145
Fulton Fish Market, 37, 161–63

Garment District, 43–44
Golf, 80–82
Governors Island, 35
Grace Church, Brooklyn, 222
Gracie Mansion, 50
Gramercy Park, 42–43
Grand Army Plaza, Brooklyn, 54
Grand Army Plaza, Manhattan, 47, 203
Grand Central Station, 45
Grant's Tomb, 52
Greenwich Village
  East, 40
  map, 188
  places of special interest, 40–42
  walking tour, 187–95
  West, 42
Guggenheim Museum, 49, 75–76
  SoHo, 49, 179
Guinness World of Records, 66

Hall of Fame of Great Americans, the Bronx, 57
Handicapped travelers. *See* Disabled travelers
Harlem, 52–53, 143
Hayden Planetarium, 51
Health care
  emergency number for medical assistance, 25
  hospitals and pharmacies, 25
  insurance, 17
Helicopter trips, 17, 33
Hockey, 82
Holidays. *See* Special events; *names of specific holidays*
Horseback riding, 82–83
Horse racing, 147–48
Hospitals. *See* Health care
Hotels, 90–105
  grand hotels, 91–96, 130
Houses of worship, 143–47
  See also specific houses of worship

Ice skating, 83
Inland waterway cruises. *See* Ship, traveling by
Insurance, 13, 17
International Center of Photography, 66
International Wildlife Conservation Park (Bronx Zoo), 56
Intrepid Sea-Air-Space Museum, 66–67

Jacob K. Javits Convention Center, 44
Jacques Marchais Center of Tibetan Art, Staten Island, 59–60
Japan Society Building, 208
Jefferson Market Library, 189–90
Jewish Museum, 67
Jogging, 83
Joseph Papp Public Theater, 40, 141

Kayaking, 149
King Mansion, Queens, 58
Kingsland House, Queens, 58

Legal aid, 26
Lincoln Center for the Performing Arts, 50–51, 86, 140–41, 154
Little Italy, 38
  Chinatown and
    map, 170
    walking tour, 170–76
Local services, 63–65
Local transportation. *See* Transportation
Lower East Side, 39, 67, 126, 133
Lower East Side Tenement Museum, 67
Lower Manhattan
  maps, 2, 162
  places of special interest, 34–40
  walking tour, 161–69

Macy's Thanksgiving Day Parade, 128
Madison Avenue and upper midtown
  map, 210
  walking tour, 209–16
Madison Square Garden, 43, 87
Mail, 24

Maps
  in this guide
    Brooklyn Heights, 218
    Greenwich Village, 188
    Little Italy and Chinatown, 170
    lower Manhattan, 2, 162
    midtown, 196
    New York, 2–3
    Rockefeller Center and Fifth Avenue, 196
    SoHo, 178
    TriBeCa, 184
    United Nations and the East Side, 204
    upper midtown and Madison Avenue, 210
    Wall Street, 162
  sources for, 26, 34, 53, 60, 62
Meadowlands, New Jersey, 148
Medical assistance. *See* Health care
Metropolitan Museum of Art, 48–49, 52, 76, 86, 215–16
Midtown (34th Street to 59th Street)
  map, 196
  places of special interest, 43–48
  shopping, 43, 47, 197, 199–200, 202–3
  walking tour, 196–203
Money
  sending, 23
  See also Automated teller machines; Credit cards; Traveler's checks
Morgan Library, 68
Museo del Barrio, 67
Museum for African Art, 67
"Museum Mile" (upper Fifth Avenue), 48–49
Museum of American Folk Art, 67
Museum of Modern Art (MOMA), 47, 76, 202
Museum of Television and Radio, 67
Museum of the City of New York, 67
Museums, 65–68, 75–76
  See also specific museums
Music and dance, 50–51, 52–53, 86–87, 139–41

Broadway musicals, 127
   discounts on tickets, 87, 198

Nassau Coliseum, 87
National Museum of the American Indian, 67–68
Newspapers, local, 61
New York Aquarium (Aquarium for Wildlife Conservation), 55
New York Botanical Gardens, the Bronx, 56
New York Hall of Science, Queens, 59
New-York Historical Society, 68
New York Public Library, 45, 197–98
New York Stock Exchange, 35, 164
New York Transit Museum, 68
Nightclubs and nightlife, 87–90
   blues and jazz clubs, 88–89
   comedy clubs, 89–90
   country and international, 89
   pop and rock, 88
   singles' bars, 89–90
   supper clubs and cabarets, 89
Noguchi Museum, 68

Older travelers, 21–22
Our Lady of Lebanon Maronite Cathedral, Brooklyn, 221

Package tours, 14–17
   for disabled travelers, 19–20
   for older travelers, 22
   for single travelers, 20–21
   See also Tours
Palace Theater, 143
Parades, 128–29
Paramount Theater, 43
Park Slope, Brooklyn, 54
Pennsylvania Station, 43
Pharmacies. *See* Health care
Photographing New York, 151–55
Pierpont Morgan Library, 68
Plane, traveling by. *See* Airplane travel
Prospect Park, Brooklyn, 54
Public Theater, 40, 141

Queens
   biking, 79–80
   boating, 149
   churches, 145
   golf courses, 81–82
   horse racing, 147–48
   places of special interest, 57–59
   special events information, 65
Queens Historical Society, 58
Queens Museum, 59

Racetracks, 147–48
Radio, 61
Radio City Music Hall, 46, 141, 201
Religion. *See* Houses of worship
Rental accommodations, 90–91
Renting a car, 13–14
Restaurants, 61, 105–21, 125–26, 128
   afternoon tea, 121
   best bites of the Big Apple, 106–9, 130–31
   Brooklyn, 221, 223
   Chinatown, 38, 126, 173–76
   Greenwich Village, 40, 41–42, 192–95
   historical, 120–21
   Little Italy, 171–73
   Lower East Side, 39, 126
   lower Manhattan, 36, 37, 161–63, 165, 168–69
   midtown, 200–201, 208
   SoHo, 181–83
   Sunday brunch, 121
   TriBeCa, 185–86
Richmondtown Restoration, Staten Island, 60
River cruising. *See* Ship, traveling by
Riverside Church, 52, 145
Riverside Park
   biking, 79
Rockefeller Center, 46, 76, 127–28, 154, 200–201
   Fifth Avenue and map, 196
   walking tour, 196–203
Roller-skating and roller-blading, 83
Roosevelt Island, 50

Sailing, 150–51
St. Bartholomew's (church), 145
St. John the Divine, Cathedral of, 143–44
St. Mark's in the Bowery (church), 145–46
St. Patrick's Cathedral, 46, 146, 200, 201
St. Patrick's Day Parade, 128–29
St. Paul's Chapel, 36
St. Thomas Church, 201–2
Samuel Paley Plaza, 202
Sara Delano Roosevelt Memorial House, 211–12
Sending money, 23
Senior citizens. *See* Older travelers
Seventh Regiment Armory, 212
Shakespeare in the Park, 127
Sheepshead Bay, Brooklyn, 55–56
Ship, traveling by
  day cruises, 16, 33, 34–35
  ferry companies, 13, 34–35, 166–67
Shopping, 69–78
  antiques, 69–70, 133–36, 138
  auction houses, 136–38
  bed and table linens, 70
  bookstores, 70–71, 199
  boutiques and specialty shops, 71
  in Brooklyn, 222–23
  CDs, tapes, and records, 71
  china, crystal, and porcelain, 71
  in Chinatown, 173–75
  clothing, 75, 77, 131–33, 212–15
  department stores, 43, 72, 173
  discount, 77, 131–33
  fabrics and trimmings, 72–73
  food, 73, 172–73, 174, 179, 186, 190, 222–23
  in Greenwich Village, 190–94
  hours, 23
  jewelry and gems, 73–74
  kitchen equipment, 74
  leather goods and luggage, 74
  in Little Italy, 172–73
  in lower Manhattan, 75, 161–63, 168–69
  malls, 37, 75, 202–3
  menswear, 75
  in midtown, 43, 47, 197, 199–200, 202–3
  museum gift shops, 75–76
  poster and print shops, 76
  shoes, 76
  in SoHo, 179, 180–83
  special districts, 38, 73–74, 133
  sporting goods, 76–77
  thrift shops and retro fashion, 77
  toys, 77, 183, 203
  in TriBeCa, 185
  uniquely New York, 77–78
  on the upper East Side, 206, 209–15
Shrine of St. Mother Elizabeth Ann Seton, 166
Shubert Theater, 142
Single travelers, 20–21
Sixth Avenue. *See* Avenue of the Americas
Skating
  ice, 83
  roller-, 83
SoHo, 39
  map, 178
  walking tour, 177–83
Solomon R. Guggenheim Museum, 49, 75–76
SoHo, 49, 179
Sotheby's, 138
South Street Seaport, 37, 161–63
Spanish and Portuguese Synagogue, 146
Special events, 65
  festivals, 38, 171–72, 174
  parades, 128–29
  public holidays, 128–29, 197, 201
  See also names of specific holidays and events
Special-interest packages. *See* Package tours
Sports and fitness, 78–84
  See also specific sports
Staten Island
  biking, 80
  boating, 149
  ferry service, 34, 166

golf courses, 82
places of special interest, 59–60
special events information, 65
Staten Island Zoo, 59
Statue of Liberty, 34, 129, 153–54, 167
Studio Museum of Harlem, 68
Subways, 62–63
Sutton Place, 205–6
Swimming, 83–84

Tax, sales, 61
Taxis, 13, 63, 85
Telephone, 24–25, 61
Television, 61
Temperature. *See* Climate
Temple Emanu-el, 146–47, 211
Tennis, 84
Thanksgiving Day parade, 128
Theater District, 45, 84–86, 127, 141–43
Theater Row, 141–42
Theaters, 45, 50, 84–86, 138–43
  Broadway musicals, 127
  discount tickets, 85, 139, 168
  Shakespeare in the Park, 127
34th Street
  14th Street to, places of special interest, 42–43
  West, 43
Times Square, 44–45
Time zone, 23
Tourist information, local, 26, 53, 60–61
Tours
  bike routes, 79–80
  day cruises, 16, 33, 34–35
  guided, 16–17, 32–33
    Central Park, 48
    Federal Reserve Bank, 164
    Harlem, 53
    Lincoln Center, 51
    NBC Television Studio, 200
    New York Public Library, 198
    New York Stock Exchange, 35, 164
    United Nations, 46
  helicopter, 17, 33

walking, 33, 35, 48, 159–223
  Brooklyn Heights, 217–23
  Greenwich Village, 187–95
  Little Italy and Chinatown, 170–76
  lower Manhattan, 161–69
  midtown (34th Street to 59th Street), 196–203
  Rockefeller and Fifth Avenue, 196–203
  SoHo, 177–83
  TriBeCa, 183–86
  United Nations and the East Side, 204–8
  upper midtown and Madison Avenue, 209–16
  Wall Street, 161–69
See also Package tours; *names of individual tours*
Train, traveling by, 43, 45
Transportation
  from the airports to the city, 12–13
  local, 34, 50, 61–63
  See also Airplane travel; Bus, traveling by; Car, traveling by; Ship, traveling by; Train, traveling by
Traveler's checks, 23
TriBeCa, 39–40
  map, 184
  walking tour, 183–86
Trinity Church, 36, 147, 165
Trump Tower, 202–3
Tudor City, 46
Turtle Bay, 207–8

Union Square, 42
United Nations, 46, 208
  East Side and
    map, 204
    walking tour, 204–8
United States Custom House, 35, 167
Upper East Side
  map, 204
  places of special interest, 48–50
  walking tour, 204–8

Upper midtown and Madison Avenue
  map, 210
  walking tour, 209–16
Upper West Side, places of special
  interest, 50–53

Vietnam Veterans Memorial Plaza,
  165

Walking tours. *See names of individual
  tours*; Tours
Wall Street
  Battery Park to, 35
  map, 162
  walking tour, 161–69
Washington Square, 41, 189
Wave Hill, the Bronx, 57

Weather. *See* Climate
West Side, upper, places of special
  interest, 50–53
West 34th Street, 43
West Village, 42
Whitney Museum of American Art,
  49–50, 76, 214
William Doyle Galleries, 138
World Financial Center, 35, 36, 169
World Trade Center, 32, 35, 36,
  129–30, 168–69

Yankee Stadium, the Bronx, 57
Yonkers Raceway, 148
Yorkville, 50

Zoos, 48, 56, 59